WESTMINSTER ABBEY RECORD SERIES

VOLUME I

ACTS OF
THE DEAN AND CHAPTER
OF WESTMINSTER
1543–1609

Part One
THE FIRST COLLEGIATE CHURCH
1543–1556

WESTMINSTER ABBEY RECORD SERIES

General Editor: Richard Mortimer, MA, PhD, FSA, FRHistS
Keeper of the Muniments, Westminster Abbey

ISSN 1365–4306

Forthcoming

Acts of the Dean and Chapter of Westminster 1543–1609
Part Two
1560–1609
Edited by C.S. Knighton

The Obedientiaries of Westminster Abbey
and their Records
Barbara Harvey

ACTS OF
THE DEAN AND CHAPTER
OF WESTMINSTER
1543–1609

Edited by

C. S. KNIGHTON, MA, DPhil, PhD

Part One

THE FIRST COLLEGIATE CHURCH
1543–1556

THE BOYDELL PRESS

First published 1997
The Boydell Press, Woodbridge

ISBN 0 85115 688 6

The Boydell Press is an imprint of Boydell & Brewer Ltd
PO Box 9, Woodbridge, Suffolk IP12 3DF, UK
and of Boydell & Brewer Inc.
PO Box 41026, Rochester, NY 14604–4126, USA

A catalogue record for this book is available
from the British Library

This publication is printed on acid-free paper

Printed in Great Britain by
Boydell & Brewer Ltd, Woodbridge, Suffolk

CONTENTS

FOREWORD

by the Very Revd the Dean of Westminster

Even after 400 years there is an anticipatory frisson when confidential records come into the public domain. Chapter minutes have always been private, yet the decisions they record uniquely reflect contemporary values and priorities and the temper of the time. The continuity, in various forms, of church life at Westminster has led to an exceptionally large and continuous archive being squirrelled away and preserved. It illustrates the many aspects of national and local history, and much of it (especially the post-Reformation period) is still under-used.

This is why it is so good to welcome the Westminster Abbey Record Series, which is being launched to publish items of historic importance and interest relating to the Abbey, most of which will be from the muniments. The acts of Chapter are a helpful thread in guiding scholars through the great mass of documents, and it is fitting that the first two volumes to be published are those from Henry VIII's first collegiate foundation and those of the Elizabethan foundation down to 1609: from the death of Copernicus to the eve of the publication of the King James version of the Bible, the latter worked on in that same Jerusalem Chamber where Chapter had almost certainly met for close on fifty years, and in which twenty times a year it still does.

None of us doubts the importance of understanding our inheritance, of all that has made us what we are; yet we should never confuse our heritage – our buildings, our statutes, the way we have been shaped by history – with our tradition, for the latter must be a living and dynamic thing, preserving those aspects of the past that we need to guard and hand on to our successors. Part of Chapter's task is to discern the difference.

Publication would not have been possible without the generous help of those grant-awarding bodies named by Dr Richard Mortimer in his preface; nor without his own immaculate scholarship and research. Today's Chapter is very grateful.

Michael Mayne

GENERAL EDITOR'S PREFACE

This book is the first volume in a new venture, the Westminster Abbey Record Series. The aim is to publish documents, calendars, lists and indexes from the Abbey's very large and continuous archive, making its contents available both to scholars and to a wider interested public. There is enormous scope. Westminster Abbey's history and archive stretch back over a thousand years: the subjects which could be illustrated include the history of art and architecture, music, genealogy and local history – not only of the London area – as well as the life of the Abbey itself, and the services and events held within it. Much of what has happened here is of national interest, and justifies its own record series.

The first document to appear is the earliest Chapter Act Book, 1543–1609, which is edited in two volumes, the introduction and text down to 1556 in this first volume, the rest of the text and index coming out in volume two next year. The third volume in the Series will be a catalogue of the medieval obedientiary rolls by Barbara Harvey.

Launching a new record series is an act of faith, on the part of a number of people and organisations. It has been made possible by generous financial support from the Marc Fitch Fund, the British Academy, the Irene Scouloudi Foundation in association with the Institute of Historical Research, and the Dean and Chapter of Westminster. The objective, however, is for the Series to be self-supporting. The publishers, Boydell and Brewer, and especially Richard Barber, have been welcoming and enormously helpful throughout. The editor of the first two volumes, Dr C.S. Knighton, has given untiringly of his time, labour and expertise. I am very grateful to all of them.

The Muniment Room, Westminster Abbey   *Richard Mortimer*
March 1996

EDITOR'S ACKNOWLEDGEMENTS

I am indebted to the Dean and Chapter of Westminster for permission to consult and publish manuscripts in their possession. I am further grateful for their generosity in depositing the sole microfilm copy of their earliest Act Books in the Suffolk Record Office for my use there. I thank those in the Muniment Room and Library who have assisted my research there over many years, especially Miss Christine Reynolds. I also acknowledge help received from the custodians and staffs of the other repositories in which I have worked. At Westminster my thanks are particularly due to Dr Richard Mortimer, Keeper of the Muniments, for inviting me to edit the early chapter acts, and for superintending every stage towards publication. Needless to say all residual imperfections are my own.

I also remember with gratitude and respect the scholarly guidance of Dr Lawrence Tanner, former Librarian and Keeper of the Muniments, Mr Howard Nixon, former Librarian, and Mr Nicholas MacMichael, former Keeper of the Muniments.

Westminster   *C.S.K.*
The Innocents' Day 1995

ABBREVIATIONS IN PART ONE

APC	*Acts of the Privy Council of England*, n.s., ed. J.R. Dasent (1890–1907)
Atherton and Holderness, 'Estates'	I. Atherton and B.A. Holderness, 'The dean and chapter estates since the Reformation', in *Norwich Cathedral. Church, City and Diocese, 1096–1996*, ed. Atherton, E. Fernie, C. Harper-Bill and A. Hassell Smith (1996), 665–87
Aylmer and Cant, *York Minster*	*A History of York Minster*, ed. G.E. Aylmer and R.E. Cant (Oxford 1977)
BL	British Library
Bodl.	Bodleian Library, Oxford
Camden, *Reges*	W. Camden, *Reges, Reginae, Nobiles et alii in Ecclesia Collegiata B. Petri Westmonasterii sepulti usque . . . 1600* (1600)
CCC	Corpus Christi College, Cambridge
Chester	*The Marriage, Baptismal and Burial Registers of the Collegiate Church or Abbey of St Peter, Westminster*, ed. J.L. Chester (Harleian Soc. x, 1876)
Collinson, *Grindal*	P. Collinson, *Archbishop Grindal, 1519–1583. The Struggle for a Reformed Church* (1979)
Collinson, 'Protestant cathedral'	P. Collinson, 'The protestant cathedral, 1541–1660', in the following, 154–203
Collinson, Ramsay and Sparks, *Canterbury Cathedral*	*A History of Canterbury Cathedral*, ed. P. Collinson, N.L. Ramsay and M.J. Sparks (Oxford 1995)
CPR	*Calendar of the Patent Rolls*
CSPD	*Calendar of State Papers, Domestic*
CSPDEdVI	*Calendar of State Papers, Domestic* (revised) *Edward VI*
CSPDM	*Calendar of State Papers, Domestic* (revised) *Mary I* [forthcoming]
CSPV	*Calendar of State Papers, Venetian*
CUL	Cambridge University Library
Cust and Hughes, *Conflict*	*Conflict in Early Stuart England. Studies in Religion and Politics 1603–1642*, ed. R.P. Cust and A.L. Hughes (Harlow 1989)
Dart	J. Dart, *Westmonasterium, or the History and Antiquities of the Abbey Church of St Peter's, Westminster*, n.d.
DNB	*Dictionary of National Biography*
EcHR	*Economic History Review*
EDC	Ely Dean and Chapter Records
EDR	Ely Diocesan Records

Edwards, *Secular Cathedrals*	K. Edwards, *The English Secular Cathedrals in the Middle Ages* (2nd edn Manchester 1967)
Elton, *Parliament*	G.R. Elton, *The Parliament of England, 1559–1581* (Cambridge 1986)
Elton, *Reform and Renewal*	G.R. Elton, *Reform and Renewal. Thomas Cromwell and the Common Weal* (Cambridge 1973)
Emden	A.B. Emden, *A Biographical Register of the University of Oxford, A.D. 1501 to 1540* (Oxford 1974)
Field, *King's Nurseries*	J.C.D. Field, *The King's Nurseries. The Story of Westminster School* (1987)
Foster, *Al.*	*Alumni Oxonienses. The Members of the University of Oxford, 1500–1714*, ed. J. Foster (Oxford 1891–2)
Foster, 'Function of a bishop'	A.W. Foster, 'The function of a bishop: the career of Richard Neile, 1562–1640', in O'Day and Heal, *Continuity and Change*, 33–54
Foxe (ed. Pratt)	J. Foxe, *Acts and Monuments*, ed. J. Pratt (1870)
Garrett, *Marian Exiles*	C.H. Garrett, *The Marian Exiles. A study in the origins of Elizabethan Puritanism* (Cambridge 1938, repr. 1966)
GLRO	Greater London Record Office
Grace Book Δ	*Grace Book* Δ, *containing the records of the University of Cambridge for the years 1542–1589*, ed. J. Venn (Cambridge 1910)
Guildhall	Guildhall Library, London
Haigh, 'Chester'	C.A. Haigh, 'Finance and administration in a new diocese: Chester, 1541–1641', in O'Day and Heal, *Continuity and Change*, 145–66
Haines, 'Longdon'	R.M. Haines, 'The appropriation of Longdon church to Westminster Abbey', *Transactions of the Worcestershire Archaeological Society*, n.s. xxxviii (1962 for 1961), repr. in Haines, *Ecclesia Anglicana. Studies in the English Church of the Later Middle Ages* (Toronto 1989), 3–14
Harvey, *Estates*	B.F. Harvey, *Westminster Abbey and its Estates in the Middle Ages* (Oxford 1977)
Harvey, *Living and Dying*	B.F. Harvey, *Living and Dying in England, 1100–1540. The Monastic Experience* (Oxford 1993)
Heal, *Goldsmiths*	A. Heal, *The London Goldsmiths, 1200–1800. A record of the names and addresses of the craftsmen, their shop-signs and trade cards* (Cambridge 1935, repr. Newton Abbot 1972)
Heal, *Prelates*	F.M. Heal, *Of Prelates and Princes. A study of the economic and social position of the Tudor episcopate* (Cambridge 1980)
Hembry, *Bath and Wells*	P.M. Hembry, *The Bishops of Bath and Wells, 1540–1640. Social and Economic Problems* (1967)
Hist. Parl. 1509–1558	*The History of Parliament. The House of Commons, 1509–1558*, ed. S.T. Bindoff (1982)
Hist. Parl. 1558–1603	*The History of Parliament. The House of Commons, 1558–1603*, ed. P.W. Hasler (1981)
HJ	*Historical Journal*

HK	*A House of Kings. The History of Westminster Abbey*, ed. E.F. Carpenter (1966)
HMC	Royal Commission on Historical Manuscripts
HMC, *Salisbury MSS*	*Calendar of the Manuscripts of the Most Hon. the Marquis of Salisbury . . . at Hatfield House* (HMC, 1883–)
Hoyle, *Estates*	*The Estates of the English Crown, 1558–1640*, ed. R.W. Hoyle (Cambridge 1992)
Inst. Cant. sed. vac.	*Calendar of institutions by the chapter of Canterbury 'sede vacante'*, ed. C.W. Woodruff and I.J. Churchill (Kent Archaeological Soc., Records Branch, viii, 1923)
JBAA	*Journal of the British Archaeological Association*
Jones and Underwood, *King's Mother*	M.K. Jones and M.G. Underwood, *The King's Mother. Lady Margaret Beaufort, Countess of Richmond and Derby* (Cambridge 1992)
Jordan, *Young King*	W.K. Jordan, *Edward VI: the Young King. The Protectorship of the Duke of Somerset* (1968)
Kenyon-Thompson, *Ruthin School*	K.M. Kenyon-Thompson, *Ruthin School. The First Seven Centuries* (Ruthin 1974)
Knighton, 'Collegiate Foundations'	C.S. Knighton, 'Collegiate Foundations, 1540 to 1570, with special reference to St Peter in Westminster' (Ph.D. dissertation, University of Cambridge 1975)
Knighton, 'Economics'	C.S. Knighton, 'Economics and economies of a royal peculiar: Westminster Abbey 1540–1640', in O'Day and Heal, *Princes and Paupers*, 45–64
Knighton, 'Education'	C.S. Knighton, 'The provision of education in the new cathedral foundations of Henry VIII', in Marcombe and Knighton, *Close Encounters*, 18–42
Knowles, *Religious Orders*	M.D. Knowles, *The Religious Orders in England* (Cambridge 1948–59)
LAO	Lincolnshire Archives Office, Lincoln
Lehmberg, *Later Parliaments*	S.E. Lehmberg, *The Later Parliaments of Henry VIII, 1536–1547* (Cambridge 1977)
Lehmberg, *Ref. of Cathedrals*	S.E. Lehmberg, *The Reformation of Cathedrals. Cathedrals in English Society, 1485–1603* (Princeton 1988)
Le Neve	John Le Neve, *Fasti Ecclesiae Anglicanae, 1541–1857*, comp. J.M. Horne *et al.* (1969–) [cited without volume number] vii, *Ely, Norwich, Westminster and Worcester Dioceses* (1992)
Loades, *Conspiracies*	D.M. Loades, *Two Tudor Conspiracies* (Cambridge 1965)
Loades, *Reign of Mary*	D.M. Loades, *The Reign of Mary Tudor. Politics, government and religion in England, 1553–1558* (2nd edn 1991)
LP	*Letters and Papers, Foreign and Domestic, of the reign of Henry VIII*, ed. J.S. Brewer, J. Gairdner and R.H. Brodie (1862–1932)
MacCulloch, *Cranmer*	D.N.J. MacCulloch, *Thomas Cranmer. A Life* (1996)

Marcombe, 'Durham: old abbey writ large'	D. Marcombe, 'The Durham dean and chapter: old abbey writ large?', in O'Day and Heal, *Continuity and Change*, 125–44
Marcombe, *Last Principality*	*The Last Principality. Politics, religion and society in the Bishopric of Durham, 1494–1660*, ed. D. Marcombe (Studies in Local and Regional History, no. 1, Nottingham 1987)
Marcombe and Knighton, *Close Encounters*	*Close Encounters. English Cathedrals and Society since 1540*, ed. D. Marcombe and C.S. Knighton (Studies in Local and Regional History, no. 3, Nottingham 1991)
McKitterick, *Perne*	*Andrew Perne. Quatercentenary Studies*, ed. D.J. McKitterick (Cambridge Bibliographical Soc. Monographs, no. 11, 1991)
Mellows, *Peterborough*	*Peterborough Local Administration. The foundation of Peterborough Cathedral A.D. 1541*, ed. W.T. Mellows (Northamptonshire Record Soc. xiii, 1941 for 1939)
Mellows and Gifford	*Peterborough Local Administration. Elizabethan Peterborough*, ed. W.T. Mellows and D.H. Gifford (Northamptonshire Record Soc. xviii, 1956 for 1943–4)
Murray Smith	E.T. Murray Smith (née Bradley), *The Roll-Call of Westminster Abbey* (3rd edn 1903)
Nichols, *Hist. county of Leicester*	J. Nichols, *The History and Antiquities of the County of Leicester* (1795–1815)
n.s.	new series
O'Day and Heal, *Continuity and Change*	*Continuity and Change. Personnel and Administration of the Church in England, 1500–1642*, ed. M.R. O'Day and F.M. Heal (Leicester 1976)
O'Day and Heal, *Princes and Paupers*	*Princes and Paupers in the English Church, 1500–1800*, ed. M.R. O'Day and F.M. Heal (Leicester 1981)
OED	*Oxford English Dictionary*
Ollard	S.L. Ollard, *Fasti Wyndesorienses: the Deans and Canons of Windsor* (Historical Monographs relating to St George's Chapel, Windsor Castle, Windsor 1940)
O.W.	Old Westminster (former pupil of Westminster School)
Parker Corr.	*Correspondence of Matthew Parker, D.D., Archbishop of Canterbury*, ed. J. Bruce and T.T. Perowne (Parker Soc. 1853)
Pearce, *Monks*	E.H. Pearce, *The Monks of Westminster. Being a register of the brethren of the convent from the time of the Confessor down to the Dissolution* (Notes and Documents relating to Westminster Abbey, no. 5, Cambridge 1916)
Pepys	*The Diary of Samuel Pepys*, ed. R.C. Latham and W. Matthews (1970–83)
Perkins, *Worship and Ornaments*	J. Perkins, *Westminster Abbey, its Worship and Ornaments* (Alcuin Club, xxxiii, xxxiv, xxxvii, 1938–52)
Pine, *Singers*	E. Pine, *The Westminster Abbey Singers* (1953)
Porter, *Reformation and Reaction*	H.C. Porter, *Reformation and Reaction in Tudor Cambridge* (Cambridge 1958)

PRO	Public Record Office
Procter and Frere	F. Procter and W.H. Frere, *A new History of the Book of Common Prayer, with a rationale of its offices* (1901, repr. 1902)
Read, *Cecil*	C. Read, *Mr Secretary Cecil and Queen Elizabeth* (1955)
Reg. PX	*Register of Sermons preached at Paul's Cross, 1534–1642*, by M. MacLure [originally part of *The Paul's Cross Sermons, 1534–1642* (Toronto 1958)], rev. by P. Pauls and J.C. Boswell (Centre for Reformation and Renaissance Studies, Victoria University, University of Toronto, Occasional Publications vol. 6, Ottawa 1989)
Robinson, *Abbot's House*	J.A. Robinson, *The Abbot's House at Westminster* (Notes and Documents relating to Westminster Abbey, no. 4, Cambridge 1911)
Robinson, *Statutes*	J.A. R[obinson], *Notes regarding the earliest form of the Statutes of the Collegiate Church of St Peter, Westminster* (privately printed 1906)
Rosser	A.G. Rosser, *Medieval Westminster* (Oxford 1989)
ROW	*The Record of Old Westminsters*, ed. G.F.R. Barker, A.H. Stenning, *et al.* (1928–)
Sargeaunt	J. Sargeaunt, *Annals of Westminster School* (1898)
Seymour, *Ordeal by Ambition*	W. Seymour, *Ordeal by Ambition. An English family in the shadow of the Tudors* (1972)
Sheils, *Puritans*	W.J. Sheils, *The Puritans in the Diocese of Peterborough, 1558–1610* (Northamptonshire Record Soc. xxx, 1979)
Shirley, *Thirlby*	T.F. Shirley, *Thomas Thirlby. Tudor Bishop* (1964)
Skeeters, *Bristol*	M.C. Skeeters, *Community and Clergy. Bristol and the Reformation c.1530–c.1570* (Oxford 1993)
Soden, *Goodman*	G.I. Soden, *Godfrey Goodman, Bishop of Gloucester, 1583–1656* (1953)
Stanley	A.P. Stanley, *Historical Memorials of Westminster Abbey* (5th edn 1882)
Statutes (1)	Mellows, *Peterborough*, 75–104/104–21 [Latin/English text of Henrician statutes for new foundations]
Statutes (2)	*Appendix* to the *First Report of Her Majesty's Commissioners appointed to inquire into the state and condition of the Cathedral and Collegiate Churches in England and Wales* (1854), 79–108 [text of Elizabethan statutes for Westminster]
STC	*A Short-Title Catalogue of Books printed in England, Scotland and Ireland . . . 1475–1640*, ed. A.W. Pollard and G.R. Redgrave, 2nd edn by W.A. Jackson, F.S. Ferguson and K.F. Pantzer (1986–91)
Thompson, *English Clergy*	A.H. Thompson, *The English Clergy and their Organization in the Middle Ages* (Oxford 1947)
TLMAS	*Transactions of the London and Middlesex Archaeological Society*
TRHS	*Transactions of the Royal Historical Society*
VCH	*Victoria County History*

Venn	*Alumni Cantabrigienses. A Biographical List of . . . the University of Cambridge*, ed. J. and J.A. Venn, part 1 (to 1751) (Cambridge 1922–7)
Vis. Art.	*Visitation Articles and Injunctions of the period of the Reformation*, ed. W.H. Frere and W. P. McC. Kennedy (Alcuin Club, xiv–xvi, 1910)
Walcott, 'Inventories'	M.E.C. Walcott, 'The inventories of Westminster Abbey at the dissolution', *TLMAS* iv (1873), 313–64
WA Library	Westminster Abbey Library
WAM	Westminster Abbey Muniments
WAM Reg.	WAM Register (Lease) Book
WCA	Westminster City Archives
Wells Act Book	*Wells Cathedral Chapter Act Book, 1666–83*, ed. D.S. Bailey (Somerset Record Soc. lxxii and HMC, 1973)
Westlake, *St Margaret's*	H.F. Westlake, *St Margaret's Westminster. The Church of the House of Commons* (1914)
Westlake, *Westminster Abbey*	H.F. Westlake, *Westminster Abbey. The Church, Convent and College of St Peter, Westminster* (1923)
Wriothesley	*A chronicle of England during the reigns of the Tudors, from A.D. 1485 to 1559, by Charles Wriothesley, Windsor herald*, ed. W.D. Hamilton (Camden Soc., n.s. xi, xx, 1875, 1877)
WRO	Wiltshire Record Office, Trowbridge

Works published in London or by issuing societies unless otherwise stated. References to *CSPDEdVI, CSPDM, CSPV* and *LP* are to entry numbers. 'The Abbey' is Westminster Abbey, the place and the continuing institution; 'the abbey' is the Benedictine monastery there.

MARK CONVERSIONS

The mark was a unit of account, not an actual coin

1 mark		13s	4d
4 marks	£2	13s	4d
5 marks	£3	6s	8d
10 marks	£6	13s	4d
11 marks	£7	6s	8d
20 marks	£13	6s	8d
25 marks	£16	13s	4d
40 marks	£26	13s	4d
50 marks	£33	6s	8d
80 marks	£53	6s	8d
1000 marks	£666	13s	4d

INTRODUCTION

I. THE CHAPTER AND ITS ACTS

(i) *General*

The chapter act or minute book is a distinctive archival product of colleges of secular clergy; nothing wholly similar is generated by monastic chapters, even those of cathedral priories. The earliest *acta* of secular cathedrals and other collegiate churches were recorded periodically in liturgical books. By the fourteenth century these institutions had found it necessary to maintain separate registers of their corporate decisions. Some chapters laid down rules for their acts; elsewhere the format depended on the inclination of individual deans and chapter clerks.[1] The most recent judgement on chapter acts as an historical source is that those of Canterbury would be 'less than fully informative even if they were complete and undamaged'.[2] Westminster's acts have survived more completely than those of Canterbury, failing to record only brief periods at the terminal points of the chapter's existence between the first foundation and the civil war. In assessing the information the acts yield, it should be remembered that they are not a journal of events, nor a report of discussions, but a record of decisions taken. The development of that record must be considered in the context of the unique constitutional history of the church of Westminster in the sixteenth century, and by relation to the experience and interests of those who governed it.

---

[1] For the evolution of chapter acts generally see Edwards, *Secular Cathedrals*, 28–31. D.M. Owen, *The Records of the Established Church in England* (British Records Association, Archives and the User, no. 1, 1970), 54 n. 73 lists printed chapter acts of cathedral and collegiate churches of the 16th century. Cf. also the subsequent *Wells Act Book*. Most closely related to the present edition are *The Chapter Acts of the Dean and Canons of Windsor, 1430, 1523–1672*, ed. S.M. Bond (Historical Monographs relating to St George's Chapel, Windsor Castle, Windsor 1966) which contains transcription and calendared entries, *Extracts from the two earliest Minute Books of the Dean and Chapter of Norwich, 1566–1649*, ed. J.F. Williams and B. Cozens-Hardy (Norfolk Record Soc. xxiv, 1953), a calendar, and Mellows and Gifford, 43–55, transcript of Peterborough acts 1585–1604. The only general listing of surviving MS act books is in the Pilgrim Trust Survey of Ecclesiastical Archives (typescript at BL, Lambeth Palace, Bodl. and CUL: cf. Owen, *op. cit.*, 10 n. 6). For variations in composition of acts of 19th century cathedrals see P.L.S. Barrett, *Barchester. English Cathedral Life in the Nineteenth Century* (1993), pp. xviii–xix.

[2] Collinson, 'Protestant cathedral', 172.

(ii) *Westminster Abbey: constitutional changes 1540–1560*

Westminster Abbey made its surrender on 16 January 1540.[3] On December 17 following the church was re-established as a cathedral for a new diocese of Westminster, and by the same instrument the first bishop, dean and canons were nominated.[4] Westminster and the other cathedrals of Henry VIII's creation are known as the 'new foundations', in distinction to the nine 'old' secular foundations, and include the former cathedral priories of Canterbury, Durham, Winchester and others, together with those former abbeys now made cathedral churches for the first time. Westminster's nearest equivalents are the cathedrals of Bristol, Chester, Gloucester, Oxford and Peterborough.[5] The establishment at Westminster consisted of a dean and twelve canons (who constituted the chapter), twelve minor canons, a gospeller and epistoler, twelve singing men (lay vicars), ten boy choristers, a master of the choristers, a schoolmaster, under master and forty scholars, two sextons (sacrists), twelve almsmen, an auditor and thirteen domestic servants. In addition the college included ten readers and twenty students resident at Oxford and Cambridge.[6] The king's commissioners issued statutes to most of the new foundations in 1544; those for Westminster have not survived, but there is record of their receipt at the time (**19** n. 46).

The diocese of Westminster was abolished on 1 April 1550, and the area of its former jurisdiction reverted to the diocese of London.[7] The dean and chapter, however, remained in being, and indeed the whole collegiate body continued to function regardless of the disappearance of the bishop. This irregular condition was notionally rectified by act of parliament in 1552 which declared Westminster to have become a second cathedral for the diocese of London.[8] On 26 September 1556 the dean and chapter surrendered their church to Queen Mary, who restored the Benedictine observance.[9] When the monks left for the second and perhaps last time in July 1559,[10] the church and its property reverted to the crown.[11] On 21 May 1560 Queen Elizabeth I founded a new collegiate church (here called the 'second' to distinguish it from the Henrician cathedral) which in most respects re-established the arrangements of 1540, but most importantly

---

3 PRO, E 322/260 (*LP* xv, 69). WAM 16473 is an imperfect 18th century copy.
4 WAM LXXXI (*LP* xvi, 379(30)).
5 For the new foundations see Lehmberg, *Ref. of Cathedrals*, 81–97; Marcombe, 'Durham: old abbey writ large'; D.M. Owen, 'From monastic house to cathedral chapter: the experiences at Ely, Norwich and Peterborough', in Marcombe and Knighton, *Close Encounters*, 4–17; Skeeters, *Bristol*, 123–6.
6 WAM 6478, ff. 1–5v.
7 *CPR* 1549–51, pp. 171–2.
8 5 & 6 Edw. VI c. 36. WAM 6490; Reg. III, ff. 228–230v.
9 WAM Reg. III, f. 307. For the chronology of the monastic restoration see Knowles, *Religious Orders*, iii, 425.
10 Wriothesley, ii, 145–6.
11 1 Eliz. I c. 24.

without the superimposition of episcopal control.[12] New statutes were subsequently drafted.[13] Although the dean and chapter of Westminster, in common
with all others, was uprooted by the republican government in 1649, its constitution has been substantially unaltered since Elizabeth's charter.

The medieval abbey of Westminster had enjoyed exemption from episcopal
and provincial authority, a status enshrined in Archbishop Langton's arbitration
of 1222.[14] In 1534, by virtue of the Dispensations Act, churches such as Westminster which had known no ecclesiastical superior save the pope became in
effect royal peculiars.[15] This was reflected in the style of the abbot and convent,
which became *regie majestati immediate subjecti*.[16] The erection of the bishopric and
cathedral in 1540 necessarily extinguished whatever peculiar status may have
been deemed to inhere in the church of Westminster beyond the surrender of
the abbot and convent. Despite this there are indications that the first collegiate
church, while still part of the diocese of Westminster and (from 1550) of London, began to exercise peculiar jurisdictions of the former abbey. These had
been in Westminster itself and in properties belonging to St Martin-le-Grand.[17]
In April 1549 the privy council complained to the dean and chapter about the
maladministration of their steward at St Martin's,[18] and no doubt in consequence a new commission was sealed for jurisdiction there (**88**), the activities of
which are recorded from 25 February 1550, and continue until 1559.[19] Of much
more significance is the resumption of peculiar jurisdiction in Westminster itself.
On 17 March 1555 on a page in the probate register last written upon in 1539,
the dean and chapter announced that there followed acts of testamentary jurisdiction *infra exemptam jurisdictionem ecclesie cathedralis sive collegiate divi Petri Westm'*
which is said to be *ad Romanam curiam nullo medio pertinente*. Business then continues
until 18 September 1556, shortly before the surrender of the secular chapter.[20] It
must be assumed (in the absence of any more positive evidence) that this renewal
of exemption was the result of the repeal in January 1555 of the Henrician

---

12 WAM LXXXVII (*CPR* 1558–60, pp. 397–403).
13 WAM 25122 (earliest version), 25123, 25124; *Statutes (2)*. See Robinson, *Statutes*, 6, 15–16;
   HK, 452–3.
14 WAM 12743. For the earlier history of Westminster's exemption see M.D. Knowles, *The
   Monastic Order in England* (Cambridge 1940), 579–80, 589–91.
15 25 Hen. VIII c. 21.
16 CUL, EDR G/1/7, f. 105v (presentation to the living of Bassingbourn, 1536).
17 For St Martin's see J.H. Denton, *English Royal Free Chapels 1100–1300. A Constitutional Study*
   (Manchester 1970), 28–40.
18 WAM 13242.
19 WCA, Reg. Wyks, ff. 163–75.
20 WCA, Reg. Bracy, ff. 72–92v. See *Indexes to the Ancient Testamentary Records of Westminster*, ed.
   A.M. Burke (1913), 72, though the date of the opening act is there misunderstood as 1554,
   as in *A Calendar of grants of probate and administration and of other testamentary records of the
   Commissary Court of the venerable the Dean and Chapter of Westminster*, ed. J. Smith and F.C.
   Coleman (printed for probate purposes only 1864), p. vi.

legislation.[21] Westminster's theoretical status as a second cathedral in London diocese had been largely ignored by the crown, which since 1550 had presented to the chapter of Westminster without reference to episcopal authority.[22] The bishop of London nevertheless had to give his consent to the dissolution of Westminster Cathedral in 1556.[23] In restoring the monks Queen Mary could not reconstitute the Confessor's foundation, which like all the English religious houses had become canonically extinct by virtue of Paul IV's bull *Praeclara* of 1555; but she did (it was claimed) restore the rights and jurisdiction of the former monastic foundation, and in effect founded a new exempt abbey.[24] The Elizabethan supremacy act brought papal jurisdictions once more into the crown's hand.[25] Westminster's present exemption may therefore be said to owe as much to Queen Mary as to her more honoured sister.

(iii) *The first chapter meetings*

The first chapter was not much prepared for the administrative duties with which it was entrusted, since few of its members had experience of secular colleges. The first dean and six of his chapter colleagues were former monks (such transfers occurred in varying proportions in all the Henrician foundations). Of the six newcomers, one (Redman) was master of the King's Hall at Cambridge, and three others (Bellasis, Haynes and Leighton) were deans or canons elsewhere.[26] For reasons unexplained there was an unusually long delay between the foundation of the cathedral and its endowment. In most cases the respective grants were made within a few weeks, but the dean and chapter of Westminster had to wait until 5 August 1542 for their endowment.[27] During this interval of almost two years the chapter had no property, and so no control of its income. The abbey's former properties were administered by the court of augmentations,

---

[21] 1 & 2 Ph. and Mar. c. 8. Cf. S.J. Loach, *Parliament and the Crown in the reign of Mary Tudor* (Oxford 1986), 111 & n. 28.

[22] The crown (as patron) should have addressed presentation to the bishop, who would then institute and direct the chapter to install. But on 20 October 1551 Edward VI sent a *mandamus* to the dean and chapter for the admission of Thomas Bricket as canon (WAM Reg. III, f. 178v), as which he was installed the same day: below, no. **184** (f. 272v). Cf. also no. **110** & n. 210. All other appointments to the chapter between 1550 and 1556 likewise by-passed episcopal authority, save that of Hugh Griffith, who was instituted by the bishop of London (Ridley) in succession to himself as canon of Westminster on 6 March 1553, with episcopal *mandamus* of same date to the dean and chapter (Guildhall MS 9531/12, ff. 317–317v; WAM Reg. III, f. 179v) followed by installation on July 4: below, no. **184** (f. 273). Cf. also no. **138** & n. 264. For all appointments see Le Neve, 69, 72–7, 79–80, 82.

[23] WAM 12792. Guildhall MS 9531/12, f. 407.

[24] *CPR* 1555–7, pp. 348–54, 546. WAM 7344. Knowles, *Religious Orders*, iii, 423, 426, 452.

[25] 1 Eliz. I c. 1.

[26] Pearce, *Monks*, 176 (Elfrede), 182 (Malvern), 183 (Dalianns), 185 (Essex), 185–6 (Charyte), 188 (Faith), 189–90 (Boston). *DNB* (Belasyse, Heynes, Redman). Emden, 349 (Leighton).

[27] WAM LXXXIII (*LP* xvii, 714(5)). For details of all new foundation charters and endowments see Knighton, 'Collegiate Foundations', 25.

which paid the salaries of the newly created body and all the domestic expenses of the church, including the bread, wine and candles for liturgical use.[28] For this reason the dean and chapter's own chief records do not begin until after August 1542. Most previous citation of the chapter acts has dated them from 3 March 1542.[29] The first extant entry in the book (**1**) is dated March 3 without year. Above this later hands have added 'H.8.33' and '1542', but these dates are not reconcilable. 3 March 33 Henry VIII would have fallen within 1541 as then calculated (the new year 1542 not beginning until March 25). The next act (**2**) is dated March 4, again without year. The third entry (**3**) is, however, dated by its writer 29 March 34 Henry VIII, which is 1543 by old and new styles. The first three entries are thus March 3, March 5, and 29 March 1543, so it is improbable in the first place that entries should have been discontinued for precisely a year from 3 and 5 March 1542. The case for dating all these March entries as 1543 is supported by the signature to no. **1** of Francis Turpin, who was not first named to a canonry until 5 December 1542 in place of the deceased Thomas Baxter.[30] Baxter was still alive on 23 October 1542.[31] Baxter may have been absent from the chapter had it met in March 1542; it is possible that Turpin may have added his signature to a minute made before his appointment.[32] But the greater likelihood is that Turpin signed in March 1543 when he was a member of the chapter, rather than to an act made when he was not. More certain is the evidence of the rear of the Act Book, which on 10 February 34 Henry VIII (i.e. 1543 by modern reckoning) was begun as a register of sealing fees (**187**). Allowing for the loss of the first nine folios of chapter business, it is thus reasonable to assume that the main series of acts was begun at about the same time as the approach *a tergo*. Act no. **2** orders a survey of estates, but this cannot have been made in March 1542 because there was not yet an estate to be surveyed. The lease register of the dean and chapter contains no entry before 20 October 1542.[33] The chapter seal was acquired in 1543 – the first payment for it is dated January 6, the last on June 27.[34] It may yet be objected that act no. **1**, by making the most basic liturgical and business dispositions, has about it an inaugural air. But no. **2** refers to an act of March 2, which must have been on one of the now excised folios (presumably f. 9); act no. **1** cannot therefore be reckoned as the first of which we have evidence. No doubt the removal (for whatever cause) of the original opening pages made it desirable to start afresh with elementary regulations.

[28] PRO, SC 6/Hen. VIII/2414–17; LR 2/111, ff. 56–76; E 314/22/1. WAM 37038, 37041.

[29] Westlake, *Westminster Abbey*, i, 208 and *HK*, 113 being the most substantial modern histories. Only Pearce (*Monks*, 185) gives 3 March 1543 (*s.a.* Essex [*alias* Baxter], on the unstated premise that the act on f. 10 (**1**) is signed by his successor).

[30] *LP* xvii, 1251(16). Patent delivered December 8 (and therefore so dated in Le Neve, 78).

[31] WAM 37036, f. 1.

[32] For retrospective signatures see below, pp. xxiii–xxiv.

[33] WAM Reg. III, title and f. 5.

[34] WAM 37046, ff. 2v, 6v. No. **2** shows that the seal was to hand by March 5.

Thereafter the acts are continuous until the demise of the secular chapter in 1556 (**182**). Certain supplementary matter from this first period is entered in later parts of the manuscript (**183–7**), more fully noted below (p. xxvi). Chapter acts resume shortly after the Elizabethan foundation (**188**), but are then absent for a year until the incumbency of Dean Goodman (**189**). The first volume was filled by 1609 (**545**), and the sequence continues in a volume which carries the record to the summer of 1642, whereafter the dean and chapter was dispersed and the Abbey came under parliamentary control.[35]

(iv) *Time and place of meetings*

The first extant act (**1**) orders a further meeting every Saturday in the chapter house. Such meetings either never took place with that regularity, or their occurrence was not invariably minuted. Conversely not all meetings that *are* recorded took place on Saturdays. A meeting scheduled for 1 o'clock on (Tuesday) 5 February 1544 had to be abandoned because only the dean and seven canons were present (**15**). Another chapter appears to have been dissolved for the same cause on Monday 11 February following (**18**). On the following day it was decided that, pending the ruling of the anticipated royal statutes, the dean and four canons should constitute a quorum (**19**). The 1544 statutes enjoined fortnightly chapters for regular business, with two general chapters each year.[36] The fortnightly cycle was required by chapter order of January 1546 (**48**) and subsequently (**59, 60**). Some meetings were still called off, even though the minimum number required by no. **19** appeared (**61, 62, 65, 71, 75**). Among many reforms made by Dean Cox in 1549, a return to weekly meetings, after 8 o'clock matins on Saturdays, was ordered (**94**).

The second collegiate church made less frequent regulations for its meetings, and the statutes are not specific on this point. The Saturday meeting is in 1563 significantly referred to as the choir chapter, at which one of the canons was to preside (**199**). These assemblies had therefore by this date (if not before) come to be distinct from the chapter meetings proper. These were poorly attended on occasion in 1568 and 1569 (**241, 251**), and throughout the 1570s, 1580s and 1590s, when the 'no quorum' formula is repeated with withering regularity. In 1570-1 the problem was blamed on the delinquency of the chapter clerk, who absconded with the petty cash (**258–60**). By 1585 it was decided to concentrate business on two main chapters in the year, one at the time of the audit in early December, the other after Easter (**374**). In 1593 there was no quorum at the December special chapter, but on this occasion the plague was a reasonable excuse (**443, 444**). Even those who turned up to meetings might be disposed to drift away; it became necessary to stipulate that only those who stayed to the end of the proceedings would qualify for the all-important dividends of fees and fines (**429**). A meeting in 1569 at which five items were decided in three hours

---

[35] An edition of Act Book II is intended later in this series.
[36] *Statutes (1)*, 101/119.

was then prorogued for a further four hours at a later day (**246**). By the end of the century the half-yearly meetings were commonly spread over two days (e.g. **541**, **543**).[37]

Although no. **1** and later acts refer to meetings in the chapter house, this cannot be the monastic chapter house, which at the dissolution was retained by the crown, first as the chamber of the House of Commons (as which it had previously been regularly requisitioned) and later (1547–1866) as a record office. It remains in public ownership. The act books are without comment on the location of meetings until 20 December 1637 when it is described as 'usuall' and December 13 when for the first time meeting in Jerusalem Chamber is specified.[38] It is likely that the tradition of meeting in this famous room in the Deanery was by then long established. But for the whole period of the first collegiate church the former Abbot's House was in the occupation of Bishop Thirlby and then the Lords Wentworth, the second of whom returned it to the church of Westminster in 1557 – that is to the monastery as at that time restored.[39] Only from 1560, therefore, did the dean occupy the present Deanery, and only since that time can it be presumed that Jerusalem was available for chapter meetings. Stanley states that meetings were held there since 1555, but his source[40] refers to no. **179** below, an order of 7 February 1556 (new style) that 'the howse in the whiche Mother Jone dothe dwell in shalbe a chapter howse'. But (if the wording of the act is continuous), Joan's house faced Westminster Hall, and so must have been on the opposite side of the church to the Abbot's House. Nor does it seem likely that Jerusalem could have afforded domestic accommodation in itself. The most likely explanation is that no. **179** means Joan's house was to be for the use of a member of the chapter. There remains a puzzle about the whereabouts of chapter meetings from 1543 to 1556. A payment in 1543 for mending windows in the church and chapter house[41] would seem to indicate that the meeting place was (a) not within the church itself, and (b) set apart for that purpose.

(v) *Signatures*

A man's signature to the Act Book does not necessarily mean he was present in chapter on the date at the head of the act. J. Pekyns signs to no. **8** of 4 May 1543, although he was not appointed until May 18.[42] Keble signs to no. **63** of 15 June 1547, at which time he had been instituted but not yet installed.[43] De

37 Cf. Canterbury, where concentration on two business meetings a year was intended to prevent a small number of activists from sharing the dividends among themselves: Collinson, 'Protestant cathedral', 173.
38 WAM Chapter Act Book II, ff. 65, 67v.
39 WAM 6485. Robinson, *Abbot's House*, 13–14. Cf. no. **156** below.
40 Stanley, 378 n. 3; his source is Walcott, 'Inventories', 359 note d (p. 47 in separate issue).
41 WAM 37046, f. 6v.
42 Nomination May 16: *LP* xviii, I, 623(70).
43 Instituted (by bishop of Westminster), May 25: Guildhall MS 9531/12, f. 246. Installed

Salinas signs to no. **154** of 13 May 1554, the day before his *mandamus* for installation (which took place on May 18).[44] Moreman signs also to no. **154**, but his patent is not dated until the following May 22.[45] No. **8** concerns the payment of canons' stipends to the day of death, and so was of special importance. The act to which Keble signed concerned a gift to his patron, the duke of Somerset. No. **154** concerned de Salinas personally but not Moreman. Bricket and Nowell sign to no. **109** of 8 November 1550, though both were appointed in 1551.[46] It is likely that Bricket and Nowell, who were the first to join the chapter since the making of no. **109**, were required to assent to its extensive provisions at the time of their installation. Most notably acts of 1574 and 1581 concerning services and sermons are signed retrospectively by almost all canons appointed during the residual currency of Act Book I (**291**, **346**). The only sure indication of presence is an attendance list (e.g. **36**, **62**, **246**) or when, in the absence of a quorum, the signatories are said to be the only attenders.[47]

H. Perkyns signs to no. **153** although he had been deprived on the previous day.[48] But Perkyns was an unconventional signatory, and from time to time registered a dissenting opinion: against the wearing of hoods (**88**), or grants with which he disagreed (**257**, **261**, **273**).

II. The Manuscript and the Edition

(i) *Description of the manuscript*

Act Book I is a bound paper volume, 11 x 8½ ins, foliated +1–+23 (and +24 excised), so numbered in a modern pencilled hand and forming the first quire, which has a stepped index cut 1½ ins from the right edge, with rubricated initials; ff. 1–9 excised; ff. 10–313, so numbered in ink and contemporary with the currency of the acts – no. **444** of 1593 carries a cross-reference to an earlier entry identified by this foliation – with occasional errors of numeration and excisions noted as they occur in the text here printed. The volume has a limp leather cover over a limp vellum sheet; the cover decorated with metal stamps and tacketed across the spine using twisted vellum strips through pads of leather on vellum, the back cover extended to form a flap to cover the fore-edge. The

---

June 21: below, no. **184** (f. 272v). Le Neve (p. 73) gives date of no. **63** for installation but f. for no. **184**.

[44] *Mandamus* May 14: WAM Reg. III, f. 181. Installation below, no. **184** (f. 273v).

[45] *CPR* 1553–4, p. 128.

[46] Le Neve, 72, 82.

[47] Retrospective signing has also been noted in the contemporary privy council registers: D.E. Hoak, *The King's Council in the reign of Edward VI* (Cambridge 1976), 13–14, 18–19. Cf. also G. Haslam, 'Jacobean phoenix: the duchy of Cornwall in the principates of Henry Frederick and Charles', in Hoyle, *Estates*, 278. No doubt similar practice may be shown for many corporate bodies.

[48] See n. 299 to no. **153**.

whole book is protected by a chemise of indeterminate date, probably sheepskin, 24 x 21 ins at maximum extent when flat.[49]

The inner cover bears record of the ownership of William Coupper, grocer, 1524 (**II**). Much of the index pages contain names, presumably this man's clients (not here reproduced). The grocer himself appears to have been a tenant of the abbey,[50] but no explanation can be offered of why or when the book came to be used by the dean and chapter. That it was already bound when acquired by the dean and chapter seems evident from the indications of its former use, and is further demonstrated by the entering of material in its latter pages (**184–7**) in the 1540s.[51]

(ii) *Previous treatments*

A transcript of Act Book I was made for the dean and chapter in 1904 by Mr A. Rogers of Cambridge University Library.[52] A single negative microfilm of the original was made following a chapter decision of 1950.[53] Until the 1970s the early act books were kept in the Chapter Office; but they are now kept in the Muniment Room.[54] The present edition is based on a new transcription; it has not been thought necessary to record variant readings in the Rogers transcription or in extracts which have been previously printed.[55]

---

[49] I am indebted to Mr Douglas East, bookbinder to the dean and chapter, for the description of the binding here followed.

[50] See below, no. **51** & n. 103, no. **114** & n. 224.

[51] WAM Reg. III (1542–56) was acquired in parchment sheets, and had been bound (for 1s 8d) by 1543: WAM 37046, ff. 4v, 7. By contrast episcopal registers were commonly kept in separate quires and not bound until the completion of each pontificate: D.M. Smith, *Guide to Bishops' Registers of England and Wales. A Survey from the Middle Ages to the abolition of episcopacy in 1646* (Royal Historical Soc. 1981), p. x.

[52] WA Library 5.C.3 (formerly Gal.0.3.3); this was corrected by Dean Armitage Robinson. Some extracts had been transcribed by an 18th century librarian, H. Brooker: WAM 63853.

[53] *HK*, 353.

[54] For the archive in general see principally L.E. Tanner, 'The nature and use of the Westminster Abbey Muniments', *TRHS*, 4th ser. xix (1936), 43–80.

[55] Among published extracts may be noted: J.W. Clark, 'On ancient libraries', *Proceedings of the Cambridge Antiquarian Society*, n.s. iii (1899 for 1894–8), 50–1 (**85**) [mis-dated 15 Dec. 1548 for 14 Jan. 1549], 51 (Goodman) (**296**), 51 (rules) (**397**), 52 (**430**); Robinson, *Abbot's House*, 51 (**11, 46, 85**) [the last mis-dated 15 Dec. 1548 for 14 Jan. 1549], 57 (**262, 263**), 58 (**218**) [mis-dated 24 for 29 Dec. 1565]; Perkins, *Worship and Ornaments*, iii, 45 (**85**), 93–4 (**286**); Pine, *Singers*, 46 (**12**) [mis-dated 25 for 26 Jan. 1544], 47 (**14**), 47–8 (**66**), 48 (subsidy) (**50**) [mis-dated 20 Feb. 1545 for 20 Mar. 1546], 48 (granary) (**69**) [mis-dated 6 for 9 July 1547], 49 (**49**), 54 (lecterns) (**50**) [mis-dated 15 Dec. for 14 Jan. 1549], 54 (plate) (**109**), 55 (scholarships) (**127**), 55 (services) (**94**), 56 ('chapel' *recte* 'chapter' minutes) (**185**, at f. 278v), 56 (discipline) (**92, 115**), 61 (**154**) [corrupt but includes later marginalia not in this edn], 66 (**176**) [mis-dated 1555 for 1556], 77–8 (**202**) [mis-dated 23 Mar. 1563 for 1 May 1564], 78 (**213**), 93–4 (**529**), 94–5 (**533**); *HK*, 113 (plate) (**109**) [not first entry as stated but of 8 Nov. 1550], 113 (services) (**1**), 113 (hours) (**14**), 113 (sermons) (**2**), 113 (Henry VII) (**7**), 113–14 (master of the choristers) (**12**), 114 (chapters) (**7**), 114 ('new statutes' *recte* chapter

(iii) *Conspectus of present edition*

Although the main series of chapter acts occurs in chronological sequence through the volume, it is preceded by some miscellaneous notes of contemporary and later date, and occasionally interspersed with supplementary sequences which formerly stood apart, but which were eventually reached and surrounded by the main series. For technical reasons the edition of Act Book I is issued in two parts. The argument for splitting the coverage between the first and second collegiate churches was felt to be so persuasive as to outweigh the consideration that the resulting parts would be of unequal length. But the opportunity is therefore taken to rectify the mild and accidental disorder of the original – without, it is hoped, destroying the authenticity of the edition. Part One contains all material deriving from the first collegiate church; Part Two contains matter from 1560 to 1609.

In summary (omitting blanks, excisions and irregularities of foliation):

MS ff.	*Contents*	*Edition no.*
unnumbered	miscellaneous notes	**I–III**
+1–+23v	⎧ grocer's index	[omitted]
	⎨ miscellaneous notes	**IV–VII**
	⎩ modern index to acts	[omitted]
10–102	acts 1543–56	**1–182**
104–271	acts 1560–1603	**188–528**
272	order about fees 1553	**183**
272v–274	admission of canons 1547–54	**184**
274v–276	acts 1603–4	**529–531**
277v–282v	admission of inferiors 1548–56	**185**
283v–298	acts 1604–1609	**532–545**
299	memorandum on goods seized 1553	**186**
303–303v	election of scholars 1572–6	**546**
304–8	table of contents	[omitted]
311v	order for sermons 1564	**547**
rear cover, 313–312	register of seal fees 1543	**187**

Entries **I–VII, 1–187** are in Part One; **188–547** in Part Two.

---

orders) (**32**) [mis-dated 15 Dec. for 22 Jan. 1545], 114 (attendance) (**69**), 114 (hospitality) (**94**), 114 (wheat) (**109**) [mis-dated 1546 for 1550], 117 (plate 1550) (**109**), 117 (plate [mis-dated 1551 for] 1552) (**125**), 117 (services) (**94**), 117–18 (discipline) (**92, 115**), 119 (goods seized) (**186**), 120 (discipline) (**176**) [mis-dated 1553 for 1556], 137–8 (housing) (**340**), 138 (library) (**397, 430**), 141 (usher) (**521**), 141–2 (choir) (**524**) [mis-dated 'following year' (to 1601) for 1603], 142 (plague) (**525**), 143 (fabric) (**529**), 145 (household dissolved) (**543**), 145 (moderating expenses) (**544**), 145–6 (Sutton) (**542**) [mis-dated 1607 for 1608], 419, (**12**).

(iv) *Editorial conventions*

Abbreviations are expanded silently where commonplace or where the particular writer's preferred forms are elsewhere explicit; but the MS is in many different hands, and uniformity is impossible throughout. The very frequent 'Westm'' for Westminster is left as abbreviated, as are other proper names for which the form is not certain, and the prefixes 'Mres' for Mistress, and 'Mr' (which in the period of this MS shifts in representation from 'Master' to 'Mister'). The letters 'c' and 't', 'i' and 'j', 'u' and 'v' are transcribed according to modern usage; but in some cases a juxtaposition (e.g. 'aucthorise') requires special treatment. Words ending '-on' are not rendered '-ion' unless there is a mark of abbreviation more distinctive than a final flourish, and 'on' (for 'one') is retained; similarly words are not accorded a final '-e' unless the loop or tail is pronounced. The double 'ff' is rendered 'F' where an upper-case initial has been editorially imposed, but otherwise is retained. Thorn is rendered as 'th' except in text notes at entries nos **1** and **114** where points of distinction are made. Numerals are left as in the MS, save that 'iiij^{xx}' (for '80') is given in the more common format $\overset{xx}{\text{iiij}}$. Suprascript letters are normally lowered, though retained for date formulae. Sums of money are represented as 'vj li. xiij s. iiij d.' (for £6 13s 4d).

Capitalization, punctuation and paragraphing are editorial; but the spacing of the earlier entries reflects the appearance of the MS without adhering to its precise arrangement.

The accidental omission or compression of single letters within a word is normally corrected without comment. More substantial textual faults, corrections and elisions are noted in the text notes, which form a separate alphabetical sequence for each entry in which they occur (except for nos **184** and **185** where the length of these entries makes it necessary to place the text notes at the foot of the pages to which they refer). Most corrections are introduced by 'repl.' (for 'replacing') which is flagged to the first word of the matter subject to the correction. Interlined addenda are noted '(number of words) inserted', words counting backwards from and including the word flagged (and words are counted as here printed, i.e. 'shalbe' is one word and 'by cause' is two). Marginalia in ink, which are contemporary or closely contemporary with the text, are included; but pencilled marginalia of later date are omitted.

Names following '*Signed:*' are editorial and standard; the dean's signature (when occurring) stands first and is so printed; other signatures are printed as approximately appearing vertically then left to right, which does not necessarily represent the order of signing (cf. p. xxiv above) nor any order of precedence, save that the subdean's name generally appears second (or, in the dean's absence, first). All variant forms (as of other MS spellings) are given in the index. But certain non-standard entries show the MS form of signature, and all comments made by signatories are transcribed.

In the footnotes the details of leases, appointments to offices and presentations to benefices have, wherever possible been collated with the corresponding entries in the Register Books. For leases the date, term and annual rent, together with any special provisions of interest, are given in the notes when not stated in the Act Book, or where variant from the details there. If no registered copy was made the data is sometimes available from original leases or other documents; but these additional sources (though frequently extant in profusion) have not normally been cited in addition to the register. The Act Book contains progressively more complete details of leases; the extent of information here supplied consequently diminishes.

Full details of the appointment of deans and canons are available elsewhere,[56] and a biographical register of these persons is projected for the present series. Such particulars are therefore largely absent from this volume.

III. Survey of contents

(i) *Principal entries*

Apart from references to the bishop's house (**11**) and to an untraced episcopal injunction (**14**) the only reflection of Westminster's brief status as a cathedral is a negative one (**25**). In other respects the acts of 1543–56 are constitutionally indistinguishable from those which follow from 1560. The installations of Deans Cox and Weston are recorded in the main series for the first collegiate church (**93, 139**), while those of the canons and others of the collegiate body are the subject of special sequences (**184, 185**). After 1560 the installations of canons are rarely noted in the acts (**194, 288, 316, 360, 450**) and those of the deans not at all. Regulations for the chapter meetings themselves (**1, 7, 19, 20, 59, 60, 94**) are frequent during the earlier period (cf. p. xxi above), as are those for the conduct of the services (p. li below) as well as the imposition of fines for absence from both these categories of events (**1, 14, 34, 36, 48, 94**) – although the actual levy of fines for neglect of duty is only twice registered (**36, 56**). Related to these concerns, but an issue of central importance in its own right, is residence. In cathedral and collegiate churches this term has the meaning of residential duty as well as occupation of domestic lodgings. That the one was deemed contingent upon the other is nowhere more pointedly expressed than in an act of 1581 where it was noted that the canons were 'forced . . . to dwell two of them in one howse' and consequently 'few of them are there resydente for anie longe tyme' (**340**). The canons of Westminster had a semi-permanent housing crisis which began with difficulties in adapting the monastic buildings to their separate and familial occupations (**26, 46, 51**), and was compounded by the temptation to lease housing in the precincts to paying tenants, despite the chapter's resolutions and occasional action to the contrary (**87, 416, 510, 513, 539**).

In the old foundation cathedrals and greater collegiate churches the canons

---

[56] Le Neve, 69–83.

had no obligation to reside, but might choose (and by their fellows be admitted) to do so for such periods as were locally defined, to which certain duties and corresponding emoluments were attached.[57] By contrast in the new foundations of Henry VIII there was no distinction between residentiaries and others in that all the members of the chapter were required to reside for some portion of the year. The 1544 statutes order the dean to be physically and operationally resident in his house in the precincts except when away on the king's or the church's business, or if forcibly detained, and with a yearly allowance of 80 days' leave for private affairs. The canons were permitted similar absences, with the proviso that no more than half should be away at any one time. But in addition canons were only to be counted as resident by keeping a household (of at least four servants) in the precincts for a period of 21 days in the year. During that time they had to attend matins and evensong daily (from at least the end of the first psalm to the conclusion of the service). Only by performing this duty might they qualify for the quotidian or daily allowance which formed part of their prescribed payment.[58] At Peterborough each canon's designated stipend was £20, comprised of £7 16s 8d *per annum* ('prebend' or *corpus*) and 8d *per diem*, and thus represents the maximum available for permanent residence: £7 16s 8d + (365 x 8d) = £20.[59] At Westminster this arrangement is explicit in one of the preliminary schemes for the establishment,[60] but never in the treasurers' accounts of the first collegiate church, where the full stipend of £28 5s per canon per year is invariably accounted in discharge of liability.[61] But it is clear from the acts (e.g. **69**) that the canons' quotidian remained 1s, and the composition of their payment was £10 + (365 x 1s) = £28 5s. In attempting to re-define and improve on

---

[57] See generally Edwards, *Secular Cathedrals*, 33–96. For particular cases see especially A.K.B. Roberts, *St George's Chapel, Windsor Castle, 1348–1416. A study in early Collegiate Administration* (Historical Monographs relating to St George's Chapel, Windsor Castle, Windsor [1947]), 107–10; *Ministers' Accounts of the Collegiate Church of St Mary, Warwick, 1432–85*, ed. D. Styles (Dugdale Soc. xxvi, 1969), pp. xxix–xxxi; R.B. Dobson, 'The later middle ages, 1215–1500', in Aylmer and Cant, *York Minster*, 52–62; D.M. Owen, 'Historical survey, 1091–1450', in *A History of Lincoln Minster*, ed. Owen (Cambridge 1994), 137–40.

[58] *Statutes (1)*, 81, 82–6 / 107, 108–10.

[59] Mellows, *Peterborough*, 71. The canons of Westminster and the other new foundations are commonly called 'prebendaries' in the 16th to 19th centuries, and their sources of income 'prebends'. But (except at Durham and initially at Norwich) no specific estates were attached to the stalls, which were distinguished only by number; and at Westminster that usage is not continued after 1660: Thompson, *English Clergy*, 77 & n. 1. *Lists of Deans and Major Canons of Durham, 1541–1900*, comp. P. Mussett (Durham 1974), pp. iv–v. Atherton and Holderness, 'Estates', 666. Le Neve, 66.

[60] PRO, E 315/24, f. 37 (*LP* xiv, II, 429). This proposes for the canons £10 *per annum* and 1s *per diem* [= £28 5s as established] and for the dean £20 *per annum* and 10s *per diem* [= £222 10s but £232 10s is the total there stated and as established]. Sums as established are in WAM 6478, f. 2 without breakdown.

[61] WAM 37045, ff. 2, 5, 7; 37043, f. 9; 37044, ff. 1, 6; 37064, f. 3; 37060, f. 4; 37112, f. 3; 33603, f. 3; 37382, f. 1v; 37387B, f. 2; 33604, f. 3; 37660, f. 1v; 37714, f. 1v [for 1542 x 1556 (with omissions) as listed in Knighton, 'Collegiate Foundations', 62].

these regulations, the dean and chapter in 1549, shortly after Cox's installation, ordered that in addition to the statutory 21 days of residence a year, *all* members of the chapter were to keep 12 days consecutively in the (three) other quarters, during which presence at 'som parte' of divine service was obligatory (**94**). In the following year it was decided that the 21 days must be kept between October 1 and April 1, but presence was required at only one of the three daily services. The 12 days to be kept in the quarters in which the 21 were not no longer needed to be consecutive (**109**). A short while later it was admitted that some words of no. **109** were 'ambyguose and doubtefull', and further explanation was made that absentees would lose not only their quotidians but also the dividends of fines, fees and sales; the 'lesser' residence was also increased from 12 days to 20 (**128**). Despite these various provisions exceptions could be made. Dean Benson was allowed by royal licence to be absent for all but three months of the year;[62] the dean and chapter themselves decided that a canon whose wife lay sick at Salisbury might be counted as resident at Westminster (**116**).

But without residence the full potential of capitular promotion could not be realised. Shortly before the chapter was re-established in 1560, a prospective (and eventual) appointee, Richard Cheyney, wrote to Sir William Cecil that he was reluctant to accept a prebend at Westminster which, since he did not intend to reside, would be worth only £10 a year to him.[63] In the Elizabethan college the distinction between 'prebend' and quotidian was retained, although the requirements of residence changed. The statutes stipulated that four of the canons should be in residence at any one time; each of the twelve canons was to perform four residences of 29 days in the year. The emolument was £7 6s 8d (prebend) + £2 13s 4d (livery) + (365 x) 8d commons.[64] A chapter order of 1574 (the only one on the subject between 1560 and 1609) illustrates a revised order of priorities, and makes a new and minimalist definition of residence: each year every canon must preach once, communicate once, and attend in choir properly habited on four occasions – anyone failing to complete this modest schedule will receive only the prebend of £10 (**291**). There is some indication that in the 1560s non-resident canons (who included several bishops) were indeed paid only that.[65] The treasurers' accounts show the amounts – and so may be calculated the number of days – for which canons who did reside were allowed commons, as the quotidians are then and thereafter called;[66] but it is not clear if cash

---

[62] *CPR 1547–8*, p. 163 (1 July 1547). It will be seen that the dean was absent from the two meetings next following (**66** continued as **68, 69**), yet present at all but one (**77**) of the remaining chapters of his decanate for which attendance is stated or to which signatures are applied (but cf. the caution on p. xxiv above).

[63] CCC, MS 114, p. 505 (*Parker Corr.*, 138–9).

[64] *Statutes (2)*, 83–4, 101. The dean's emolument is shown as £100 (prebend) + £4 15s (livery) + [365 x] 7s 8d commons [= £232 10s]. See further Robinson, *Statutes*, 6–17.

[65] WAM 33620, f. 2; 38204, 38206.

[66] WAM 33624–8 (f. 1v *passim*); 33629, f. 2v; 33631, f. 1v [for 1564–71 as listed and analysed in Knighton, 'Collegiate Foundations', 240].

equivalents in part or whole were paid to those canons who fulfilled the requirements of residence but opted out of the common meals. More stringent accounting for the commons was instituted by chapter order of 1565 (**211**). Admission to the canons' table was a valued perquisite, extended occasionally and with some circumspection to the head master and other lay officers (**206, 304, 447, 498**); special provision was also made for young men of the better sort and their servants (**221, 236**). Those below the salt had to be discouraged from bringing their friends in to join the common table (**372**) or taking their rations out to sell in the street (**521**).

For deans and canons the most important benefits of corporate life were the dividends of fees for application of the college seal, of rent income in kind, and above all of the fines levied on making or renewing leases.[67] Since most of these transactions passed unrecorded, such evidence of them as we have is always of particular interest. It happens to be one area in which the early records of the dean and chapter are more revealing than those of their monastic predecessors.[68] The rear of Chapter Act Book I was opened as a register of seal fees on 10 February 1543 (**187**); although only a few entries were made on that date, and the registration was then discontinued (whether from prudence or inertia), it establishes that the standard fee was £1 or £2. In one case the fee is waived because of roadwork done. Later entries in the main series (**174, 180, 182**) show that by 1556 the £1 fee is most usual – £2 may represent payment for two seals or include an element of fine. An act of 1567 enforces application of the fees (**229**) and on his appointment (1605) Dean Neile noted that £1 had long been customary (**535**). Rents were received mostly in cash, but included some produce and livestock; the share of wheat rent among the residentiaries was the subject of several orders (**29, 68, 94, 109**). The acts are unspecific about receipts from wood sales, but these are occasionally mentioned (**49, 355, 362, 419**); there are also orders for woods to be harvested by tenants or others for various purposes (**235, 365, 429, 472, 521**). Entry fines were subject to negotiation at each new or renewed tenancy; there were as yet no published calculations.[69] The acts supply some insight into the process. An agreement of 1585, on the advice of the chapter's legal counsel, gave the tenants of Steventon in Berkshire the security of

---

67 In this context 'fine' is an agreed cash payment not a penalty. Fees were also levied on other occasions, principally the installation of new members of the collegiate body, but these were not the exclusive perquisite of the dean and chapter (**69, 142, 146, 191**).

68 For fines levied by respectively the abbot and convent of Westminster see B.F. Harvey, 'The leasing of the abbot of Westminster's demesnes in the later middle ages', *EcHR*, 2nd ser. xxii (1969), 22 & n. 1; Harvey, *Estates*, 158–9. An additional instance (to the abbot in 1539) is given in G. Alexander, 'Victim or spendthrift? The bishop of London and his income in the sixteenth century', in *Wealth and Power in Tudor England. Essays presented to S.T. Bindoff*, ed. E.W. Ives, R.J. Knecht and J.J. Scarisbrick (1978), 140.

69 See E. Kerridge, 'The movement of rent, 1540–1640', *EcHR*, 2nd ser. vi (1953), 19–21. For later practice see particularly P. Mussett, 'Norwich Cathedral under Dean Prideaux, 1702–24', in Marcombe and Knighton, *Close Encounters*, 91–4.

fines at a fixed rate (**382**). In the following year a potential tenant of woods must pay 20 marks in advance of the negotiation; but this is returnable if no lease is agreed (**392**). A chapter in 1597 ruled that all those then assenting to a lease to the queen might share the £100 fine (the largest received in this period) even though only the dean and six canons could wait to see the deed sealed (**480**) – this notwithstanding an earlier decree (**429**) restricting dividends to those who stayed to the end of meetings. The acts specify the fines paid with some frequency from 1543 to 1556, but only rarely from 1560 to 1609. By contrast the dividends are little recorded in the first period (**29, 68**) but quite often in the second (**201, 214, 220, 222, 232, 270, 277, 281, 286**). In special cases the fine might be waived: as when the lease was at the request of the lord protector's lady (**79**), in a grant to the chapter's own officer, who was required instead to draw up a terrier (**47**), or when (for whatever reason) a tenant was admitted on payment of seal fees only (**57**).

Tenants often renewed their leases before the terms were close to expiry. This may in some cases have been because the landlord discovered a fault in the original grant and required to charge for rectifying it. In January 1556 the dean and chapter ordered that all new leases should carry a certain clause (**177**) and in the following month a sitting tenant was obliged to pay to have the clause added to his lease (**180**). The successor chapter in 1564 and 1566 fined other tenants to be dispensed from obtaining the same additional clause (**209, 219**). On the other hand in 1585 a defective lease was revised and newly sealed, no doubt for a fee, but apparently without fine (**382**). Some tenants, however, may have wished to renew leases simply to extend their terms and so acquire greater security for themselves and their families.[70] Where the Act Book entries allow comparison between fines agreed and the terms and rents of leases to which they applied, the sums involved would seem modest by comparison with those exacted by lay landlords or some ecclesiastical ones. The fine is commonly equivalent to a year's rent, rarely more than that of two (except in the last year of the first collegiate church, 1555–6). Although details are much rarer after 1560, the level of fine seems notably lower than the four or five years' purchase then common for initial grants of 21 years or three lives on crown lands.[71]

---

[70] Cf. D. Thomas, 'Leases of crown lands in the reign of Elizabeth I', in Hoyle, *Estates*, 174.

[71] See J.E.C. Hill, *Economic Problems of the Church. From Archbishop Whitgift to the Long Parliament* (Oxford 1956), 30–1; *The Agrarian History of England*, gen. ed. H.P.R. Finberg, iv, *1500–1640*, ed. I.J. Thirsk (Cambridge 1967), 267, 327, 336; Marcombe, 'Durham: old abbey writ large', 139; Haigh, 'Chester', 161–3; Heal, *Prelates*, 58–9, 185–6, 281–5; Knighton, 'Economics', 53–4; W.J. Sheils, 'Profit, patronage or pastoral care: the rectory estates of the archbishopric of York, 1540–1640', 94–6, and D. Marcombe, 'Church leaseholders: the decline and fall of a rural elite', in O'Day and Heal, *Princes and Paupers*, 257–8; G. Haslam, 'The Elizabethan duchy of Cornwall, an estate in stasis', in Hoyle, *Estates*, 96–9; Atherton and Holderness, 'Estates', 667 & n. 10.

Entry fines recorded in Act Book I
(omitting seal fees, fines waived and uncertain instances)

No.	Year of act	Tenant	Years of Lease term	Rent £	Rent s	Rent d	Fine £	Fine s	Fine d	
5	1543	Baugh	60	8	6	8	10	0	0	(a)
5	1543	Parsons	40	3	6	8	10	0	0	
5	1543	Wrenford	80	26	0	0	53	6	8	(b)
5/6	1543	Nutting	96	20	0	0		13	4	
							per annum of increase			
7	1543	Brocket	60	17	0	0	20	0	0	(c)
				and produce						
12	1544	Whashe	40	[not stated]			13	6	8	
44	1545	Barnard	[not stated]	[not stated]			2	13	4	
77	1548	Neste	21	4	6	8	6	13	4	
77	1548	Smyth	21	8	0	0	8	0	0	
77	1548	Symons	20	8	6	8	6	13	4	
85	1549	Grene	60	4	0	0	6	13	4	
96	1549	Mason	50	8	0	0	10	0	0	
101	1549	Smalbone	40	20	10	6	13	6	8	(d)
103	1550	Pynchyn	21	20	0	0	20	0	0	
108	1550	Porter	40	5	2	8	2	0	0	(e)
113	1551	Chauncy	40	12	13	4	26	13	4	(f)
122	1552	Rychardes	21		5	0	2	0	0	
132	1553	Clargier	40	3	18	0	3	6	8	
151	1554	Baugh	31	[not stated]			8	0	0	
167	1555	Weston	60	3	6	8	20	0	0	(g)
167	1555	Polley	90	55	0	0	20	0	0	
174	1555	Weston	51	7	6	8	20	0	0	
174	1555	Sorrell	41	1	13	4	13	6	8	
174	1555	Cowike	80		1	8	5	0	0	
174	1555	Harberde	61	4	6	8	12	0	0	(h)
175	1555	Weston	70	4	6	8	6	13	4	
175	1555	Cawod	60	[not stated]			6	13	4	
175	1555	Henslowe	70	27	0	0	6	13	4	

No.	Year of act	Tenant	Years of Lease term	Rent £	s	d	Fine £	s	d	
180	1556	Churche	[new clause]	–			6	13	4	
180	1556	Busby	41	25	0	1	26	13	4	
180	1556	Sutton	71	3	6	8	5	10	0	
209	1564	Smyth	[dispensation]	–			10	0	0	
219	1566	Parker	[dispensation]	–			40	0	0	
263	1571	Naylor	61	50	0	0	50	0	0	
392/403	1586	Smith	20/21	1	16	0	13	6	8	(i)
464	1595	all urban tenants	–	–			two fat birds			
480/481	1597	The queen	21	50 and produce	0	0	100	0	0	

(a) Cf. **187**	(e) Rent as Reg.	(i) £13 13s 4d fine in Reg.
(b) Cf. **187**	(f) 60 years in Reg.	
(c) Cf. **187**	(g) 90 years in Reg.	
(d) 50 years in Reg.	(h) 67 years in Reg.	

Entry fines were cherished principally as a mitigation of long leases. The 1544 new foundation statutes had prohibited chapters from letting rural properties for more than 21 years or urban tenements for more than 60; but this was an unrealistic provision.[72] Elizabethan legislation attempted to restrict all ecclesiastical bodies to leases of 21 years or three lives.[73] The dean and chapter of Westminster had an endowment of approximately £2,600 *per annum* which, although less than three-quarters of that which the monks had in 1535, gave them an income commensurate with that of all but the most substantial lay magnates. It was, for an ecclesiastical corporation, a peculiarly dispersed estate, its country properties spread over many counties and with the largest concentration in southern Worcestershire, Gloucestershire, Oxfordshire and Berkshire.[74]

---

[72] *Statutes (1)*, 80/106.

[73] 13 Eliz. I c. 10, 18 Eliz. I c. 11. See Elton, *Parliament*, 147, 217.

[74] Harvey, *Estates*, esp. appendixes I (pp. 335–64), III (pp. 402–12) and map II (pp. [472–3]). Knighton, 'Economics', 49–51. The 1535 valuation was £3,470 2s 0¼d: *Valor Ecclesiasticus temp. Henr. VIII auctoritate regia institutus*, ed. J. Caley (1810–34), i, 424. Possessions assigned to the cathedral in 1542 amounted to £2,598 4s 5d, of which £2,164 2s 2d derived from properties held by Westminster Abbey and St Martin-le-Grand, the remainder from the dissolved houses of Merton (Surrey), Mount Grace (Yorkshire), Pershore and Evesham (Worcestershire), Newstead (Nottinghamshire), Bardney, Grimsby and Haverholme (Lincolnshire): WAM 6478, ff. 6, 8–12.

There was, however, very little of the direct spoliation to which ecclesiastical landowners were notoriously subject between the Reformation and the civil war. The only substantial alteration came in 1545 and 1546 when Henry VIII took back lands which had previously sustained university readers and students on the original foundation (**33**, **39**), for which the dean and chapter would attempt to secure better compensation (**41**). An exchange of property with a prominent courtier in 1548 is also recorded (**82**). The dean and chapter were, nevertheless, unremittingly prevailed upon by their neighbours, the greatest in the land, to grant leases and offices beneficial to the recipients, which the dean and chapter were normally too weak or too wise to refuse.

One of the first such suits was made in the name of the young Princess Elizabeth (**30**). Half a century later Elizabeth was to make a particularly awkward request on behalf of one of her ladies (**480**, **481**, **486**). Elizabeth's fourth and final step-mother, Catherine Parr, sought special consideration from the dean and chapter (**38**); so too did Protector Somerset (**76**), his troublesome brother (**72**, **78**) and tiresome wife (**79**, **80**). The next head of government, the duke of Northumberland, also became a Westminster tenant (**117**). Other occupants of the dean and chapter's properties were secretaries of state Sir William Cecil (**112**) and his son the future first Lord Salisbury (**467**), Sir William Petre (**149**) and Sir John Bourne (**158**), lord keeper Egerton (**488**) and chancellor of the exchequer Sir John Fortescue (**431**), Hobart C.J. (**545**) and Birch J. (**263**), and an Armada captain, Lord Sheffield (**544**). The dean and chapter were landlords for innumerable courtiers and government servants. One such was Thomas Keys (**239**), a humble palace official who was misguided enough to marry one of Queen Elizabeth's relatives. Here too are prominent royal doctors Butts (**111**), Huick (**202**) and Hammond (**374**) – the first a key figure at Henry VIII's court and with some notable Westminster connexions;[75] the construction industry is represented by Elizabeth's surveyor (**225**) and comptroller (**269**) of works. Something of a local hero was Cornelius Vandon, a Dutchman who became yeoman of the guard to Henry VIII and his three children, and who built an almshouse at Westminster (**243**). Westminster tenants also included William Heather, benefactor to Oxford music (**532**) and the carver Gerard Christmas (**541**).

Conversely the dean and chapter could enlist prominent men as their stewards, such as Sir Anthony Denny, one of Henry VIII's most trusted courtiers (**32**), Sir John Thynne, Somerset's secretary (**64**) and the earl of Arundel, one of Mary's councillors (**164**). The Cecils were the Abbey's best friends at court; after the first Lord Burghley's death the dean and chapter prudently sought the patronage of his sons Thomas (who inherited the title) and Robert (who

---

[75] As a promoter of reformist clerics he advanced the career of the future dean of Westminster William Bill: E.W. Ives, *Anne Boleyn* (Oxford 1986), 311–12. He gave (very intimate) evidence at the proceedings (in the Abbey precincts) which released Henry VIII from his marriage to Anne of Cleves: J. Strype, *Ecclesiastical Memorials* (Oxford 1822), i, II, 461 (*LP* xv, 850).

inherited the power) (**498**). The Russells were also associated with successive regimes at Westminster,[76] and rented a house in the precincts (**332**). Later the Howards joined the rent-roll (**541**). The chapter were also able to retain legal and business advisers of the highest calibre, such as Nicholas Bacon (**5**) and Thomas Mildmay (**9**).

It must also be noted that of those mentioned in the Act Book three of the tenants (Seymour of Sudeley, Somerset and Northumberland) were beheaded for treason and one (Stourton: **164**) hanged for murder; one sometime presentee (Cardmaker: **7**) and one former canon (Ridley) were burned for heresy, and one prospective verger (Rossey: **149**) was disembowelled.

(ii) *Deans and canons*

Between 1540 and 1609 there were 90 individuals in the Westminster chapter.[77] Of the original thirteen [*1, 8–19*] only H. Perkyns survived until Mary's purge of 1554. He and two of those who had been subsequently appointed to the first collegiate church (Nowell [*30*] and Alvey [*34*]) returned at the start of the second in 1560. Two deans (Goodman [*5*] and Andrewes [*6*]) had previously been canons. Aldrich [*63*] vacated one stall and was reappointed to another. Their collective lifespan stretches from the birth of Thomas Elfred [*16*] in or just before 1477 to the death of William Robinson [*90*] in 1642.[78] The Act Book normally records the annual elections of canons to chapter office. The earliest appointments are noted periodically (**6, 31**); the first general election took place in 1545, when canons were appointed subdean, receiver and treasurer, with minor canons named as precentor and sacrist (**46**). The receiver was principally concerned with receipt of net revenue, the treasurer with its internal disbursement. The receivership became a lay office in 1549, initially during the tenure of John Moulton (**97**); although the duties were on occasion thereafter discharged by a canon (**215, 217**), it was never again regularly so held. From 1560 an archdeacon was annually elected (**188**) to preside over the office, instance and probate jurisdiction.[79] The acts include elections of a steward and a divinity

---

[76] Not just the Elizabethan college: Abbot Feckenham was a friend of the first earl of Bedford and preached at Countess Anne's funeral in the Abbey: D. Willen, *John Russell, First Earl of Bedford. One of the King's Men* (Royal Historical Soc. Studies in History Series, no. 23, 1981), 42.

[77] In this section only numbered *1–7* (deans) and *8–90* (canons). Full details of appointments are in Le Neve, 69–83. Prebendal stall numbers I–XII are given to show succession; but at Westminster these numbers did not indicate precedence, which was determined by seniority of appointment: cf. no. **207** where Reeve (stall IX) is called senior resident of the month – presumably by years standing rather than stall number, unless the holders of X–XII happened to be the only other residents.

[78] Elfred said his first mass in 1498/9: Pearce, *Monks*, 176. The average age of Westminster monks at ordination is posited as 22 in Harvey, *Living and Dying*, 118–21. For Robinson's death see Le Neve, 76.

[79] Cf. p. xix above. From June 1560 the jurisdictions of Westminster and St Martin-le-Grand

lecturer or reader from 1564 (**209**) although these posts were also occupied from 1560.[80] Those with financial responsibilities were appointed with retrospective effect for the year which had begun at the preceding Michaelmas. Vacancies might, of course, be supplied in mid-term, as in March 1554 when a new subdean was required to replace a Marian deprivee (**153**). By no means all canons served in one or other of these posts; indeed the offices were most often filled by those for whom the Westminster stall was their principal attainment. Individuals are also frequently mentioned in connexion with their housing. From these and other references it is possible to say something of all the appointees.[81]

[*1*] William Benson (in religion Boston) (dean 1540–9) was the last abbot of the Confessor's foundation; he was, as Knowles tersely noted, 'a king's man'.[82] He was certainly an incomer: the first abbot appointed from outside the ranks of the Westminster community since 1214. His abbacy has been criticized in particular for the disadvantageous exchange of property with the crown in 1536, and for concentrating the administrative offices in his own hands; it must be said that in both these respects he followed recent precedent,[83] and a centralized financial system has its merits. But the early pages of the Act Book, which appear to be mostly in Benson's hand, are a poor memorial to his new role as dean; the writing is wretched and the organization of the material haphazard.[84] The Act Book records decisions under Benson to grant long leases to the duke of Somerset (**76**) and his brother Seymour (**78**) and the gift of stone to the duke (**63**). Financial worries are said to have killed him.[85] But personally he was rich; he left over £600 in cash, and in addition to his official residences he had a

---

were united under the archdeacon; wills for both areas under the new regime begin on 25 June 1560, and act books survive from 1566: WCA, Reg. Bracy, f. 152; Act Book I.

[80] WAM 33617, f. 9.

[81] For reasons stated above (p. xxviii) a full biographical register is not here presented. Acts instanced are selective. Biographical details are to be found as follows: *DNB*: *1, 2, 3, 4, 5, 6, 7, 8, 9, 11, 24, 30, 31, 32, 33, 34, 35, 37, 43, 45, 47, 48, 51, 54, 57, 59, 60, 61, 64, 66, 67, 68, 70, 75, 80, 81, 83, 84, 85, 86*; Emden: *2, 3, 9, 10, 13, 14, 20, 22, 23, 30, 37, 39, 40, 43, 44, 50, 51*; Foster, *Al.* (if not in Emden): *7, 24, 47, 58, 60, 61, 62, 69, 70, 71, 72, 73, 74, 75, 77, 78, 79, 81, 83, 85, 86, 88, 89*; Venn: *1, 2, 3, 4, 5, 6, 7, 8, 9, 11, 12, 19, 20, 24, 25, 26, 27, 28, 31, 32, 33, 34, 35, 37, 42, 45, 46, 47, 48, 49, 53, 54, 55, 57, 59, 60, 61, 63, 64, 65, 66, 67, 68, 69, 70, 71, 75, 76, 78, 79, 80, 82, 84, 87, 89, 90*; Garrett, *Marian Exiles: 2, 14, 22, 30, 31, 32, 34, 45, 53, 54, 69*; Ollard: *2, 3, 8, 30, 35, 39, 50, 57, 64*; Pearce, *Monks: 1, 13, 14, 15, 16, 17, 18*; F.O. White, *Lives of the Elizabethan Bishops of the Anglican Church* (1898): *2, 31, 45, 47, 48, 51, 57, 59, 64, 66, 67, 68, 80*; or as specified.

[82] Knowles, *Religious Orders*, iii, 243.

[83] *HK*, 108–9. But cf. Harvey, *Estates*, 93 & n. 3 (multiple holding of obediences), 337 & n. 2 (exchange of 1531).

[84] Benson's first signature is by initials only (**1**), the second likewise, partially extending the forename (**2**); but the third (**5**) has the surname in full, and this seems to be the hand which has recorded most entries on ff. 10–52 (**1–91**). Cox's acts from f. 56 (**94**) begin a much neater section; a similar change is seen in the Ely chapter order book in 1557 when Andrew Perne [*33*] took over the deanery from the ex-prior: CUL, EDC 2/1/1, f. 55.

[85] *HK*, 115–16 following Heylin (for which see further n. 112 to no. **63** below).

house in Long Ditch which was left to Hugh Latimer on the understanding that John Moulton the receiver might have rooms there.[86] References in early acts to the dean's house (**11**, **46**, **85**) are to the residence of the Henrician deans; the abbot's lodging became the bishop's house in 1540, and Benson moved to more modest but perhaps less rat-infested premises.[87] On his death [*2*] Richard Cox (dean 1549–53) took his place. Cox was almoner and tutor to Edward VI; he was already dean of Christ Church, and retained this and other benefices during his time at Westminster. He had already had a formative role at Westminster as one of the draftsmen of the general new foundation statutes.[88] His arrival at the deanery was marked by a series of chapter orders (**94**, **109**, **128**) which attempted to clarify uncertainties in the statutes and previous local regulations. But his many other duties must have made Westminster only occasionally his concern; his imprisonment in his house there at the start of Mary's reign may have been his most concentrated period of residence. His best remembered appearance in the Abbey pulpit came after exile and return, when at the State Opening of Elizabeth's first parliament he preached in the restored monastery (as it yet was) denouncing monks.[89] Later, as bishop of Ely, he would be more charitable to the restored secular college at Westminster (**219**). Meanwhile [*3*] Hugh Weston (dean 1553–6) had come and gone. Mary's dean made a considerable mark among the muniments generally, though in these acts chiefly in the profusion of Westons, brothers and other kinsmen, who received leases or grants of office during his decanate (**143**, **148**, **167**, **174**, **175**, **182**). Dean Weston is generally remembered for his part in Cranmer's trial, and for being deprived of his deanery of Windsor for immorality.[90]

The first head of the Elizabethan foundation [*4*] William Bill (dean 1560–1), was simultaneously master of Trinity College, Cambridge and provost of Eton; he survived only a year in the enjoyment of these prestigious appointments. Only one chapter act was entered in his time (**188**) but a later one mentions his gift of tapestries (**218**). He was also Elizabeth's almoner, as which he appeared at

---

[86] PRO, PROB 11/32, ff. 290–291v. He also left a house in Peterborough (for which see Mellows, *Peterborough*, p. xxvii and cf. Pearce, *Monks*, 189 following WAM 33313) which was his birthplace: PRO, SP 1/182, f. 204 (*LP* xviii, II, App. 2). But that he had previously been abbot of Burton-upon-Trent is established by an entry on the pardon roll which may be the only contemporary record of his pre-Westminster monastic career: *CPR* 1548–9, p. 159. Cf. MacCulloch, *Cranmer*, 20.

[87] For the houses see nn. 35 and 36 to no. **11** below. For the rats see Harvey, *Living and Dying*, 135 & n. 78 commenting on an entry in Robinson, *Abbot's House*, 39–40.

[88] Lehmberg, *Ref. of Cathedrals*, 91–2. For the statutes see below, no. **19** & n. 46.

[89] For his imprisonment see n. 266 to no. **139** below. The 1559 sermon is reported in *CSPV* vii, 15. For Cox's career generally (but chiefly as Elizabeth's bishop of Ely) see G.L. Blackman, 'The career and influence of Bishop Richard Cox, 1547–1581' (Ph.D. dissertation, University of Cambridge 1953); also Heal, *Prelates*, 296–7 and *passim*.

[90] That Weston was a Balliol man (so supposed on the basis of bequests: Emden, 616) seems evident from PRO, SP 11/8, no. 67 (*CSPDM*, 442).

the Abbey at Queen Mary's funeral on 14 December 1558.[91] By contrast with the brief tenure of Bill, the reign of [5] Gabriel Goodman (stall XII, 1560–1; dean 1561–1601) was almost co-eval with that of the queen. His appointment was marked by the usual revision of existing orders, and by another improvement in the smartness of the record (**189**). The acts record a donation of books by Goodman (**296**) and, in the last entry before his death, the chapter's allowance to him of free oats for his horses (**520**). He was founder of a school and college at his native Ruthin, which would be a continuing responsibility for the Westminster chapter (**538**). He also established for the school and college of Westminster a country retreat. From 1563 it became frequently necessary to escape the plague in the city. A house at Putney was first hired for this purpose (**197**) and in subsequent years adjournment was ordered to Wheathampstead or elsewhere in the country (**202, 248, 252, 263**). A permanent solution was found when Goodman, in his capacity as prebendary of Chiswick in St Paul's Cathedral, made the house of his prebendal estate available to Westminster as a refuge and general holiday house (**267**). In Westminster itself the plague continued to trouble those who remained: in 1574 the chapter ordered that its victims were to be kept out of the precincts (**293**) and in 1603 they were moved to a rare instance of *reportage* by citing the weekly mortality rate (**526**). Nevertheless Goodman had been prompted to establish one of Westminster's most agreeable dispositions.[92] It was enjoyed by his successor [6] Lancelot Andrewes (stall XI, 1597–1601; dean 1601–5). Although his walks to 'distant Chiswick' appear to have strained the imagination of Sir Geoffrey Elton,[93] they are well attested; and the acts, which record his presence at Chiswick in the summer of 1603 with scholars preparing for the next election, indicate that the walking was for pleasure and not for lack of adequate transport (**525**). Although Andrewes was dean for only a short time, the acts are a record of his attention to such matters as good order at the servants' meals (**521**) and in the choir (**524, 529**) and the education of the choristers (**533**). He left behind some wainscot – but not, it seems, as a gift (**538**). He had gone to be bishop of Chichester, and would move on to Winchester; one major occasion of return to the Abbey was to preach at the 1621 State Opening.[94] His successor [7] Richard Neile (dean 1605–10) was

[91] PRO, LC 2/4(2), f. 31v. Misplacing of SP 11/2, no. 1, a warrant for distribution of alms by Bill, as of 1 Jan. 1554 (*recte* 1559: *CSPDM*, 961) misled the *DNB* to suppose Bill had also been almoner to Edward VI. The error was noted in L.E. Tanner, 'Lord high almoners and sub-almoners, 1100–1957', *JBAA*, 3rd ser. xx–xxi (1957–8), 77–8.

[92] For Goodman see R. Newcome, *A Memoir of Gabriel Goodman, with some account of Ruthin School* (Ruthin 1825); Soden, *Goodman*, 39–40 and *passim*; also Kenyon-Thompson, *Ruthin School*, which (pp. 190–7) prints Goodman's will.

[93] G.R. Elton, 'Lancelot Andrewes', repr. in *Studies in Tudor and Stuart Politics and Government* (Cambridge 1974–92), iv, 166.

[94] For Andrewes see P.A. Welsby, *Lancelot Andrewes, 1555–1626* (1958, repr. 1964), 73–89 (for his time at Westminster), 276–8 (for bibliography to 1958). Of much recent work see especially K. Fincham, *Prelate as Pastor. The Episcopate of James I* (Oxford 1990), *passim*; P.G.

another high-flyer (landing eventually at Bishopthorpe) and an enthusiastic ad-
ministrator.[95] In his first year he raised the scholars' commons allowance (**534**)
and steered the chapter to decisions on the registration of documents, on the
making of new choir stalls and their orderly occupancy, and for an experimental
use of sea-coal in the kitchen (**538**). Later reforms included more sermons (**541**)
and reduction in kitchen expenses (**544**). An inventory of all movables was
ordered (**539**). Neile's acts continue into Book II.

First named among the canons[96] was [*8*] Simon Haynes (stall I, 1540–52); he
was also one of the first to be elected to administrative duty (**2**). But his chief
activity was as head of his own chapter at Exeter, where his advanced protestantism and the severity with which he handled his colleagues made him un-
popular.[97] At Westminster, where the society was probably more congenial, his
amenities included a garden with the old dovecote (**46**). [*9*] John Redman (stall
II, 1540–51) was the most eminent of the founding chapter; he was licensed to
preach in the diocese of Westminster,[98] but his main work was at Cambridge,
where he was master of the King's Hall, and then of its successor foundation,
Trinity College (**62** & n. 111). [*10*] Edward Leighton (stall III, 1540–7), despite
an apparently successful ecclesiastical career which included the clerkship of the
closet, was obliged to sign away his Westminster income to his creditors (**28**).
[*11*] Anthony Bellasis (stall IV, 1540–52) was another early chapter officer, being
appointed in meeting no. **2** to inform the choir of decisions made in no. **1**. He
played a key role in Thomas Cromwell's service as 'something like the patronage
secretary'. But as head of his own collegiate body at Sherburn in county
Durham, his estate management was 'reckless and irresponsible'.[99]

[*12*] William Britten (stall V, 1540–52) has the doubtful distinction of being
the only canon mentioned in the acts as having been fined for missing a preaching duty (**56**). [*13*] Denis Dalyons (stall VI, 1540–3) had been prior of Westminster; he was probably dead before the extant acts were made, since his name

Lake, 'Lancelot Andrewes, John Buckeridge and *avant-garde* conformity at the court of
James I', in *The Mental World of the Jacobean Court*, ed. L.L. Peck (Cambridge 1991), 113–33;
N.R.N. Tyacke, 'Archbishop Laud', in *The Early Stuart Church, 1603–1642*, ed. K. Fincham
(Basingstoke 1993), 62–4. The 1621 sermon is printed in *Collected Works*, ed. J.P. Wilson and
J. Bliss (Library of Anglo-Catholic Theology, 1841–54), *Ninety-Six Sermons*, v, 203–22,
discussed in Welsby, *op. cit.*, 224.

95 For Neile see A.W. Foster, 'A biography of Archbishop Richard Neile' (D.Phil. dissertation,
University of Oxford 1978); *idem*, 'Function of a bishop', 40–53; *idem*, 'Church policies of
the 1630s', in Cust and Hughes, *Conflict*, 196–216; R.L. Arundale, *Richard Neile, Bishop of
Lincoln 1614–1617* (Lincoln 1987); N.R.N. Tyacke, *Anti-Calvinists. The Rise of English Armini-
anism c.1590–1640* (Oxford 1987), 106–24; M. Tillbrook, 'Arminianism and society in
County Durham, 1617–42', in Marcombe, *Last Principality*, 202–5, 208–10.

96 But cf. n. 77 above.

97 See particularly N.I. Orme, *Exeter Cathedral as it was, 1050–1550* (Exeter 1986), 95–101.

98 Guildhall MS 9531/12, f. 253v. See also MacCulloch, *Cranmer*, 343–4.

99 Elton, *Reform and Renewal*, 24–5 & n. 55. D. Marcombe, 'A rude and heady people: the local
community and the rebellion of the northern earls', in Marcombe, *Last Principality*, 126.

never occurs there and his successor J. Pekyns [*22*] signs to no. **8**. By contrast [*14*] Humphrey Perkyns *alias* Charity (stall VII, 1540–54; stall II, 1560–77), the most distinguished of the last monks of the pre-1540 abbey, outlived all his original colleagues in the secular chapter, where he became a fixture until first dislodged by Queen Mary and later when his health failed in old age (**301**). In his youth he had been on the fringe of the circle of Robert Joseph, the 'little Benedict' of Evesham, where the old monastic spirituality and the new human-ist scholarship briefly met.[100] [*15*] Thomas Baxter *alias* Essex (stall VIII, 1540–2) has been already noticed (p. xxi above). [*16*] Thomas Elfred (stall IX, 1540–6) became subdean in the first election (**46**). [*17*] John Rumney *alias* Malvern (stall X, 1540–1) was the first member of the new chapter to be replaced. [*18*] William Harvey *alias* Faith (stall XI, 1540–4) was named as surveyor soon after the chapter assumed charge of its business affairs (**6**). [*19*] Gerard Carleton (stall XII, 1540–9) became head of one of the sister new foundations in 1543 as dean of Peterborough.[101] At Westminster one of his perquisites was lead from the infirmary chapel roof (**54**). [*20*] Edmund Weston (stall X, 1541–54) and [*21*] Francis Turpin (stall VIII, 1542–5) appear only briefly in the acts (**24**, **3**). [*22*] John Pekyns (stall VI, 1543–54), the brother of Humphrey Perkyns [*14*],[102] was the first whom the acts record as appointed the chapter's proctor in convocation (**70**). [*23*] Thomas Reynolds (stall XI, 1544–56) was one of those who negotiated the surrender of lands to the crown when the university readerships and student-ships were discontinued (**33**). The most notable occupant of a canonry in Henry VIII's cathedral at Westminster [*24*] Nicholas Ridley (stall VIII, 1545–53) is among the least in evidence here; he never signs the acts, and his appointment is only interesting for technicalities in his vacating it (**138** n. 264).[103] By contrast [*25*] Bernard Sandiforth (stall IX, 1546–54) was one of the most active members of the chapter (**64**, **69**, **73**), and was also vicar-general of the diocese of West-minster from 1546.[104] [*26*] Edward Keble (stall III, 1547–54) was afflicted by family problems (**116**) and then financial disaster which led him to become an inmate of the Westminster sanctuary (**140**). He seemed to find, or cause, trouble, at every place he acquired preferment.[105] [*27*] Giles Eyre (stall XII, 1549–51), who was dean of Chichester for the same years, had a house provided for him at Westminster (**111**) but was not notably active in it. [*28*] Hugh Griffith (patent

---

100 *The Letter Book of Robert Joseph, monk-scholar of Evesham and Gloucester College, Oxford, 1530–3*, ed. H.C. Aveling and W.A. Pantin (Oxford Historical Soc., n.s. xix, 1967 for 1964), 233–4. Cf. Knowles, *Religious Orders*, iii, 100–7.

101 For Carleton's dealings as dean of Peterborough with William Benson [*1*] see Mellows, *Peterborough*, pp. xxvi–xxviii.

102 Relationship established by endorsement to inventory of Pekyns's house: WAM 6608.

103 For Ridley see principally *The Works of Nicholas Ridley, D.D., sometime Lord Bishop of London, Martyr, 1555*, ed. H. Christmas (Parker Soc. 1841); J.G. Ridley, *Nicholas Ridley* (1957).

104 Guildhall MS 9531/12, f. 263v.

105 See n. 267 to no. **140** below; also C.A. Haigh, *Reformation and Resistance in Tudor Lancashire* (Cambridge 1975), 24, 181.

1550; stall VIII, 1553–6) receives mention because of uncertainty about the stipend due to him on succession to Ridley [*24*] when the bishop relinquished his *commendam* (**138**). He has two distinctions: the only Westminster canon instituted by a bishop of London, and the last man to graduate in canon law from an English university.[106] [*29*] Thomas Bricket *alias* Birkhed (stall XII, 1551–4) appears to have received his canonry following a direct appeal to Sir William Cecil (**110** n. 210). [*30*] Alexander Nowell (stall II, 1551–4; stall VII, 1560–4) was the first head master of Westminster to be a canon, and a man of so many parts it is surprising his invention of bottled beer is invariably mentioned among them.[107] Some indulgence should perhaps be allowed a man whose house is in 'utter ruyne and dekaye' (**143**). Another celebrity [*31*] Edmund Grindal (stall V, 1552–4) is mentioned here only in connexion with one of his servants (**138**).[108] [*32*] James Haddon (stall IV, 1552) was a member of the chapter for no more than two months, and unsurprisingly has left no record in its acts; he does not seem to have been installed.[109] [*33*] Andrew Perne (stall I, 1552–6), to whom a house was assigned (**149**), later and for more than thirty years dean of Ely, was a Cambridge character, ridiculed for his relentlessly accommodating churchmanship.[110] He naturally retained his canonry at Westminster when others lost theirs in Mary's purge (**153** n. 299). Among those then departing was [*34*] Richard Alvey (stall IV, 1552–4; stall V, 1560–74). On his return from exile he became master of the Temple and rejoined the Westminster chapter; although on one occasion showing dissent to his colleagues' decisions (**216**), he gave them a set of silver spoons with his monogram (**285**). [*35*] Francis Mallet (stall VI, 1554–6) was Queen Mary's almoner.[111] At Westminster his house was designated (**169**) and the acts also include an unexplained note, perhaps of a dividend payment to him (**174**). [*36*] John Baker (stall III, 1554–6) was one of those forced to share a house with a colleague (**167**, **171**). [*37*] Henry Cole (stall IX, 1554–6) is seen peaceably purchasing the domestic effects of his deprived predecessor Sandiforth [*25*] in 1555 (**165**). Cole (provost of Eton and while still canon of Westminster) attended Cranmer in his last days at Oxford, and preached at the

---

106 Le Neve, 79. Griffith proceeded D.Cn.L. at Cambridge in 1556: *Grace Book* Δ, 114.

107 See R. Churton, *Life of Alexander Nowell* (Oxford 1809). *A Catechism written in Latin by Alexander Nowell, Dean of St Paul's*, ed. G.E. Corrie (Parker Soc. 1853) includes (pp. 223–9) text of sermon which Nowell preached in the Abbey at the State Opening in 1563 (for which see Elton, *Parliament*, 358). For his head mastership see Sargeaunt, 4–5.

108 See *The Remains of Edmund Grindal, D.D., successively Bishop of London and Archbishop of York and Canterbury*, ed. W. Nicholson (Parker Soc. 1843); Collinson, *Grindal*.

109 Cf. no. **184** (f. 273) where the installation of Grindal [*31*] is followed by that of Perne [*33*]. Haddon's sole contribution to Westminster history would appear to be through publication of a famous incident in the career of the future Abbot Feckenham: Garrett, *Marian Exiles*, 170.

110 For this and other insinuations see *Puritanism in Tudor England*, ed. H.C. Porter (1970), 207–8. He is chiefly commemorated in McKitterick, *Perne*.

111 As such he can be identified as author of PRO, SP 11/12, no. 1 (*CSPDM*, 677), enclosing a new year's gift to the queen.

execution.[112] [*38*] Alphonso de Salinas (stall VII, 1554–6) had the companionship of a fellow-Spaniard, King Philip's confessor, while he was at Westminster (**166**). But de Salinas was the only Marian canon not found other preferment in 1556, and the Elizabethan chapter did its best to avoid paying a pension settled on him by the restored abbey (**234, 238**). [*39*] William Pye (stall XII, 1554–6) headed the chapter's commission to arrest a defaulting rent-collector (**176**) but was himself involved in a questionably legal manoeuvre to secure a chapter living for the dean (**147** & n. 276). A miserable fate awaited [*40*] John Ramridge (stall IV, 1554–6), who signs to no. **154**. Having escaped from the Tower, to which Elizabeth I sent him, he was murdered by thieves in Belgium. Mary's appointees to the chapter are not well-known; their careers at Westminster were short, and elsewhere were for the most part terminated by the queen's death. Of one, however, a depiction may remain: [*41*] John Richarde (stall II, 1554–6).[113] [*42*] Thomas Wood (stall X, 1554–6), at Mary's death in the process of promotion to the episcopate, would later face the threat of a Tower racking after the accession day bells had prompted incorrect memory of the previous queen.[114] For [*43*] John Moreman (stall V, 1554) imprisonment had come during Edward VI's reign when he (and a sermon of his which had given offence) were lodged in the Fleet.[115] Of [*44*] John Smith (stall V, 1554–6) the most that can be said is that he was probably not the incumbent (**45**) or precentor (**84**) named here.

[*45*] William Barlow I (stall I, 1560–6) heads the roll of Elizabethan canons. He was one of several bishops in the chapter during the first years of the second collegiate church.[116] [*46*] John Hardyman (stall III, 1560–1) was appointed archdeacon in the first act of the restored chapter (**188**). He is found acting in this capacity in March 1561, but later in the year was deprived of his canonry and the archdeaconry which was dependent upon it.[117] [*47*] Richard Cheyney (stall IV, 1560–2) was bishop of Gloucester and Bristol from 1562. His interest in Westminster has already been noted (p. xxx above).[118] [*48*] Edmund Scambler

---

112 MacCulloch, *Cranmer*, 597, 600–1. For Cole's authorship of a paper once thought to be Cranmer's see P.A. Sawada, 'Two anonymous Tudor treatises on the general council', *Journal of Ecclesiastical History* xii (1961), 197–214.

113 Westminster Cathedral, Queen Mary's manual, f. 11v; reproduced and identification of Richarde suggested in J.M. Bickersteth and R.W. Dunning, *Clerks of the Closet in the Royal Household* (Stroud 1991), facing p. 66. Illumination ascribed to Levina Teerlinc: R.C. Strong, *The English Renaissance Miniature* (1983), 60.

114 PRO, SP 12/59, no. 43 (*CSPD* 1547–80, p. 348).

115 PRO, SP 10/9, no. 48 (*CSPDEdVI*, 418).

116 See particularly E.G. Rupp, 'The early career of Bishop Barlow' in *Studies in the making of the English Protestant Tradition* (Cambridge 1947), 62–72; Hembry, *Bath and Wells*, 79–87, 105–23; R.B. Manning, *Religion and Society in Elizabethan Sussex* (Leicester 1969), 50–9.

117 PRO, SP 12/16, nos 38–40 (*CSPD* 1547–80, p. 172) for proceedings as archdeacon. Deprivation noted in WAM 6495. Cf. R.V.H. Burne, *Chester Cathedral. From its founding by Henry VIII to the accession of Queen Victoria* (1958), 44.

118 For his problems as bishop see Heal, *Prelates*, 251, 253; Skeeters, *Bristol*, 127–9, 134–7;

(stall VI, 1560–1), from 1561 bishop of Peterborough (where one of his main irritants would be Percival Wiborne [*54*]), appears only in connexion with the vacation of his stall (**194**).[119] [*49*] William Latymer (stall VIII, 1560–83) was, by contrast, a regular chapter member, serving as archdeacon (**209**) and acting as receiver (**217**). Like Barlow I [*45*] he had been chaplain to Anne Boleyn, whose piety he chronicled. Anne Boleyn's daughter made him dean of Peterborough.[120] [*50*] Richard Reeve (stall IX, 1560–94) is mentioned as preacher (**207**) and went with the dean to court when help was needed for repairs to Henry VII's chapel (**234**). Much later he was deputed to be on hand at Windsor (where he was also canon) when Westminster muniments were shown in evidence (**356**). [*51*] William Downham (stall X, 1560–4) was bishop of Chester from 1561; despite favours from the queen as a former chaplain, he suffered much financial trouble there.[121] [*52*] William Young (stall XI, 1560–79) appears to have been one of the few non-graduates appointed to Westminster after 1560. He is most prominently featured as master of a delinquent servant (**232**). [*53*] Thomas Wattes (stall XII, 1561–77), also archdeacon of Middlesex, was able to lend £25 to the Westminster chapter (**287**). He divided his time between London and the archiepiscopal peculiar of Bocking in Essex, of which he was jointly dean with Still [*67*].[122] The most noted enthusiast in the second chapter was [*54*] Percival Wiborne (stall III, 1561–1606), who was regularly present at Westminster despite extensive activities in Northamptonshire and, for a time, in the Channel Islands. At Rochester, where he was also a canon, he came close to deprivation for his extreme views.[123] A pleasanter moment is glimpsed at Westminster when he and Andrewes [*6*], then still a canon, exchanged houses 'by mutuall consent' (**488**) – probably the only matter on which these two ever agreed. [*55*] John Beaumont (stall VI, 1562–5) was brother of the master of Trinity (Robert, an O. W.). John's appointment was made *vice* Scambler [*48*] despite a previous patent for the same

C. Litzenberger, 'Richard Cheyney, bishop of Gloucester: an infidel in religion?', *Sixteenth Century Journal* xxv (1994), 567–84.

[119] See W.J. Sheils, 'Some problems of government in a new diocese: the bishop and the puritans in the diocese of Peterborough, 1560–1630', in O'Day and Heal, *Continuity and Change*, 168–72; Sheils, *Puritans*, 6–7, 28–33.

[120] 'William Latymer's Chronickille of Anne Bulleyne', ed. M. Dowling, *Camden Miscellany* xxx (Camden Soc., 4th ser. xxxix, 1990), 23–71 (for biographical details pp. 27–9 & n. 3); cf. G.W. Bernard, 'Anne Boleyn's religion', *HJ* xxxvi (1993), 2–3. For Latymer at Peterborough see Mellows, *Peterborough*, pp. xxix–xxx.

[121] See Haigh, 'Chester', 155–9.

[122] A. Hoffmann, *Bocking Deanery. The story of an Essex peculiar* (1976), 42–3.

[123] For Northamptonshire see Sheils, *Puritans*, 23–8 and *passim*; P. Collinson, *The Elizabethan Puritan Movement* (1967), 141–4. For the Channel Islands see Collinson, *op. cit.*, 151, 293; also HMC, *Salisbury MSS*, xiii, 145 (recorded at Jersey in June 1577). For Rochester see C.S. Knighton, 'The reformed chapter, 1540 to 1660', in *Faith and Fabric. A History of Rochester Cathedral 604–1994*, ed. W.N. Yates and P.A. Welsby (Woodbridge 1996), 70, 72.

vacancy issued to Robert Rolles.[124] This may explain why Beaumont's installation is one of those for which special entry was made in the acts (**194**). [*56*] Thomas Norley (stall IV, 1563–70) paid a rare visit to a long meeting in 1569 (**246**). [*57*] Edmund Freake (stall X, 1564–72) served as divinity reader (**202**). He became bishop of Rochester and then Norwich (where Mrs Freake did much to vindicate the queen's views on marriage among the higher clergy).[125] [*58*] John Hill (stall VII, 1564–7) was perhaps a former King's Scholar (**185** (f. 278v)). He was one of those who offered a differing opinion when signing the acts (**213**). [*59*] Matthew Hutton (stall VI, 1565–7) passed through the Abbey on his progress to the deanery of York (where he was a strong presence), the bishopric of Durham and then back to York as archbishop.[126] The Westminster chapter used his talents while they were available: he was appointed proctor in convocation – but with Hill [*58*] in reserve in case Hutton could not stay to attend (**222**) and was nominated with the dean to a sub-committee to choose a parish incumbent (**227**). [*60*] Thomas Browne (stall I, 1566–85) was head master. The acts record his admission to commons before he joined the chapter (**206**) and election as proctor (**262, 263**). He lent (and was repaid) £20 to the dean and chapter (**287**). [*61*] John Pory (stall VII, 1567–70) was appointed treasurer (**237, 243**) and to assert the church's right to funeral furnishings (**245**). His nephew and namesake would become a pupil and collaborator of Richard Hakluyt [*85*], and achieved an honoured place in American constitutional history.[127] [*62*] Walter Jones (stall VI, 1567–77) served as proctor (**263, 272**). There are some uncertainties about his career; but his identification as canon of Southwell is established from family letters in the Abbey muniments.[128] [*63*] Thomas Aldrich (stall VII, 1570–3; stall V, 1574–6) was one of those who investigated the disappearance of the chapter clerk in 1570 (**254**); but his own irregular tenure at Westminster – his readmission is specially recorded (**288**) – seems to have mirrored a controversial career at Cambridge.[129] [*64*] William Wickham or Wykeham (stall IV, 1570–1) had a short spell at Westminster coinciding with disruption of business after the chapter

124 *CPR* 1560–3, p. 320. Le Neve, 76, regards patent as 'possibly ineffective', and Rolles is not included in the present sequence.

125 See A.L. Rowse, *The England of Elizabeth. The Structure of Society* (1950, repr. 1964), 412; A.H. Smith, *County and Court: Government and Politics in Norfolk, 1558–1603* (Oxford 1974), 208–27.

126 For his deanship see M.C. Cross, 'From the Reformation to the Restoration', in Aylmer and Cant, *York Minster*, 205–6, 209–10. See also P.G. Lake, 'Matthew Hutton – a puritan bishop?', *History* lxiv (1979), 182–204.

127 Pory jr was first speaker of the Virginia assembly, North America's earliest legislature: W.S. Powell, *John Pory, 1572–1636. The Life and Letters of a Man of Many Parts* (Chapel Hill 1977), 4 & n. 5 (for Pory sr), 9–16 (for Hakluyt).

128 WAM 10804–26. He resided mostly at York: HMC, *Salisbury MSS*, xiii, 145. He may thus confidently be identified as the D.C.L. who was assistant vicar-general in the archdiocese: R.A. Marchant, *The Church under the Law. Justice, administration and discipline in the diocese of York, 1560–1640* (Cambridge 1969), 41–2, 94–5.

129 See Porter, *Reformation and Reaction*, 149–54.

clerk's disappearance (**254, 258**). Wickham's advancement to the bishopric of Lincoln was followed with special appropriateness by translation to Winchester. [*65*] Robert Ramsden (stall IV, 1571–5), chaplain to and probably tutor in the household of Sir William Cecil,[130] was assigned administrative duty soon after appointment to Westminster (**266**). [*66*] John Young (stall X, 1572–1605) is named as proctor in convocation less than a month after appointment to the chapter (**272**). He became bishop of Rochester in 1578, a dignity later held by successive deans of Westminster. Young offered the doubtless excellent maxim that a man should spend no more than a third of his income on food and drink, though it would appear he was unable to confine himself to these limits.[131]

[*67*] John Still (stall VII, 1573–93), once thought to be the author of *Gammer Gurton's Needle*, was dean of Bocking jointly with Wattes [*53*]; as archdeacon of Sudbury he sided with the puritan gentry of Suffolk against the distant authority of Bishop Freake [*57*] in Norwich. Parker, whose chaplain he was, proposed Still for the deanery of Norwich, but with such reservation that the promotion was understandably not made.[132] At Westminster Still's principal record in the acts is his recommendation of a candidate for a chapter living, despite the fact that the man (who happened to be from Still's own college) had failed his ordination examination at the first attempt (**345**). Still eventually went on to become a successful bishop of Bath and Wells.[133] [*68*] William Chaderton (stall IV, 1575–9) also became a bishop – first of Chester, where he succeeded Downham [*51*] whose finances he only slightly improved upon. He was a friend of Andrewes [*6*] the future dean, but perhaps not of a former one.[134] [*69*] John Rugge (stall V, 1576–82) appears to have lost interest in chapter attendance after the first few months of membership (**305 x 313**). He resided mostly at Wells, where he was archdeacon. He also made a determined but unsuccessful attempt to secure the archdeaconry of Norwich.[135] [*70*] Edward Grant (stall XII, 1577–1601), whose installation was enacted (**316**), was the first Old Westminster to return as head master, and (according to the school's main historian) the first to leave his mark there.[136] He left his mark on the chapter in the person of his son Gabriel (canon 1613–38). Edward was on the library committee (**397**) and twice proctor (**332, 485**). [*71*] Griffith Lewis (stall VI, 1577–1607) was elected archdeacon (**321**) and

[130] R.W. Beckingsale, *Burghley. Tudor Statesman, 1520–1598* (1967), 248.

[131] Heal, *Prelates*, 86, 257.

[132] D.N.J. MacCulloch, *Suffolk and the Tudors. Politics and Religion in an English County, 1500–1600* (Oxford 1986), 51. *Parker Corr.*, 449–50.

[133] Hembry, *Bath and Wells*, 183–206.

[134] See Haigh, 'Chester', 156–7; Heal, *Prelates*, 212–13, 314–15. He is alleged to have criticized Cox [*2*] in a sermon at Paul's Cross: J. Strype, *The Life and Acts of Matthew Parker* (1711), 473, referring to a sermon at Paul's Cross in 1574 (not recorded in *Reg. PX*).

[135] *The Letter Book of John Parkhurst, Bishop of Norwich, compiled during the years 1571–5*, ed. R.A. Houlbrooke (Norfolk Record Soc. xliii, 1974 and 1975), 39, 142 & n. 292.

[136] Sargeaunt, 51–2. Grant's House, it should be noted, is *not* named after him: Field, *King's Nurseries*, 56.

had a grant of building timber from one of the dean and chapter's properties close to his deanery of Gloucester (**472**). [*72*] John Reade (stall II, 1578–87) was also archdeacon (**374**) and was appointed with Lewis [*71*] to deal with Gloucestershire business (**362**). [*73*] John Wickham (stall XI, 1579–92) served as treasurer (**382**). [*74*] Thomas Wagstaff (stall IV, 1579–86) signs for the first time in 1580 (**332**) and several times thereafter, but is not otherwise evident. [*75*] Nicholas Bond (stall V, 1582–1608) was chaplain of the Savoy, and also president of Magdalen College, Oxford (where his charges would include Henry, prince of Wales). He was associated with the benefactions of the countess of Sussex (**424**) and served as treasurer and on the library committee (**355, 397**). [*76*] Edward Buckley (stall VIII, 1583–1621) had his installation recorded (**360**) and his appointment as archdeacon (**465**). He appears to have taken chiefest satisfaction in a refutation of popery at Paul's Cross in 1590.[137] [*77*] Thomas Montford (stall I, 1585–1633) was treasurer, proctor and archdeacon at various times (**403, 408, 413**). He was chaplain to the earl of Warwick and canon of St Paul's. [*78*] Richard Webster (stall IV, 1586–1601 or 1602) was on the library committee (**397**) and elected archdeacon (**419**). He was also archdeacon of Middlesex and a canon of Hereford. [*79*] Richard Wood (stall II, 1587–1609) was a canon of Canterbury and St Paul's, and dean of Bocking. At Westminster he was on the library committee and archdeacon (**397, 447**). He was also specially permitted to fence off an area at the west of the Abbey to use as his garden (**459**). [*80*] Richard Bancroft (stall XI, 1592–7) was proctor for the Westminster chapter (**437**); he was granted a house which he rebuilt and which was long known by his name (**435, 476**). He vacated his canonry to become bishop of London, from where he moved to Canterbury in 1604.[138] [*81*] Thomas Ravis (stall VII, 1593–1607) would also become bishop of London, having previously held the bishopric of Gloucester. He was the first O. W. bishop. His advancement had an uncertain start when his election to Christ Church, recorded here (**546**) was not effective until Burghley and the queen lent support to Westminster's rights to scholarships.[139] As canon, Ravis became treasurer (**447, 534**); he also held the prime Abbey living of Islip (**494**). [*82*] Cuthbert Bellott (stall IX, 1594–1620) was obviously a controversial appointee, since it was necessary to admit him 'without contradiction' (**450**). [*83*] Hadrian Saravia (stall XI, 1601–13) is of special interest, not only as one of the small band of foreigners who have become dignitaries of the Church of England, but as one of the first in a wave of preachers distinguished by extreme deference to the power of the monarchy. He was also one of the translators of the Bible.[140] At Westminster he was given

---

137 *Reg. PX,* 68, following note in *An Apologie for Religion, or an Answere to an Unlearned Pamphlet Intituled: Certaine Articles, or Forcible Reasons* (1602: *STC* 4025), 96.
138 See principally S.B. Babbage, *Puritanism and Richard Bancroft* (1962).
139 Sargeaunt, 58–9.
140 Porter, *Reformation and Reaction,* 352–3. W. Nijenhuis, *Adrianus Saravia (c. 1532–1613). Dutch Calvinist, First Reformed Defender of the English Episcopal Church Order on the basis of the Ius*

the post of archdeacon (**534, 539**). [*84*] William Barlow II (stall XII, 1601–13) was, like his namesake of 1560 [*45*] destined to be a bishop (of Rochester 1605 and Lincoln 1608). His appointment to Westminster was probably a reward for the difficult assignment of preaching at Paul's Cross following the earl of Essex's rising. On 10 November 1605 he occupied the same pulpit charged with the task of explaining what Gunpowder Plot was.[141] In the following month his Westminster colleagues elected him subdean (**534**). The geographer [*85*] Richard Hakluyt (stall IV, 1602–16) was archdeacon of Westminster (**530**). He is perhaps the only member of the chapter whose fame is unconnected with religion; he is certainly the only one whose work is mentioned by Shakespeare.[142] [*86*] Christopher Sutton (stall X, 1605–29) was appointed because James I particularly admired his preaching style. He gave the sermon at William Camden's funeral in the Abbey. His colleagues there were concerned because he had long been without a canonical house (**542**). [*87*] John Fox (stall III, 1606–23) (who was not the martyrologist) was canon of St Paul's and, at Westminster, treasurer (**544**). [*88*] Hugh Goodman (stall VII, 1607–23) was at Westminster and Christ Church with Hakluyt [*85*], next to whom he signed the acts for the first time (**541**). He had been master of the school at Ruthin founded by Dean Goodman [*5*], and it has been suggested that he was the dean's illegitimate son.[143] [*89*] George Darrell (stall VI, 1607–31), brother of Sir Matthew, the cofferer of the household, was himself also canon of Lincoln. [*90*] William Robinson (stall V, 1608–42), was the last canon appointed during the currency of Act Book I, and signs to the last entries (**543–5**). His half-brother would join him in the chapter in 1621: his name was William Laud.

(iii) *Discipline*

The authority of the dean over the whole collegiate body is established in the statutes: even his chapter colleagues were required to show obedience to him as *caput et dux* in a way which distinguishes the new foundations from the old.[144] But uncertainty about contradictions in the statutes permitted a measure of leniency

---

Divinum (Leiden 1980), 139–40 (for Westminster). J.P. Sommerville, 'Ideology, property and the constitution', in Cust and Hughes, *Conflict*, 50, 54–5. Collinson, 'Protestant cathedral', 179–80 & n. 148 (citing further sources).

[141] *Reg. PX*, 75–6, 85–6. *STC* 1454, 1455. The first sermon is reprinted in *In God's Name. Examples of Preaching in England from the Act of Supremacy to the Act of Uniformity, 1534–1662*, ed. J. Chandos (1971), 110–19.

[142] The allusion (*Twelfth Night*, III, ii) is owed to K.G. Feiling, *In Christ Church Hall* (1960), 9. Hakluyt was an O.W. For his personal history see *The Original Writings and Correspondence of the two Richard Hakluyts*, ed. E.G.R. Taylor (Hakluyt Soc., 2nd ser. lxxvi, lxxvii, 1935); J.A. Williamson, 'Richard Hakluyt', in *Richard Hakluyt and his successors*, ed. E. Lynam (Hakluyt Soc., 2nd ser. xciii, 1947), 1–46.

[143] Soden, *Goodman*, 29, 42 & n. 4; Kenyon-Thompson, *Ruthin School*, 79. At Ruthin his predecessor was John Price, former under master of Westminster.

[144] *Statutes (1)*, 81/107. For the old foundation deans see Edwards, *Secular Cathedrals*, 137–48; Thompson, *English Clergy*, 75–6.

and self-regulation (**69**). Towards the canons there is no overt display of decanal authority. Over the subsidiary or inferior members of the foundation the dean was similarly paramount, but his responsibility for appointments was the subject of contention only finally resolved by George VI.[145] By the 1544 statutes the dean and chapter were jointly charged with appointing the minor canons, lay vicars, lay officers and the butler, but the lower servants (if they may be so termed) were to be chosen by the dean alone. The almsmen, like the dean and canons, were and would remain crown appointments.[146] In March 1546 the chapter decided to share out the nomination of the subsidiary posts, the dean having two choices to every one made by each canon (**50**). This was revised in the following year when the dean was allotted the selection of all ten choristers and four of the scholars, the other 36 boys' places to be shared among the canons (**66**). Some of the nominations are specified in no. **185**. This arrangement, which has counterparts elsewhere,[147] seems to have been satisfactory enough to escape revision by Dean Cox, although in 1552 a chapter order warned that anyone taking bribes for making nominations would be allowed no further choices (**127**). The Elizabethan statutes are less precise about the nomination (as opposed to the function) of the inferiors; the servants were to be chosen by the dean, ruled by the officers (subdean, archdeacon, treasurer and steward), but if disobedient to them to be expelled by the dean.[148] But it was the joint agreement of the dean and chapter to impose this extreme sanction in 1567 on Canon Young's servant, whose fights and quarrels were 'verie offensive to good people' (**232**). This followed a warning that misbehaving servants would be expelled after a second offence proved before the dean and two canons (**228**). In 1551 one of the men of the choir was dismissed for slandering two colleagues; in this case on the authority of the dean alone (**92**, repeated **115**). An act of violence received a sharper but less enduring penalty: three days in the gatehouse and a fine to mend the victim's head (**176**).

That such instances are comparatively rare may not necessarily mean that all was otherwise well; routine discipline was handled by the precentor: at first merely 'one of the prestes' was 'monitor' (**1**); later the precentor is specified (**14**) and required to keep and submit a record of absenteeism among the choir (**48**). The precentor was chosen by the dean and chapter from the minor canons. He was chiefly a disciplinary and administrative officer rather than a musician; less grand than his namesake in the old foundations, but in some ways following the secretarial functions of the monastic precentor of Westminster.[149] To these

---

[145] *HK*, 457–8.

[146] *Statutes (1)*, 88, 90–3 / 111–15.

[147] At Ely: CCC, MS 120, pp. 288–9; at Worcester: *Documents illustrating early education in Worcester, 685 to 1700*, ed. A.F. Leach (Worcestershire Historical Soc. xxxi, 1913), 169–71.

[148] *Statutes (2)*, 89. The officers (*magistri*) are defined *ibid.*, 85.

[149] In the old foundations the precentor is a canon, normally ranking second to the dean: Edwards, *Secular Cathedrals*, 159–66. For (non-liturgical) paperwork by the monastic pre-

duties were subsequently added those of reading matins in Henry VII's chapel and supervising alms distribution (**248, 249**).

Absent or misbehaving choirmen were probably less of a worry to the dean and chapter than dishonest financial officers. They were obliged to take legal action against one defaulting rent collector (**227**) and were only prevented from proceeding against another (**176, 178**) because the man was arrested on a more serious charge. Another problem came when the chapter clerk disappeared 'towardes night' in November 1570 (**255**) – he reappeared behind bars. His absence meant that meetings of the chapter were repeatedly abandoned (**258–60**) despite an earlier attempt to recover papers from the missing man's chamber (**254**). But in general the dean and chapter were well served by their lay officers – most notably John Moulton, who had begun his career in the service of the abbey, became receiver-general in 1545 (**31**) and remained in that post until his death, indifferently serving cathedral, restored abbey and refounded college.[150]

The most disgraceful abuse of the foundation was perpetrated by Queen Elizabeth, who appears to have allowed a boy to occupy one of the almsmen's places (**503**). These were supposed to be enjoyed by persons aged and decayed in the nation's service, as indeed they commonly were. Appointment of them was the subject of the only royal letter which the chapter copied into their Act Book (**155**) and another time occasioned a message and token from two of Elizabeth's most trusted ladies to secure the queen's intention (**378**).

(iv) *Fabric*

Maintenance of the building was not the predominating concern for the sixteenth-century dean and chapter that it would become for their more recent successors. There was no large worry about the stability of the structure, nor any disposition as to its further extension or embellishment. The acts record a survey of the east end made for report to Henry VIII's council (**10**) but it was not until 1603 that the chapter felt the need to establish a fabric fund (**529**). In 1567 they had sought state aid for repairs to Henry VII's chapel (**234**). Early acts catalogue the destruction or conversion of redundant monastic buildings (**26, 46, 54, 113**), a process most pointedly continued later by the division of the dorter to serve more wakeful purposes as schoolroom and library (**430, 504**). Concern is shown for the amenities of garden and orchard (**200, 514**), and for the proper functioning of the water conduit system (**10, 11, 141**) – with strict prohibition of its use for laundering, an activity which the dean and chapter appear to have regarded with special disfavour (**340, 425**).

---

centor see *Customary of the Benedictine Monasteries of Saint Augustine, Canterbury, and Saint Peter, Westminster*, ii, ed. E.M. Thompson (Henry Bradshaw Soc. xxviii, 1904), 36, 254.

[150] It has been wrongly stated that Moulton was dismissed by Dean Cox: Westlake, *Westminster Abbey*, i, 217; *HK*, 117. This is based on misreading of the reversionary grant of the receivership to Thomas Fisher in 1550: WAM Reg. III, ff. 159v–160v.

(v) *Liturgy*

Those among the monks transformed into secular canons by Henry VIII and who had been occupied in the choir offices of Westminster Abbey would have found their new duties lighter. Most notably gone was the obligation to rise for matins at midnight.[151] On the other hand the canons of the old foundations had long since devolved their liturgical functions upon their vicars choral.[152] The canons of the new foundations were required to fulfil a somewhat intermediate function. The largest increase in duties was for the men and boys of the lay choir previously serving the Lady Chapel; they now replaced the choir monks as the principal liturgical and musical unit in the Abbey, and must have had to learn a much more extensive repertoire.[153] This, however, would have to be as quickly forgotten when it was discovered that polyphony was displeasing to God. Simple English settings of the communion service were used for the first time at the mass of the Holy Ghost inaugurating Edward VI's first parliament in 1547: the chapter's concern is expressed only to elect their proctor for the convocation to meet in St Paul's on the same day (**70**). Hitherto the music and ritual had been largely unaffected by religious as opposed to institutional changes. The first surviving chapter act (**1**) orders three masses a day, the third of which was sung with deacon and subdeacon. The institution of high mass was embodied in the new foundation by the appointment of a gospeller and epistoler; these jobs disappeared when the second Prayer Book in 1552 effectively abolished the choral celebration. By 1547 it would appear that there was only one daily mass, no more than equivalent in importance to matins and evensong (**69**). Two years later, when the first Prayer Book was issued, mass had become 'communion tyme' (**94**). There is no matter in the acts dealing with the restoration of Catholic worship after 1553, but other muniments bear much testimony to this.[154] With the return of the Prayer Book liturgy under Queen Elizabeth, a monthly celebration of communion, by one of the canons or his deputy, was the only

---

[151] Miss Harvey (*Living and Dying*, 77 & n. 22) calculates that the *claustrales* represented about one third of the Westminster community. Since the 1540 secular chapter included the former abbot, prior and other seniors, it may be doubted if more than one or two of the new canons had recent experience of the full office. For the hour of matins in the abbey see Harvey, *op. cit.*, 156. For collegiate practice see A.H. Thompson, *The Cathedral Churches of England* (1928), 196–200. Cathedral matins was fixed nationally at 6 a.m. in 1547, but for the new foundations the night office must have ceased in 1544: *Vis. Art.*, ii, 138. *Statutes (1)*, 97/117.

[152] See Edwards, *Secular Cathedrals*, 258–67.

[153] For Lady Chapel choirs in greater monasteries see F. Ll. Harrison, *Music in Medieval Britain* (2nd edn 1963), 38–45. For Westminster Abbey see Pine, *Singers*, 19–36; *idem*, 'Westminster Abbey: some early masters of the choristers', *Musical Times* xciv (1953), 258–60. For a comparable institution see R.D. Bowers, 'The liturgy of the cathedral and its music, c. 1075–1642', in Collinson, Ramsay and Sparks, *Canterbury Cathedral*, 419–24, 427.

[154] WAM 37412–13, 37417–19, 37426, 37432, 37573, 37637, 37642A, 37646B, 37650 are among the most informative.

requirement (**189**). By contrast sermons are the subject of increasing attention. The first collegiate church had provided these every Sunday in the Abbey (**2**) and also quarterly in St Botolph's Aldersgate, which was in the chapter's gift (**94**). Arrangements were also made for deputies (**32**) and for a verger to conduct the preacher to and from the pulpit (**94**). The second collegiate church made additional orders: from 1561 there were to be sermons on Christmas Day, Whit Sunday and All Saints Day – these and the Sunday sermons to be given by members of the chapter in turn, or by deputies from among their number. A quarterly sermon was to be given in St Bride's Fleet Street as well as at St Botolph's (**189**). Subsequent acts regulated the payment of deputies (**203**) and their approval in advance by the dean (**286**), the order of seniority in which canons were to preach (**207**) and what the preacher should wear (**262**). In 1564 sermons were introduced on certain holy days: the Circumcision, Epiphany, Purification and Annunciation, St Mark, Sts Philip and James, Ascension Day, St John Baptist, St Peter (when the dean was to preach), St James, Michaelmas, St Luke and Sts Simon and Jude (**547**). Further rostering of the feast day sermons was made in 1581 (**346**). A sermon was also preached on the queen's accession day (**350**). Loopholes were closed in 1607 when sermons were ordered on 'extraordinary dayes not yet provided for' (**541**). Further edification was provided by lectures endowed by the countess of Sussex (**424, 541**).

The progress of the Reformation is to be noted also in the redeployment of the monastic buildings at Westminster (**26, 46, 54, 113**) and St Martin-le-Grand (**68**), and in the disposal of Catholic liturgical equipment in the reign of Edward VI, when economy and protestantism were mutually supportive (**85, 88, 109**). The most dramatic simplification of the liturgical *décor* was achieved by the king's commissioners in 1553; it is recorded in a special entry at the end of Act Book I (**186**). Further material changes occurred under Elizabeth I, when such vestments as remained were cut up to serve a secular purpose (**262**) and the communion plate was altered to allow for ministration of the cup to the laity (**199**).

Despite the increasing emphasis on the spoken word and the dismantling of the ornaments of worship, the music of the Abbey, as in other such places, somehow survived. The choristers and their master are provided for in early chapter acts (**12, 49**). It may be noted that the men and boys of the choir remained in being during the monastic restoration (when, it is to be presumed, they resumed operations in the chapel of Henry VII) and again without a break into the second collegiate church, thus providing a continuity of liturgical service through four successive regimes at Westminster. Towards the end of the period covered by Act Book I there is renewed interest in the choir and their music. The men's wages were raised in 1583 and 1606 (**355, 539**). In 1603 'many disorders' (unspecified) in the choristers were detected and reformed (**529**). Two years later they were ordered to attend school with the king's scholars when not about their musical occasions (**533**). Also in Dean Andrewes's time the men of the choir were required to stagger their absences so that a proper balance of voices would be maintained – regrettably in this sensible arrangement the Abbey had to copy St Paul's (**524**).

When John Taylor gave up the mastership of the choristers in 1569 the chapter gave him a testimonial and appointed a lay vicar to fill the office until they found a permanent successor (**246, 248**). That was to be Robert Whyte (**250**), but he was soon to die of plague. The appointment of Edmund Hooper is also recorded (**407**), although this was later in question (**529**) and a new patent as organist was issued in 1606 (**538**).[155]

(vi) *State occasions*

Between 1543 and 1609 four monarchs were crowned in Westminster Abbey and three buried.[156] These events receive no mention here. But the State Opening of parliament had at this time a religious prelude: originally and again during Mary's reign a votive mass of the Holy Ghost, under the new order reduced to a sermon.[157] In 1547 the preacher was Nicholas Ridley (**70** n. 117). In 1571 the dean and chapter cannibalized the best of the copes given by Abbot Feckenham to make a canopy for the queen as she attended the Abbey before parliament (**262**). Another canopy was required for the same purpose in the following year (**272**). In 1584 the chapter were at first content to ask that only those of their fellows who 'may convenyently be here' need escort the queen (**370**). This entry was scored out, and the whole collegiate body ordered to attend (**371**). Another state occasion, though not one graced by the monarch's person, was November 17, the queen's accession day. At Westminster this was thought an appropriate time for canons to deliver their maiden sermons (**350**).

(vii) *Burials*

One of the earliest chapter acts (**3**) concerns the burial of a public servant in the Abbey. This was already a well-established custom and, for the dean and chapter, a useful source of revenue – not yet a problem. They had a scale of charges, from a gentleman (in the body of the church £10, in any of the chapels £13 6s 8d) to an archbishop or duke (£40). In addition there were clothing allowances to the dean, the subdean, precentor, vergers, almsmen and preacher's man.[158] In 1569 there was a quarrel with the College of Arms which led the chapter to assert their right to funeral furnishings (**245**). In 1571 they were able to apply the

---

[155] Musical matters of the period are briefly treated in J. Perkins, *The Organs and Bells of Westminster Abbey* (1937), 3–6; Pine, *Singers*, 37–95; *HK*, 416–17, 418–19, 421–2; D.A. Guest, *A Short History of the Organs of Westminster Abbey* (1969), [1–2].

[156] Henry VIII was buried at Windsor.

[157] For the ceremony in general see J.E. Neale, *The Elizabethan House of Commons* (2nd edn 1963), 336–7; D. Dean, 'Image and ritual in the Tudor parliaments', in *Tudor Political Culture*, ed. D.E. Hoak (Cambridge 1995), 262–5. An order of proceeding for the November 1554 parliament service is in PRO, SP 12/90, no. 16 (*CSPDM*, 136).

[158] WAM Reg. III, f. 147v.

proceeds of a burial to the decoration of the sacrarium (**266**). The appointment of keepers of Henry VII's chapel and the monuments (**512**, **541**) shows that tourism was already a matter requiring regulation. Few of the members of the chapter in this period have surviving monuments. That of Dean Benson in St Blaise's chapel has long since gone.[159] The next dean to die in office, Bill, is commemorated by a brass marking his grave in St Benedict's chapel.[160] Goodman's bust is there also. Of the tenants one, William Jennings (**166**), made elaborate provision for his burial in the restored abbey and the erection of a brass there, but this can no longer be seen. Among those whose memorials conspicuously survive and who in life had some connexion with the Abbey there may particularly be mentioned Frances, duchess of Suffolk (**85**), Sir William Cecil, 1st Lord Burghley (**112**), John, Lord Russell (**332**), Sir Thomas Owen (**377**, **459**) and Lord Hunsdon (**385**).

The Abbey's burial registers are not extant until 1607; among the first entries are those for John Winterburne, verger, appointed in 1599 (**509**), and John Blackburne, the scholars' butler, appointed in 1607 (**541**); they were buried in the cloisters in 1607 and 1609 respectively.[161]

(viii) *School*

Henry VIII's establishment of forty scholars and their two masters was, like the choral foundation, undisturbed by the upheavals at Westminster from 1550 to 1560. Although Westminster School regards Elizabeth I as foundress and marks November 17 by a triennial commemoration, education at Westminster no more began in 1560 than it had done in 1540. The Elizabethan *amicabilis concordia* with Trinity and Christ Church, upon which the advancement of Westminsters would so crucially depend, was prefigured by university studentships briefly existing on the Henrician foundation (**39**). These links may in turn be seen as the continuation of a monastic tradition.[162]

The chapter acts are an important source for the history of Westminster School.[163] The admission of scholars is recorded, albeit sporadically, in the time

---

159 Camden, *Reges*, sig. I, 1v.

160 J.S.N. Wright, *The Brasses of Westminster Abbey* (1969), 33–4, [35].

161 Chester, 108, 109. For burials before 1540 see Harvey, *Estates*, 365–86. The more notable burials within the Abbey between 1540 and 1607 are given in Dart, *passim*; Stanley, 180–91; Murray Smith, 85–127.

162 Cf. B.F. Harvey, 'The monks of Westminster and the university of Oxford', in *The Reign of Richard II. Essays in Honour of May McKisack*, ed. F.R.H. Du Boulay and C.M. Barron (1971), 108–30.

163 There is no distinct school archive for this period, although certain artificial collections have been assembled in the Abbey muniments: WAM 43045–51, 54000–25 are the most important. Westminster School Archives, Buttery Book, which contains lists of scholars elected to Trinity and Christ Church 1561–1822, is not a contemporary record. For the school in this period see Sargeaunt, 1–64; L.E. Tanner, *Westminster School. Its Buildings and their Associations* (1924), 1–3, 88–90; Tanner, *Westminster School. A History* (1934), 1–10; J.D.

of the first collegiate church (**67, 185** *passim*), as are the arrangements for nomination and election (**66, 69, 127**). There is also a table showing elections of Westminsters to Trinity and Christ Church between 1572 and 1576 (**546**). Housing for the second or under master is provided (**98, 131**). Of the head masters Alexander Nowell has already been noted in his capacity as a canon (p. xlii above). The surprising appointment of Nicholas Udall (whose previous head mastership had ended with a prison sentence) is among those recorded (**185** (f. 282v)). In 1564 the head master (Browne) was admitted to the canons' commons – but only if it was necessary to make up the number of four residentiaries (**206**). He later became a canon anyway. Edward Grant's appointment in 1577 is also recorded (**316**). When William Camden became head master in 1594 the queen specially requested that his servant should receive commons (**451, 452**). Camden's own commons had been allowed earlier (**447**). Ireland was similarly accommodated in 1598 (**498**).

There was a particularly close association between the chapter and the school in Elizabeth's reign. No doubt the plague-time evacuations (p. xxxix above) fostered the community spirit. So too did the taking of tutorial charge by some of the canons (**199, 208**). By 1584 this duty appears to have been discharged by college servants (**372**). The residence of the scholars and their recreation was the subject of an order in 1563 (**199**). The development of the great room known laconically as School is first mentioned in 1591: it was hoped that the building work would begin in the following year with the aid of contributions to hand and expected from 'godlie disposed persons' (**430**). By 1599 the project had evidently lapsed, but was taken in hand again because the existing schoolroom was too small and low to contain the (obviously quite tall) scholars (**504**). The acts also record the benefaction of Lord Burghley (**426**) and the support of James I (**544**) which in their several ways helped Westminsters at the universities.

(ix) *Library and muniments*

The making of a library and the buying of books from the proceeds of the sale of redundant ornaments is ordered in 1549 (**85**). Nothing more is said on the subject in the first collegiate church – though by chance a book owned by one of the tenants found its way into the collection (**110** n. 211). A gift of books by Dean Goodman is recorded (**296**) but it is not until 1587 that a schedule of library rules was made, ordering the making of desks and shelves, an inventory and a register of benefactors, and the weeding out of duplicates and triplicates; William Camden was named as keeper, in addition to his duty as under master (**397**).

The muniments were of more immediate concern to the chapter, and are consequently more often mentioned. They were to be kept locked (**2**) and items

Carleton, *Westminster School. A History* (1965), 1–7; Field, *King's Nurseries*, 9–29; Knighton, 'Collegiate Foundations', 253–300; *idem*, 'Education', 22–5.

retained by the government after the interregnum of 1540–2 were to be returned (**9**). Efforts were made to recover documents which had been kept privately by the chapter's own officers (**37, 254**). But muniments sometimes had to be taken away for use in evidence – at Windsor (**356**) or before the court of high commission (**363**). The muniments and the act book itself served essentially legal and practical purposes. Although the chapter regarded the acts as a register of their decisions (**189**), previous orders might be scored through or more heavily obliterated (**142, 537**); in one instance even this was inadequate, and a whole page was officially removed (**287**). Perhaps when they ordered an extract to be made from their fourteenth century cartulary known as Domesday (**264**) they may have wondered if their own dispositions would endure to such a time.

TEXT

MISCELLANEOUS PRELIMINARY MATTER

I. *Memorandum, 19th century.*

[first unnumbered leaf] [note by A.P. S(tanley)[1] of the contents of the book]

II. *Previous owner, 1524.*

[second unnumbered leaf] [non-Westminster business, including:
Thys boke made the 14^{io} October 1524 pertaynyng unto me William Coupper, grocer.[2]]

III. *Production in evidence, 18th century.*

This book was shown to Charles Battely, esquire, and Charles Lowe, gentleman, at the times of their severall examinations taken in Chancery on the part and behalf of Francis [Atterbury], Lord Bishop of Rochester, Michael Evans and Thomas Sprat, clerks, Lawrence Brodrick, Robert Cannon and Harry Barker, Doctors in Divinity, defendants, at the suit of the Right Honourable Nicholas Lechmere, esquire, his Majesties Attorney Generall, at the relation of Nicholas Onley, Thomas Dent, Thomas Lynford and Edward Gee, Doctors in Divinity, Samuel [Bradford], Lord Bishop of Carlisle, Robert Freind, Doctor in Divinity, and William Farrer, esquire, complainants. [*Signed*] Edward Northey.[3]

IV. *Memoranda, 16th century.*

[f. +1] [non-Westminster business]
[pen trials, including:
Honty soyte qui male ypence.]
Edwardus sextus. Memorandum that the yere of the kynges majesties reygne is alwayes renuyd upon the xxviijth day of January.

V. *Pension for a canon, 1557.*

The date of Mr Alfonsous patent.
Vicesimo die Martii anno Domini 1556 annisque regnorum Philippi et Marie iij^{tio} et iiij^{to}.

---

1 Dean 1864–81.
2 See Introduction, p. xxv.
3 This relates to the controversy over Dean Atterbury's proposed building of the new College Dormitory, which divided the chapter (as they appear in this memorandum) in the years 1718–21 before the House of Lords sided with the dean on 16 May 1721. Work on Wren's building began in the following year: Sargeaunt, 143–6. *HK*, 201.

The patent is graunted to Alphonso de Salinas[4] as appeareth by the same and the register. The embassadors, videlicet Mr Chamberleyn and Sir Thomas Chaloner[5] do certifye that one Alonso de Salinas is alyve. The lettre of atturney is made by Alonso de Salinas and not Alphonso de Salinas: he hath written his own name in the register boke Alonso de Salinas. His lettre of atturney doth not declare that authoritie is geven to his atturney to aske for and receyve the annuitie or pension from tyme to tyme, or for any certeyn tyme, but barely to ask and receive an annuitie of xxx li.[a] graunted by John abbot of Westm' of [b] the said abbot and his convent[c] and theyr successors or of any other person to whom the said monastrie shall cum.

The late abbot and[d] his convent did give the said Alphonso a bond of ccc li. with condition to pay the said annuitie, and have bound themselfes and theyr successors to pay the same. The date of the obligaton is the xx[ti] [e] of Marche 1556, videlicet the same date that the patent beareth.

> [a] Sum and 'of' inserted. [b] Repl. 'and his successors'. [c] Three words repeated then deleted. [d] Repl. 'd[id]'. [e] Repl. illegible figure.

VI. *Gift of a verge, c.1598.*

[f. +1v] Memorandum that Ralf Riddle late one of the vergers of this colledge did give his rodde to those that succeede in that office from tyme to tyme, which was since newly repaired by the colledge, and therefore yt is appointed by[a] the deane and chapter that the same shall contynue to the use of those that succeede from tyme to tyme.[6]

> [a] Repl. 'that yt shalbe'.

[f. +2] [non-Westminster business]

---

[4] De Salinas was the only member of the dissolved secular chapter of 1556 who received no compensatory promotion: Knighton, 'Collegiate Foundations', 162. He had been granted a pension of £30 by the abbot and convent on 27 Feb. 1557 secured (as here recorded) by a bond of £300 dated March 20: WAM Reg. IV, ff. 5, 17. WAM 5927. The restored dean and chapter took up the burden and paid the pension in 1559/60 and 1561/2 (WAM 33617, f. 5; 33619, f. 4v) but thereafter defaulted. Salinas had returned to Spain and was forced to sue at common pleas through the agency of a Spanish merchant in London: WAM 38705, 38710, relating to proceedings in 1567 and 1568. The memorandum entered here, in the hand of the receiver-general George Burden, dates from the early 1560s and would seem to represent a feeble attempt to evade payment on a technicality. But judgement was given in the Spaniard's favour, and he received £160 in arrears and full settlement in 1567/8 and 1568/9: WAM 38594, 38595, 33627, f. 5v; 33628, f. 5v. See below, nos **234, 238**.

[5] Sir Thomas Chamberlain was ambassador in Spain in 1560–2: *Hist. Parl. 1558–1603*, i, 589–90; Sir Thomas Chaloner was resident there 1561–5: *ibid., 1509–1558*, i, 611.

[6] Occurs as a servant of the dean and chapter 1581: WAM 39894. Appointed verger 19 May 1590: below, no. **415**; vacated in 1598: WAM 33651, f. 3v; 33652, f. 3; below, no. **494**. No plate owned by the Abbey before 1660 is still in its keeping.

VII. *Leases sealed 25 March 1555.*

Sealinges the xxv daye of Marche 1554 [*recte* 1555]. 1. In primis W. Westone for Vahnne howse.[7] 2. John Cowike.[8] 3. Langridge.[9] 4. Gertrude Cowbridge.[10] 5,6. For the sales of the wodes at Whetamesteade. 7. Henre Cole.[11] 8. Edmunde Lorde.[12] 9. John James.[13] 10. Thomas Polly.[14] 11. John Russell.[a] [15] 12. Agnes Graunt.[16] 13. H. Northei.[b] [17] 14. Lorde Sturtone.[c] [18]

> [a] Repl. 'Gertrude Cowbrid[ge]'.   [b] Repl. 'John Cowike', and the numeration corrected.
> [c] Followed by deletion.

[f. +2v] [blank]
[f. +3] [non-Westminster business]
[f. +3v] [blank]
[f. +4] [modern index]
[f. +4v] [blank]
[f. +5] [non-Westminster business]
[ff. +5v – +6v] [blank]
[f. +7] [non-Westminster business]
[f. +7v] [blank]
[f. +8] [non-Westminster business]
[f. +8v] [blank]
[f. +9] [non-Westminster business]
[ff. +9v – + 11v] [blank]
[f. +12] [non-Westminster business]
[f. +12v] [blank]
[f. +13] [non-Westminster business]
[ff. +13v – +14v] [blank]

[7] See below, no. **167** & n. 319.
[8] Cowycke, of Stepney, gent., granted three tenements in the Sanctuary and one in Thieving Lane for 80 years from the expiry of the interest of John Grene at £3 6s 8d rent 14 March 1555: WAM Reg. III, ff. 255v–256. Or lease of walls of the Sanctuary: below, no. **174** & n. 353.
[9] See below, no. **166** & n. 317.
[10] William Cowbridge, shoemaker, had lease of a tenement in St Martin-le-Grand in 1550: WAM 13018.
[11] See below, no. **165** & n. 315.
[12] See below, no. **152** & n. 298.
[13] See below, no. **167** & n. 320.
[14] See below, no. **167** & n. 321.
[15] Russell, carpenter, granted tithe of garbage corn and hay of the rectory of St Margaret's for 80 years from Lady Day following at £2 13s 4d rent 14 March 1555: WAM Reg. III, f. 267.
[16] Granted a tenement in the Sanctuary for 41 years from Christmas last at £1 5s rent 19 March 1555: *ibid*.
[17] See below, no. **249** & n. 208.
[18] See below, no. **164** & n. 314.

[f. +15] [non-Westminster business]
[ff. +15v – +16v] [blank]
[f. +17] [non-Westminster business]
[ff. +17v – +18v] [blank]
[f. +19] [non-Westminster business]
[ff. +19v – +20v] [blank]
[f. +21] [non-Westminster business]
[ff. +21v – +23v] [blank]
[f. +24v excised]

ACTS 1543–1556

[ff. 1–9 *excised*]
[f. 1] *Margin:* nychill. *This and the other excised leaves were fully written up but nothing more remains than the initial letters or parts thereof of numerous short entries.*

1. *1543. March 3. Overseers to record and distribute fines for absence of the priests and lay vicars. Chapter meetings every Saturday. Three masses daily, to be sung by rota by the minor canons.*

[f. 10] [*At the head, in later hands:* Henrici 8. 33. 1542. Jesus.][1]
The iij of Marche it is concluded and decrede that one of the prestes shalbe monitor and observer of the perditions[2] of the absence[a] of prestes and one of the clarkes to be monitor of the clarkes, and that the perditions of the prestes to be destribute amonges the prestes and perditions of the clarkes amonges the clarkes. And in case the sayd monitores do omit any of the said perditions or put in any man to be absent whiche is present in deyd, that then the sayd monitor to forfet and pay in penaltie iiij d. for every tyme that he so dothe.

Item it is decreed that every Satterday the deane[b] and prebendares, being [present][c] at home,[d] shall repare unto the chapitor house[3] and tract suche mat[ter][e] as do appertene unto the house and here corrections of the ministers.[f]

Item it is ordined and decrede that every day there shalbe thre masses sayd[g] within the churche, the fyrste[h] in St Jones chapell of the northe part of the churche,[4] to[i] begyn at seven[j] of the cloke, the other to be our Lady masse,[k] and the thyrd immediately after our Lady masse;[l] and the petye cannons, with the deken and subdeken,[m] to say the sayd masses by curse, and to begyn of Monday next ensewyng.

Signed: Benson, 'd[ecanus]', Haynes, H. Perkyns, Turpin, Elfred, Leighton.

[a] MS. 'þe thabsence'. [b] Repl. 'preben[dares]'. [c] MS. 'prebend'. [d] Four words inserted. [e] Written to edge of recto. [f] Repl. 'mo[nitores]'. [g] Repl. 'song' or 'sung'. [h] Five words inserted. [i] 'one of theme to' deleted but the last word inadvertently so. [j] Word inserted repl. 'halfe owre to viij'. [k] Five words inserted repl. 'at nyne' first corrected to 'at halfe owre to nyne'. [l] Five words inserted repl. 'at halfe owre to ten of [the cloke].' [m] Five words inserted.

---

1 For discussion of this dating see Introduction, p. xxi.
2 Penalty payments. The *OED* cites Westminster custom for this usage.
3 For place of chapter meetings see Introduction, p. xxiii.
4 The chapel of St John the Evangelist in the north transept or that of St John Baptist in the north ambulatory. The former was certainly in use in 1544, probably as a chantry: PRO, E 336/1, f. 13.

2. *March 5. The keeping of manorial courts to begin the second week after Low Sunday (April 1). Copyhold tenures. Sermons every Sunday. Keeping accounts. The rent collector for Westminster properties to find sureties for discharge of his duties. Canon Bellasis to inform the choir of decisions of the previous meeting. Muniments to be kept under lock; the dean to hand over those he has. The surveyor's fee.*

[f. 10v] The fyft of Marche.

It is decred that the*ᵃ* stewerd and surviers shall ryd to kepe the courtes in the second wyke after dominica in albis.⁵

It is decred that the sayd persons shall take order with the lattyng and settyng of copy holdes and take fynes for the same.

It is decreyd that sermondes shuld be mayd every Sonday.

It is decreyd that the accountes of Mr Haynes⁶ and Mr Carletones⁷ shuld go forward with sped.

Item Mr Dean is content to stand for Tyllswortes accompte for the collect[ion] of St Martens⁸ for Cristynmas terme, so far and so mutche as he*ᵇ* shall receyve.

Item it is decrede that the collector of Westm' shall fynd sufficient surtie by obligation.

Item it is appointed that Belassis⁹ shall declare*ᶜ* unto the ministeres of the quere the ordinances in the chapitor done the iij day of Marche.

Item it is decreyd that the charters, rentalles and other bokes tochyng the churche*ᵈ* and howse, with*ᵉ* the common seall, shalbe keppe under lokes in the tresery.

[f. 11] Item Mr Dean is content at his retorne to delyver suche instruci[ons]*ᶠ* or scripes that concerne the house as be in his handes at his retorne.

It is decreed that, notwithstonding the former acte made the second daie of March,¹⁰ Mr Bellises shall have this yer for his ffee in surveing and receiving the landes of this churche, from the feast of seint Michael last past unto the same fest next cuming exclusive, xx markes, and allso his expenses alowed according to his booke therof to be made upon his conscience.

Signed: Benson, Haynes, Bellasis, Elfred, Britten, Harvey, Turpin.

ᵃ Repl. 'Mr Dean' (inserted then deleted). *ᵇ* Word inserted. *ᶜ* Repl. 'upon' (for 'open'). *ᵈ* Repl. 'ho[wse]'. *ᵉ* Repl. 'shall'. *ᶠ* Written to the edge of recto.

⁵ Accounts for this progress are in WAM 37048, ff. 5–8.
⁶ Canon Simon Haynes.
⁷ Canon Gerard Carleton: cf. below, n. 29.
⁸ St Martin-le-Grand, London, a collegiate church appropriated to Westminster Abbey in 1503 as part of Henry VII's chantry benefaction: see M.B. Honeybourne, 'The sanctuary boundaries and environs of Westminster Abbey and the college of St Martin-le-Grand', *JBAA*, n.s. xxxviii (1932–3), 324–33 and map inset. William Tyllesworth was a London goldsmith (Heal, *Goldsmiths*, 259) and collector of rents for Westminster properties in London: WAM 33192, f. 2v.
⁹ Canon Anthony Bellasis.
¹⁰ No longer extant because of the excision of ff. 1–9.

3. *March 29. Negotiation of burial fees.*

Memorandum it whas agreid the xxix day of Marche anno xxxiiij° Henrici viij ffor the berryall of Sir Thomas Clyfford[11] at the request of Sir Anthony Browne[12] for the agrement of the brekyng of the grownde and for thynges whiche the churche shuld have, yt whas determynyd by Mr Dean, Mr Charite, Mr Elfrid and Mr Turpyn,[13] by causse ther wher no mo of prebendaris at home, that the hole mater shuld be put to Mr Browns gentyllnes.

4. *April 6. A lease brought for renewal.*

Memorandum that the vj day of Aprell anno xxxiiij° Henrici viij Kateryne Hedley browght to Mr Dean her leasse to be renewyd acordyng to the covnanttes of the indenture and desyerith to have it new sealled accordyng to the holde costome, and requyerith a day.[14]

[f. 11v *blank*]

5. *April 10. Appointment of legal counsel. Leases granted.*

[f. 12] The xth day of Aprell.

Imprimis it is ordened and consented that Mr Bakon, the solicitor of the court of thaugmentation, shalbe concellor of the house of Westm' with a fee of fowre markes by yeer.[15]

Item it is agreyd and consented that Edward Bawghe shall have hys lease of the reversion of Burton onder hyll under the chapitor seall accordyng unto the tenor of his convent seall for a fyne of x li.[16]

[*Margin*: Nota.] Item memorandum that John Parsons shall pay x li. by fore he have his lettres patentes delyvered.[17]

Item it is agredd that John Wrenford, upon a fyne of $\overset{xx}{iiij}$ markes^a shall have^b the lease of Longdon under the chapitor seall etc., ffor lxxx yeres, he beynge

---

11 Governor of Berwick. He was buried under the pavement of the quire: Dart, ii, 23. Stanley, 180.

12 Master of the horse and captain of the gentlemen pensioners: *Hist. Parl. 1509–1558*, i, 518–21.

13 Canons Humphrey Perkyns (Charity was his name in religion), Thomas Elfred and Francis Turpin. For Elfred and Perkyns see Pearce, *Monks*, 176, 185–6.

14 Richard Hedley had been collector of the monk chamberlain's rents in 1529 and 1530: WAM 18821, 30672, 30721.

15 Nicholas Bacon, later lord keeper but at this time solicitor of the court of augmentations (the government office handling former monastic revenues): *Hist. Parl. 1509–1558*, i, 358–60.

16 Baugh, yeoman, of Twyning, granted the manor of Bourton-on-the-Hill, Glos., for 60 years from Michaelmas 1550 at £8 6s 8d rent 1 March 1543: WAM Reg. III, ff. 32v–34v. For his fine see below, no. **187**.

17 John Person, of Bagnor, Berks., and Maude his wife granted renewal of the manor there for 40 years from previous Michaelmas at 5 marks rent 31 January 1543: WAM Reg. III, ff. 11–12v.

bound to the repayres of the ij chaunceles*c* that be coveryd with tylle and to fynd mans mett and horse met to them that comythe for necessa[ry]*d* besynys.*e*[18]

Item that Raffe Nottyng shall have his leasse sealled by the chapitor seall payng for a fyn of every yeere incressed in his lease*f* one marke sterlyng.[19]

Signed: Benson, Leighton, Bellasis, H. Perkyns, Turpin, Elfred, Harvey.

> *a* Sum and word repl. 'one hondrethe powndes'.   *b* Word inserted.   *c* *Sic*.   *d* Written to edge of recto.   *e* 'ffor . . . besynys' inserted.   *f* Four words inserted.

6.   *April 23. Appointment of surveyor for London and St Martin-le-Grand. Lease granted.*

[f. 12v] xxiij° *a* Aprilis anno regni regis Henrici viiij*vi* xxxv*to*.

Imprimis it is agreyd and ordined that Mr William Harvye[20] shalbe survior of all our landes within the citie of London, aswell St Martens as other, with a ffee of fyve*b* powndes.

Item it is agreyd that Raffe Nottyng shall have his lease of Cowhous*c* for lxxxxvj yeers, yeldyng for every yeer addet unto his former yeeres*d* xiij s. iiij d.

Signed: Benson, Bellasis, Britten, H. Perkyns, Turpin, Elfred, Harvey.

> *a* MS. 'xxiij° tertio'.   *b* Repl. 'v li.'   *c* Repl. abbreviated form.   *d* Four words inserted.

7.   *April 29. Leases granted. Presentation to the vicarage of St Bride, Fleet Street. The canons to attend chapter by rota. Memorial service for King Henry VII.*

[f. 13] xxix*no* Aprilis anno regni regis Henrici viij*vi* xxxv*to*.

Imprimis it is agreed that Mr Broket shall have his lease of Wethamstede for lx yeris, paying xx li. for a fyne.[21]

Item agreed that Mr Currye shall have his lease renued for lxxx yeris.[22]

Item agreed for Roger Emsons lease for the personage of Okeham.[23]

---

[18] Wrenford, of Longdon, Worcs., granted the parsonage there with the chapels of Castlemorton and Chaceley, for years stated from previous Lady Day at £26 rent 31 May 1543: *ibid.*, ff. 25v–26v. For his fine see below, no. **187**. For maintenance of the chancels of Longdon and its dependent chapels *alias* Morton Foliot and Chaddesley see Haines, 'Longdon', 12, 243 n.92.

[19] Nuttynge, yeoman, of Hurley, Berks., John Nuttinge of Hendon and Thomas Hunte of Westminster granted lands of Cowhouse and Hodford, i.e. Cowhouse manor in Hampstead, Midd., for 96 years from previous Michaelmas at £20 rent 24 December 1542: WAM Reg. III, ff. 12v–14.

[20] Canon; Faith in religion: Pearce, *Monks*, 188.

[21] John Brocket, esq., of Wheathampstead, Herts., granted the manor there for years stated from Michaelmas 1556 at £17 and 40 quarters of wheat rent 5 May 1543: WAM Reg. III, ff. 17v–19v. For his fine see below, no. **187**. See also *Hist. Parl. 1509–1558*, i, 499–500.

[22] Richard Curre, gent., Prince Edward's cook, granted a tenement or forge and gardens in Tothill St for 80 years from Midsummer following at £1 6s rent 4 May 1543: WAM Reg. III, ff. 19v–20v. For his fee see below, no. **187**.

[23] Empson, one of the lay vicars, granted the parsonage of Oakham, Rutland, for 66 years from Christmas 1545 at £14 rent 25 April 1543: WAM Reg. III, ff. 16v–17v; regnal year wrong (25) in Reg. text (f. 16v) but correct (35) in bond there (f. 17v).

Item Mr Jynnines lease to be renued in Samsons name.[24]

Item that Mr Taylor, bachelar of dyvynyte, have a presentation of St Brygittes, Mr Saxis benefyce.[25]

Item agreed every one of the prebendaryes to kepe the chapter by course, or to gyve iiij d. for his course to another man that kepith it for hym.

Item that forty pounde be employed on the observation of kyng Henry the vij[th] dirige, beside the waxe.[26]

Item decreed for Fullers lease.[27]

Signed: Benson, Redman, Britten, H. Perkyns, Turpin, Elfred, Harvey, Carleton.

8. *May 4. Canons' incomes to be paid up to the day of death.*

[f. 13v] 4[to] Maii anno 35 Henrici 8[vi].

Agreed that whan God callith any of the prebendaryes to his mercy furthe of this worlde that all[a] the emolumentes and proffytes of his prebende shal pertayn unto hym unto the day of his dethe.

Signed: Benson, Leighton, Redman, Britten, Bellasis, J. Pekyns, E. Weston, Carleton, Turpin, Elfred, Harvey, Haynes.

[a] Word inserted.

9. *December 17. The audit to begin on January 7. The endowment charter to be examined by legal counsel. Enquiries to be made about the use of the gatehouse and duties of road repairs. Redemption of leases from inhabitants of the precincts. Suit for return of lease counterparts and other muniments.*

[f. 14] xvij[mo] Decembris[a] anno xxxv[to] Henrici v[iij[vi]][b].

It is agreyd and concluded that the audete shalbegyne for suche as be nye unto the cites of London and Westm' the morow after xij[th] day alias Epiphanye, and so continew, asuell for suche as be ny Westm' and London as those that dwell forther of, to the audete be holly endet and finyshed. And precepes to be mayd with spede and conveyd by means of receveres.

Item it is agreyd that our boke of thindowment shalbe perused by Mr

---

24 Sampson Awdeley, the king's servant and one of the vergers, granted three tenements and a garden in the Sanctuary for 78½ years from previous Lady Day at £2 rent 2 May 1543: *ibid.*, ff. 22–3. For his fee see below, no. **187**. John Gymmes, deceased, had held five messuages in the Sanctuary: WAM 33192, f. 8.

25 John Cardmaker *alias* Taylor, B.D. Oxon., was admitted vicar of St Bride's 21 November 1543, vac. 1551. A noted preacher, he was executed for heresy in 1555. His predecessor in Fleet St, William Saxey, retained other benefices without interruption to his death in 1567: *DNB*. Emden, 101, 506. Skeeters, *Bristol*, 159.

26 The anniversary of the king's death was April 21.

27 Richard Fuller, yeoman of Prince Edward's household, granted five tenements and gardens in Tothill St for 60 years from Midsummer 1546 at £2 10s 8d rent 31 March 1543: WAM Reg. III, ff. 21–21v. For his fee see below, no. **187**.

Chidlay[28] or some other lerned man byfore the begynyg of the terme, to see whether we be charget with the tentes byfore the said indoment dyd passe the seall or no, and he to have for his labor by the discression of hym that procurethe the same, videlicet[c] Belassis.

Item to enquire of some lerned man whether that the prison of our libertes, being the gaythous of Westm', shuld be used as a common prisons or no.

Item Mr Dean of Peterberow[29] to desyre Doctor Perkyns[d] [and/or][e] his brother[f] Mr John Car[leton][g] to see whether we be bownd to the reparaton of the way at Stanes or no, and to begyn to mend the hye ways to Henden and other at Marche next commyng.

Item it is concludet that Mr Lyghton[30] and Mr Pekyns[31] shall common with the inh[ab]itantes within the closse for the redemtion of the leasses of the howses, and that the college shall bere in common the redemtion of the same.[h]

[f. 14v] Item Mr Hervye to make sute bytwyx this and the beginnyg of the next terme unto Mr Mildmey[32] for our rentalles or for the copie of the same and for the conterpayns and the register.

Signed: Benson, Redman, Leighton, Bellasis, J. Pekyns, Carleton, Turpin, Elfred, E. Weston.

[a] Repl. 'Septembris'.   [b] Written to edge of recto and now partially lost.   [c] Repl. 'by Belass[is]' (written to edge of recto).   [d] Two words inserted.   [e] Ellipse in MS or previous insertion rejected without deletion.   [f] Repl. 'p[ri]son'.   [g] Three words inserted written to edge of recto.   [h] Followed by 'to wit Burbages' and several words overscored.

10.   *December 18. Repair of the water conduit. Masons to survey the east of the church. The door of the Abbey gatehouse to be secured.*

xviij[vo] Decembris anno predicto.

It is ordined that the condethe shalbe amendet with all convenient spede, and that Mr Guy[33] shall make serche for some honest plumer for the same.

Item it is appointed that Mr Gwy shall cause some masons with hym to survye the east end of the churche, to thintente the kinges majesties consell may be enformed of the same.

---

[28] Probably Robert Chidley, Middlesex J.P.: *CPR 1547–8*, p. 86. The endowment patent was dated 5 August 1542: WAM LXXXIII (*LP* xvii, 714(5), pp. 392–6). £4 was paid for the enrolment: WAM 37043, f. 12v.

[29] Canon Gerard Carleton. His brother John was a receiver of the court of augmentations, and had handled much of the Westminster business during the interval between the dissolution and refoundation.

[30] Canon Edward Leighton.

[31] Canon John Pekyns.

[32] Thomas Mildmay; auditor (with his brother Walter) of the court of augmentations: *Hist. Parl. 1509–1558*, ii, 600–1. WAM 35057.

[33] Guy Gascon, head sexton or sacrist, who in this year received an additional payment of £1 13s 4d 'pro supervisione operum', and was by 1548/9 styled clerk of the works: WAM 37043, f. 10; 33603, f. 4v.

Item that the said Gwy to provide a barr for the way unto Touthyll, and the porter to kepe the key of the same.[34]

11. *1544. January 26. Plumbing for the clergy houses and elsewhere.*

[f. 15] 26 Januarii anno regni regis Henrici 8[i] xxxv[o]. It is concluded that Mr Grey, plummer, shall make the conducte hed[a] new, and shall bring home the water to as many places as it was wont to cum, and as plenteosly, and the said Grei shall have the old pipes that be under the grownd and xx li. sterling, that is to saie to my lordes kechyn,[35] to Mr Deanes kechin,[36] to Mr Burbages howss,[37] to Mr Webbes howss,[38] to Mr Doctor Brettons howss, to Mr Vaghans howss,[39] to Mr Leightons howss, to Mr Perkyns howss, to Mr Redmans howss, to Mr Carletons howss, to Mr Heynes howss, to Mr Belowses howss, to Mr Harvyes howss, to the churche and the saxtri, and to the peticanons and vicars comons, if he wilbe bownd to doo it by Ester next cummyng.

Signed: Haynes, Leighton, Britten, Carleton, H. Perkyns, Elfred, Harvey, Redman.

[a] Word inserted.

12. *Same day. Appointment of master of the choristers. Lease renewed.*

Die et anno predictis. It is concluded that Fox the master of the chorustars shall have the whole governing of the chorustars, to teache them, to provide for meate and drinke, and to se them clenly and honestly apparailed in all thinges, and he to have ther whole stipend. Also it is agreid that the said master of the chorustars shall have the howss over the gate going into the Allmery for hymself and the said chorustars rent free, he repairing it sufficiently before Ester next cummyng. And bicause the howss is now in grett rwyn, it is agreid that the said Fox shall

---

34 The ruinous state of the gatehouse had been noted in the earliest surviving survey by the dean and chapter, 23 October 1542: WAM 37036, f. 1.

35 The former abbot's lodging (now the Deanery) became at the Henrician foundation the bishop's palace (although never referred to as such): Robinson, *Abbot's House*, 13. Thomas Thirlby was the only bishop of the diocese, for whom see T.F. Shirley, *Thomas Thirlby. Tudor Bishop* (1964), which follows Robinson in all matters relating to the house. The kitchen is to the south of the abbot's hall (now College Hall); see plan inset in Robinson, *op. cit.*

36 The dean of the first collegiate church was accommodated in the former prior's house, the location of which (based on this and other entries in the Act Book) is shown by Robinson, *op. cit.*, 50–4 to be on the site of the present Ashburnham House.

37 Thomas Burbage was tenant of 'the great redde house' otherwise 'the gret place in the Elmys' (on the site of Dean's Yard): WAM 6493; 37036, f. 1; 37041, f. 21.

38 William Webbe was keeper of the Sanctuary and gaoler of the Palace; the butt of many scurrilous yarns: G.R. Elton, *Policy and Police* (Cambridge 1972), 10–11. His house was in the kitchener's garden: WAM 37041, f. 4; 37126, f. 9v.

39 Sir Hugh Vaughan had been a prominent lay servant of the abbey; for his career and properties see Rosser, 333–4. Cf. WAM 37066.

only at this time have xl s. towardes the charges of the said reparations.[40] Item it is concluded the said yer and daie that Elizabeth Whashe, widow, shall have her lease of the howses at Charing Cross which she now holdeth renewed and to have a lease granted for xl yeres, she paijng for a fine xx markes at the sealing.[41]

Signed: Haynes, Leighton, Britten, Elfred, Carleton, H. Perkyns, Harvey, Redman.

13. *Same day. Making a door in the Dark Entry.*

[f. 15v] [A]nno et die supradictis. It is concluded that before Ester next cummyng a new dore shalbe made right furthe wher the darke entrie[42] is now, and that Gye shall have the oversight of the pulling downe a pece of the prevy dorter and of the buylding up of the said new dore.

Signed: Haynes, Redman, Leighton, Britten, H. Perkyns, Elfred, Harvey, Carleton.

14. *January 29. The precentor to fine minor canons and lay vicars absent from service.*

Anno predicto die 29 mensis predicti. It is concludid that the chantor shall have the ordryng of the quere to*a* chekke the prestes and seculars absent and to multe theym as hath bene afore acustumed and as was apointed by my lorde of Westm',[43] that is for matens j d., masse j d., pryme and howres eche of them ob., evensong j d. Also that if any of the prestes or syngyngmen go forth of the quere and there tary forth any space without licence, than his negligence to be countid an absence, although he cum in agayn afore the ende of the service.

Signed: Benson, Redman, Haynes, Leighton, Britten, E. Weston, H. Perkyns, Elfred, Carleton.

a Repl. 'that'.

15. *February 4 for 5. A chapter meeting summoned.*

[f. 16] Memorandum that the forth day of February was monysshed to appere at the chapter to be holden at Westm' the nexte day folowenge at one of the clocke at after none by Gwye Gaskon all the prebendaryese*a* for the redresse of dyverse necessary causes of the churche, but at the forsaide day and howre appointed there appered only suche persons as whose names hereafter foloweth. Fyrste was presentt Wylliam Benson. Mr Bellasyse appered but havenge*b* busynes necessary

---

[40] Robert Foxe took over from William Grene as master of the choristers at Lady Day 1543: WAM 37045, ff. 5v, 8; not 1542 as stated in Knighton, 'Collegiate Foundations', 352.

[41] William Washe had eight tenements in Charing Cross St in 1542; *Alice* Wasshe, widow, was subsequently tenant there: WAM 37036, f. 8; 37043, f. 8v; 43930, f. 14v.

[42] The vaulted passage connecting the south-east corner of the Great Cloister with the Little Cloister and other buildings.

[43] Bishop Thirlby: see n. 35 above.

of the churches he myght nat tarye. Johannes Pekyns. Thomas Elfryd. Edmund Weston. Gerarde Carleton. Humfre Perkyns. Simon Heynes.

^a Repl. 'cumpany'.   ^b Repl. 'beinge'.

16.   *February 5. Wheat rent.*

Anno predicto 5° die Februarii. It ys agreyde that wyddowe Stasy shall paye whete for her ferme accordyng to her indenture from tyme to tyme herafter save that for this yere only that is to saye for that that^a nowe ys and shalbe dewe bytwyxt this and mydsomer she shall paye fyfteyne quarters of good and lawfull whete, thother fyfteyne in reddy money at xij s. the quarter, and ferder it is agreyde that Mr Bellasys shall take a order with her for the last yere^b past as he shall thynk good accordyng to his dyscretyon.⁴⁴

Signed: Benson, Haynes, J. Pekyns, Elfred, E. Weston, H. Perkyns, Carleton.

^a Word inserted.   ^b Word inserted.

17.   *February 6. Lease agreed.*

[f. 16v] The vjth day of Februarii. Hyt is agreed that Mr Foulk Appauyll shall have a tenemente callyd the Castell taverne with diverse other tenementes adjonyng to the same which comethe to the yerly value of xij li. iij s. iiij d., out of the wyche he is allowyd towardes the repayres xx s. yerly, so he muste pay xj li. iij s. iiij d., and he to have hytt for iiij^{xx} yeres apon this^a condition that mysteres Stafferton bryng yn her old lease with hyre open and free consente.⁴⁵

Signed: Benson, Haynes, Redman, E. Weston, Elfred, Carleton, Harvey.

^a Repl. illegible words.

18.   *February 10 for 11. A chapter meeting summoned.^a*

Memorandum that the x^b day of Februarii anno 35 I W. Benson appointed a chapter the Munday folowenge, videlicet the xj day of Februarii, wheare I appered and v more prebendaryese, videlicet Mr Redman, Mr Pekyns, Mr Weston, Mr Elfrede and Mr Carleton. Per W.B.

^a Whole entry in the dean's hand.   ^b Corrected from 'xj' (11th was Monday).

⁴⁴ Joan Stace, daughter of the wife of Ralph Nutting, had lease to her and Andrew Durdaunt of the manor of Yeoveney for 90 years from previous Michaelmas at £17 rent 20 October 1538: WAM 16810.

⁴⁵ Katherine Staverton or Stafferton of London, widow, granted the Castle tavern and other buildings within the Sanctuary, Foulke Apphowell *alias* Lancaster being the occupant, for *84* years from previous Michaelmas at £11 0s 4d rent 17 March 1544: WAM Reg. III, ff. 41v–43. Her husband, a London grocer, had died as a 'debtor' (though evidently a man of substance) in the Sanctuary in 1534: Rosser, 157 & n. 186.

19. *February 12. Arrangements for summoning canons to chapter.*[a]

[f. 17] xij^mo Februarii. Wheras[b] there be as yet no certayn statutes mayd in the new erected howse by the kinges majestie,[46] and that certayn urgent busynesse dayly dothe occure in the kinges majesties new erected howse of Westm', the prebendares beyng for grett of times[c] times absent, therfor unto suche tyme as it may please his majestie to apoint statutes for the sayd house it is thought meyt by the dean and chapitor of the sayd howse of Westm' that Guy[d] Gascon or some soch other[e] shalbe the apparator to gyve at the commaundment of the dean monyshion unto[f] suche as have not houses personally if he can have sure knowlage that they be within the citie of Westm', and to suche as have houses to be warned at ther houses in Westm'; in cace they do not come at the tyme apointed that then the dean being present with iiij prebendares of the sayd housse with hym shall take such order as they shall thynk mete, and the same to stand in as great force and sternth as if the dean with all the chapitor had ben present.

> [a] Whole entry deleted. [b] Repl. 'F[orasmuch]'. [c] 'of them / times' inserted repl. 'now'. [d] Repl. 'if'. [e] Four words inserted. [f] Word inserted repl. 'shall' (monish).

20. *February 12. Further orders for chapter attendance.*

[f. 17v] Anno predicto the xij day of Februarye. It is agreed by the dean and prebendaries that the said dean or his deputie shall apoint one to gyve warnyng unto the said prebendaries to repayr together unto the chapter howse or other where for ordring of siche thynges as be necessary. And if all the said prebendaries or the more parte be monyshed and opon half a days warnyng do not cum at[a] the tyme lymyted, then aswell the said persones so warned as all other not warned to stand unto syche directions and ordres as shall be takin by the said dean or[b] hys deputie and iiij or iij[c] of the prebendaryes being present for suche causes as shall occurre touchyng the affayres of the said cathedrall churche.

Signed: Benson, Redman, Bellasis, H. Perkyns, Elfred, Carleton, Harvey, Britten, Haynes, J. Pekyns, Leighton.

> [a] Word inserted. [b] Repl. 'and'. [c] 'or iij' inserted.

21. *March 8. Appointment of receiver-general.*

[f. 18] Memorandum that the eygth day of March yt was agreyd by the deane and chapyter that maister Deane and maister Belysus shuld enter communicatyon wyth John Multon off and ffor such busynys as the foresayde deane and

---

[46] Statutes were promised in the foundation charter, and though no copies survive they were certainly to hand by the end of 1544, because accounts for the Michaelmas quarter include payments for writing them (WAM 37047, ff. 8, 12v, 13), probably in June or July when most of the other new foundation cathedrals received equivalent texts: *The Statutes of the Cathedral Church of Durham*, ed. A.H. Thompson (Surtees Soc. cxliii, 1929), p. xl. *Documents relating to the foundation of the chapter of Winchester*, ed. G.W. Kitchin and F.T. Madge (Hampshire Record Soc. i, 1889), 144. Mellows, *Peterborough*, p. lxxx. CUL, EDC 1/E/2.

maister Belysus shall thynke meate for the colledge to have concernyng that matter*a* and to conclude wyth the sayde John for hys yerely*b* stypend.[47]

Signed: Benson, Bellasis, J. Pekyns, H. Perkyns, Elfred, E. Weston, Haynes.

a Three words inserted repl. 'and to conclude from tyme to tyme'. *b* Word inserted.

22. *March 21. Lead to be stored or sold.*

[f. 18v] The xxj*ti* daye of Marche anno predicto. It is agreed by the deane and chapter that the leade which is in the storehouse the one halffe to be sold and the reste to be caste in shettes and laid upp for the store of the churche and the mony which is made of the firsaid leade to be pute to the use of the churche as reparations as all other buyldynges within the precyncte.

23. *April 4. Payment for business.*

[f. 19] iiij*to* Aprilis anno predicto. It is ordered that xlvij li. shalbe bystowed unto certayn persons for there payns takyng about bysynesses of the churche of Westm' like as it dothe apere more playnly by certayn bylles apparent of the same.

Signed: Benson, Bellasis, E. Weston, Elfred, Harvey.

24. *May 3. Appointment of receiver-general. Courts to be kept. Appointment of collector of rents in Westminster. Henry VII's obit. The audit.*

iij*o* Maii. It is agreed that John Multon fynding sufficient suertes for m li. shall have xl li. ffee to receive all the landes abrode in the contre in all partes of this realme and to sollicit our causes and sutes as nede shall require.[48] It is agreed that the lete shalbe kept for good ordre and trew assise of vitail be kept, and other faultes be amended and corrected from tyme to tyme. Item it is agreed that Edwarde Hendy, servant to Mr Doctor Heyns shalbe collector of all renttes in Westminster and from thens unto the Temple Barre growing dewe from than-nunciation of our Lady laste paste,*a* and he to have x li. sterling yerly for his stipende. Item it is agreed that King Herry the*b* vij*thes* anniversary shalbe kepte this yer after the same forme and manner as it was kepte the laste yer. Item it is agreed that Mr Redmain, Mr Bretton, Mr Pekyns, Mr Weston, Mr Elfride and so mani of the prebendaris as wilbe present shall upon Monday next and so furth afterward*c* here the accomptes of all accomptantes, and iij of them present shall have actorite to alow and disalow billes of rekening unto suche accomptes be fineshed, and thei shall have of the comen charge of the churche dayly meate and drinke whan they sitt and be occupied in the said busynes.

[47] See following note.
[48] Patent for life, with bond of 1000 *marks*, the sureties being Moulton himself, William Freeman of Batsford and Edward Baugh of Twyning, Glos., 2 October 1544: WAM Reg. III, ff. 27–8.

Signed: Benson, Redman, E. Weston, Bellasis, Britten, Leighton, Elfred, J. Pekyns, Haynes, Harvey.*d*

a Nine words inserted repl. 'from the feiste of the nativitie of sainte Jhon Baptiste nexte ensuyng or now folloing'.   *b* Repl. 'theightes a[nniversary]'.   *c* Four words inserted.   *d* Repetition erased.

25. *June 27. Leases to be sealed.*

[f. 19v] xxvij Junii anno domini mccccxliiij*to*. It is agreyd by Mr Dean and the chapitor that certayn leasses here folowyng shuld passe by chapitor seall. Boltones lease of certayn tenementes in Long dyche for*a* lx yeres.[49] Gwy Gascon for a tenement in Long dyche lxx yeeres.[50] Mr Smalwodes lease of tenementes*b* in Long dyche lxx yeeres.*c* [51] Alexander Wakes lease of ij tenementes in Brokwharfe lxj.[52] Edmond Wyldgrys of tenementes in Kyngstrete xxiiij yeeres[53] [*Margin*: Delyvered to Mr Elfred.] Jane Calverley of thre tenementes in Kyngesstrete lx.[54] A lease for the vicar of Myntyng for xxj yeeres.[55] Raff Stanow for the parsonage in Newport Pownd xlj.[56] The confirmation of my lordes graunt to Stratford in the Bow.[57] Walter Hull for v tenementes in Thevyng lane lxiij

---

[49] Richard Bolton, the king's servant, granted five tenements in Long Ditch, with a cottage and garden adjoining, for years stated from previous Christmas at £3 4s 8d rent 6 March 1544: *ibid.*, ff. 69v–71.

[50] Grant for years stated from Midsummer following at 13s 4d rent 23 June 1544: *ibid.*, ff. 31–32v; years correct in Reg. text but wrongly (60) marginated there (f. 31v).

[51] Robert Smallwood, brewer, granted six tenements in Long Ditch for 40 years from Michaelmas following at 10s rent 20 May 1530: WAM Reg. II, f. 262v. His widow Joan and son John had lease of tenements in Long Ditch in 1559: WAM 36021. Robert had been one of the first two M.Ps for the city of Westminster: Rosser, 399. *Hist. Parl. 1509–1558*, iii, 328.

[52] Alexander Wake of London, winedrawer, granted two tenements at Broken Wharf in the parish of St Mary de Monte Alto *alias* Mounthaunt, London, for *41* years from Midsummer following at £1 16s rent 28 May 1544: WAM Reg. III, ff. 62v–63v.

[53] Edmund Wyllgres of Westminster, fishmonger, granted the tenement where he dwelt, next to the Saracen's Head, for years stated from Lady Day following at £2 rent 16 March 1544: *ibid.*, ff. 36–7.

[54] Jane Calverley of Westminster, widow, granted three tenements in King St by the Sanctuary gate for years stated from previous Lady Day at £6 rent 16 June 1544: *ibid.*, ff. 58v–59v.

[55] William Kyngestone, vicar of Minting, Lincs., granted corn tithes of the parish for years stated from previous Michaelmas at £3 rent 24 March 1545: *ibid.*, ff. 57v–58.

[56] Stannowe, gent., of London, granted rectory of Newport Pound, Essex, for years stated from previous Lady Day at £18 rent, reserving the advowson to the dean and chapter, 7 May 1544: *ibid.*, ff. 63v–65.

[57] Licence to parishioners of Stratford-atte-Bowe, Essex, to avoid coming to Westminster Cathedral for Pentecost procession, dated 20 May 1542 ratified by dean and chapter 1 December 1544: Guildhall MS 9531/12, f. 260.

yeeres.[58] Jaksones leasse of thre tenementes for lxij yeeres.[59] The [lease of]*d* Nicholas Mole of certen tenementes in Gutter layn lx yeres.[60]

Signed: Benson, Redman, Leighton, Bellasis (*quater*), Britten, Harvey, E. Weston, Carleton.

a Word inserted. *b* Repl. 'a'. *c* Word inserted. *d* Ellipse in MS.

26. *November 5. Demolition of the monastic refectory. Ground assigned to a canon's house.*

[f. 20] v*th* November anno regni regis Henrici viij xxxvj. It is agreyd bi master Deaine and the chapiter that Guy Gasken, servant unto the said deaine and chapiter shall*a* forthwith in all hast for the awoiding of ferther inconveniences take downe the frater howse,[61] and also that Mr Deaine of Peterborow[62] shall have the vacant grownd betwixt Mr Readmans and Mr Turpins howse with the stable apon the walle of the said Mr Deaine of Peterborows howse.

Signed: Benson, Leighton, Elfred, H. Perkyns, Carleton, E. Weston.

a Repl. 'that he'.

27. *November 11. The audit.*

11*a* Novembris anno predicto. It is agreyd by Mr Dean and the chapter that Mr Doctor Parkyns and Mr Weston shall here the accompttes*b* in the audytte and the sayd audytte to be kepte for thys presentte yere in Mr Carletons howse.

a Repl. '10'. *b* Repl. 'audytte'.

28. *Same day. A canon assigns his stipend to city merchants.*

[f. 20v] Be it knowen to all men that I Edwarde Leyghtone,[63] one of the prebendaries within the cathederall churche of Westminster have appoynted

58 Not traced.
59 George Jackson, of St Clement Danes, London, brewer, and Alice his wife, granted three cottages opposite the bishop of Norwich's palace for years stated from previous Lady Day at £1 rent 3 April 1544: WAM Reg. III, ff. 59v–60v.
60 Nicholas Mowld, citizen and goldsmith of London (Heal, *Goldsmiths*, 207) granted tenements in Gutter Lane called King's Alley for years stated from previous Lady Day at £4 16s 8d rent 24 February 1544: WAM Reg. III, ff. 66v–67v.
61 On the south side of the cloister. Its destruction occasioned the chief loss to the monastic buildings of Westminster.
62 Canon Gerard Carleton.
63 Leighton, although substantially beneficed, was in financial difficulties which resulted in imprisonment for debt in 1546. He attempted to solve his problems by effectively selling his Westminster canonry to Edward Keble; but the latter (so Leighton claimed – and in view of what is known of Keble, probably correctly) forged his bond of payment, which lost Leighton his canonry and his cash: WAM 9418. Knighton, 'Collegiate Foundations', 327–8; *idem*, 'Economics', 47–8, 62 n. 18. The deed here registered represents an earlier attempt to mortgage his income. One of the payments to the Fullers (1544) is recorded in WAM 37048, f. 13.

Thomas Fuller and Nicolas,*ᵃ* citizins and mersers of London, and their assignes*ᵇ* to receve all my portion and stipende within the saide churche of Westminster apperteyning to my prebende ther whiche is risen dewe from the feaste of the nativitie of our Lorde laste before the date hereof unto this presente daye, and that shall rise dewe unto me for the same hereafter unto suche tyme as the forsaide Thomas Fuller and Nicolas or ther executores shall cum in before the deane of the saide churche and chapiter and knowledge them selffes to be agred that I*ᶜ* the saide Edwarde Leyghton or sum other my assignes shall receve it.*ᵈ* And further I knowledge my selff to be contentt that thaquittaunce of the saide Thomas and Nicolas or of*ᵉ* ther executores or assignes*ᶠ* or of any of them shalbe as sufficient for the discharge*ᵍ* of*ʰ* the deane and chapiter from tyme to tyme agaynste me and myne executores in this behalff as thowe I shuld make and write the same quittaunces withe my awne hande. And furthermore I covenauntt and agree nott to revoke*ⁱ* this my dede unto suche tyme as the saide Thomas and Nicolas or ther executores shalbe agreed therto. In witnes wherof I the saide Edwarde Leyghton have written this warrauntt and subscribed my name with my owne hande the xj^th^ of Novembre in the xxxvj^th^ yer of the regne of king Henry theight. Per me Edwardum Leyghton predictum. [*Margin*: I Wylliam Benson, deane, was presentt at this agrementt bytwyxte the partyese withyn wryeten. Per W.B. W. Bretton. Gerard Carleton. Edmund Weston. Humfrey Perkyns. Be me Thomas Elfryd.]

ᵃ Sic. *ᵇ* Three words inserted, 'their' repl. 'to'. *ᶜ* Repl. the sai[d]'. *ᵈ* Three words inserted. *ᵉ* Two words inserted repl. 'of of'. *ᶠ* Word deleted then repeated. *ᵍ* Repl. 'receit'. *ʰ* Repl. 'to'. *ⁱ* Repl. illegible word.

29. *December 6. Dividend of wheat rent.*⁶⁴

[f. 21] 6° die Decembris anno predicto. It is agreyd by Mr Dean and the chapter that the rent whette shalbe devydyde at x s. the quarter in this maner folowyng, that is to saye that Mr Dean to have therof twenty quarters, the resydewe to be devydyde amonge the resydensyariis equally whos names herafter folowyth: Mr Hayns, Mr Redman, Mr Bellassys, Mr Bretten, Mr Perkyns, Mr Elfred, Mr Carleton, which amountyth to every oon vij quarters and oon busshell.

Signed: Benson, Bellasis, Britten, H. Perkyns, Elfred, Carleton.

30. *1545. January 19. A bellringer appointed on Princess Elizabeth's nomination.*

[f. 21v] 19° Januarii anno regni regis Henrici 8 36°. It is agreed by the dean and the chapter that Jhon Penycote shall have thoffice and rowme of a bell rynger whiche shall happen nexte to be vacantt by deathe of any of thincumbenttes that

⁶⁴ 40 quarters from Wheathampstead manor and 30 quarters from Sawbridgeworth rectory per annum: e.g. WAM Reg. III, ff. 18, 167.

nowe be and this is att the sute and requeste of the Lady Elizabethe, doughter to our soveraine lorde the kyng.[65]

Signed: Benson, Redman, Leighton, J. Pekyns, H. Perkyns, Elfred, Carleton.

31. *January 20. Appointment of rent collector, receiver-general and treasurer, and their duties defined.*

[f. 22] 20 die Januarii anno predicto. It is agreed that where Mr Dean and the chapter have grauntid to Edward Hendye the collection of the rentes in[a] Westm' and about unto Temple Barre, he to have for his fee x li. by yere, and also provided that he shall not be charged with the vacations nor rent that can not be levied upon the tenantes and[b] that to be tried by his othe or by neibors ther-aboute[c] and that he shall answer for all siche tenantes as shall be putte in by hymself without any exception of theyr povertie or ronnyng awaye. Also it is agreed that Johan Multon shall occupie the office of the receyvershippe and[d] to have xl li. for his labor yerely opon his acoumpte makyng,[e] and for the same fee also to sollicite our suetes. And to have a patent sealed of the said office, he fyndyng sufficient suretye to be bond in m li.[66] Also it is agreed Mr Doctor Perkyns to be the tresores[f] for this yere to take the money of the receyver and se the laying of it up in the chiste thereto apointed with Mr Dean and Mr Doctor Bretayn,[g] who shall have every one a key of the sayd chiste and se the laying up and taking out of the money, and that the said Mr Perkyns shall se the repayres of high ways[67] and all other reparations within the cities of Westm' and London, and further that he shall paye all the mynisters and other paymentes within the churche, havyng for his labor vj li. xiij s. iiij d., and to make his acompte quarterly to Mr Dean and the cumpanye. [68]

Signed: Benson, Leighton, Haynes, Carleton, Britten, Elfred, H. Perkyns, Red-man, J. Pekyns, Bellasis, E. Weston.

[a] Repl. 'of'.   [b] Repl. 'but to'.   [c] Four words inserted.   [d] Repl. 'for this yere next cum-myng'.   [e] Five words inserted repl. 'as he had the laste yere'.   [f] *Sic.*   [g] Deleted signature of Redman below.

---

[65] Elizabeth was then aged 11. For Penycote see also below, n. 131.
[66] For Moulton's patent see above, n. 48. He had exercised the office since the death of the previous receiver, William Russell, in July 1543: WAM 37043.
[67] For road-mending as an aspect of the devotional life cf. E. Duffy, *The Stripping of the Altars. Traditional Religion in England 1400–1580* (1992), 367–8. It was a general obligation placed on the new foundation chapters, and at Westminster £40 per annum was allowed for this purpose: 31 Hen. VIII c. 9. WAM 6478, f. 4v. In the year of this Act Book entry £20 was spent re-making the highway between Tottenham Court and Kentish Town, and £13 0s 7¾d on paving in Petty France: WAM 37064, f. 4v.
[68] This appointment is the first to be made in accordance with the statutes received in 1544 (above, n. 46). Perkyns's account for 1544/5 is WAM 37064. Henceforth the chapter officers were elected at the audit in late November or early December, with (for those who rendered accounts) effect from the previous Michaelmas. The first such election is below, no. **46.**

32. *January 22. Sir Anthony Denny*[69] *appointed high steward, and to be consulted about the Gatehouse prison and the court. Canons to officiate and preach in turn or provide deputies.*

[f. 22v] 22 die Januarii anno predicto. It is agreed by the dean and the chapter that Mr Denye shall have the stuardshippe of all the liberties of*[a]* Westm' within*[b]* the countie of Middelsex with a fee of foure markes, with a clause of distresse within any of our landes and tenementes within the cite of Westm'. Also that Mr Dean and Mr Haynes shall speke with Mr Deny concernyng the prison, concernyng the kepyng of the courte, and they to commen and conclude*[c]* with hym of all thees and*[d]* other siche*[e]* thynges expedient for the house, and that the hole*[f]* cumpanye is content to ratifie siche thinges as they by theyr discretions shall condescende*[g]* and agre opon with the said Mr Deny. [*Margin*: Also it is agreed that opon all siche days as the prebendaryes shuld*[h]* execute that every man kepe his course or elles he that executith for hym to have of hym xij d. for his labor, and also the same ordre to be kepte touching the sermons, every man to do it hymself in his course or to get one*[i]* of*[j]* the cumpany to doo it for hym if it may, or elles sum other able man, under payne of vj s. viiij d.]

Signed: Benson, Redman, Haynes, Leighton, E. Weston, Britten, H. Perkyns, Carleton, Elfred.

[a] Four words inserted repl. 'within' inserted then deleted.   *[b]* Repl. 'and nere about with/ within the citie and nere about there adjoynyng unto and'.   *[c]* Three words inserted repl. 'have communication'.   *[d]* Two words inserted.   *[e]* Word inserted.   *[f]* Word inserted.   *[g]* Repl. 'the' (? incompleted word).   *[h]* Repl. insertion erased.   *[i]* Four words deleted in error.   *[j]* Repl. 'to do'.

33. *February 1. A deputation to confer with the bishop and others about an order from the king.*

[f. 23] The fyrst daye of February. It is agreed by Mr Dean and the chapter that Mr Reynoldes and Redmayn shall repayre*[a]* to my lord of Westm' and Chichester[70] and Mr Chancelor of thagmentations[71] to common and conclude*[b]* with theym concernyng the kynges majesties plesor acording to the tenure and effecte of the lettres late directed from theym.[72]

---

[69] Chief gentleman of the privy chamber, keeper of Westminster and Whitehall palaces, and one of Henry VIII's most trusted courtiers. This entry places his appointment as high steward earlier than given in *Hist. Parl. 1509–1558*, ii, 27–9 (citing WAM 33192 [m. 5d]). His seat was at Cheshunt, where the church had been appropriated to Westminster Abbey: Harvey, *Estates*, 405. Jones and Underwood, *King's Mother*, 196–7. There survives a letter from him to the dean and chapter asking to place a scholar at the school: WAM 43046.

[70] Richard Sampson, bishop of Chichester.

[71] Sir Edward North.

[72] This concerned the university students and readers which the dean and chapter were obliged to support. The chapter responded with a certificate where they admitted ignorance of what the students actually studied: WAM 43048. The university connexion was soon disestablished: see below, no. **39** & n. 78, and Knighton, 'Education', 26–34.

Signed: Benson, Haynes, Redman, Leighton, J. Pekyns, H. Perkyns, Elfred, Reynolds, E. Weston, Carleton.

^a Repl. 'be auctorised to common and conclude'. ^b Two words inserted.

34. *February 3. Fines for absence and their distribution.*

3º die Februarii. It is decreed that all the prebendaryes being within the cite of Westm' or London shall opon lawful and resonable monition gyvyn be present at all siche tymes as it^a shall be apointed apon payn of a crowne toties quoties onlesse manyfeste excuse can be alledgid that they be in the kynges or quenys^b affayres or elles be syke that they can not cum, or violently deteyned,^c the said crowne to be devydid amonges the cumpanye than^d present.

Signed: Benson, Redman, Leighton, Bellasis, J. Pekyns, H. Perkyns, Elfred, Carleton, E. Weston, Reynolds, Haynes.

^a *Supra*: 'any chapter'. ^b Two words inserted: 'affayres' also here inserted then deleted. ^c Three words inserted. ^d Word inserted.

35. *Same day. Two leases.^a*

[f. 23v] 3 die Februarii [anno]^b predicto. It is agreed by Mr Dean and the chapter that William Tilesworth, goldsmythe, shall have ij leasis, one of Fordovehaley and another tenement now in the tenure of one Martyn, acordyng^c to siche covenantes as be comprised in the indentures redde in the chapter house the day above writtin, provyded that he shal be bonde in obligation of c li. for perform-ance of the same covenantes.[73]

Signed: Benson, Redman, Leighton, Elfred, Carleton, E. Weston, H. Perkyns, J. Pekyns, Reynolds.

^a Whole entry deleted. ^b MS. 'die' in error. ^c Repl. 'the fyrste'.

36. *February 6. Commons and wages of the minor canons. Fine for absence.*

[f. 24] 6 die Februarii. Decreed by Mr Dean and the chapter that Johan Multon for the tyme and the tresourer after that he hath the money delyverid unto his handes shall from tyme to tyme delyver to the cater^a of the peticanons for keping of theyr commons as shall be thought nede, and to abate somyche in the payment of theyr wages quarterly.

Signed: Benson, Redman, Leighton, J. Pekyns, H. Perkyns, E. Weston, Elfred, Reynolds.

^a Repl. 'stuard'.

Memorandum hoc die predicto abfuit Mr Doctor Brettayn contra decretum de absentia etc., quare debet v s., presentibus tunc magistro decano, Redmayn, Perkyns, Pekyns, Reynoldes, Leyghton, Weston, Elfrede.

---

[73] See below, no. **100** & n. 184.

37. *February 9. Payment to the treasurer. Custody of records.*

[f. 24v] ix° die Februarii. Hit was decreyd by Mr Deane and the chapiter that John Multon shall delyver unto Mr Doctor Parkyns tresaurer for this yere xx li. sterlyng towardes the necessary afferes of this house, and his bill subscribyd with his hand shalbe a sufficyent discharge unto the sayd John Multon yn this behalf.

Signed: Benson, Redman, H. Perkyns, J. Pekyns, Reynolds, Elfred, E. Weston.

Also Mr Pekyns, Mr Weston and Johan Multon be apointed to serche and gether together the evydence which was in Russelles[74] handes, Mr Harvys[75] etc.

38. *March 6. A reversion to the queen's servant contrary to a previous order.*

[f. 25] The vj[th] [a] daye of March[b] was brought unto Mr Deane and the chapiter the quenes graces lettres yn the favor of one of hir pages of hir prevy chamber namyd George Crosyar for the preferment to[c] the reversion of the[d] ferme of the parsonage of Stanford yn the vale of the white horse in Barkshire[76] which, not withstandinge ower[e] formere decre agaynst[f] reversions[77] was grauntyd to satisfye the quenes request, thies[g] beyng present, for xxxj yeres.

Signed: Benson, Leighton, J. Pekyns, E. Weston, Elfred, H. Perkyns, Reynolds.

   [a] Altered from (?) 'ij'.   [b] Repl. 'F[ebruarii]'.   [c] Repl. 'for'.   [d] Three words inserted.
   [e] Repl. 'the'.   [f] Repl. 'was grauntyd'.   [g] Repl. 'yn'.

39. *March 13. Lands surrendered in exoneration of maintaining university students.*

xiij° Martii. Master Deane assemblyng the company bi there consentes[a] sealyd the deade of gyfft of certayne landes unto the kynges majestie for the exoneration of the exhibition of twenty[b] scholars yn Oxford and Cambrige.[78]

Signed: Benson, Leighton, H. Perkyns, Elfred, Redman, E. Weston, Reynolds.

   [a] Three words inserted.   [b] Repl. 'certayn'.

[74] William Russell: see above, n. 66.
[75] Canon William Harvey died between 8 July and 22 November 1544: GLRO, DL/C/355, f. 50. *LP* xix, II, 690(63).
[76] Granted for *40* years from end of lease to Richard Plotte (18 years from Lady Day 1535) at 40 marks rent, reserving the advowson to the dean and chapter, 16 May 1545: WAM Reg. III, ff. 52–53v.
[77] Not extant. But may refer to the statutory prohibition of renewals 'per modum renouationis alicuius termini cum expletus fuerit' (*Statutes (1)*, 80/106) as assumed in Knighton, 'Economics', 54. Reversions of more than 21 years were illegal under 32 Hen. VIII c. 28.
[78] See above, n. 72. The surrender is not registered, but the expenses of the transaction are recorded: WAM 37064, ff. 4v, 5. In the following year further properties were surrendered in exoneration of the obligation to maintain the five readers in each university: WAM 18400; Reg. III, ff. 76–77v. In all lands worth £567 18s 11½d were returned to the crown: WAM 12960.

40. *March 17. Almsgiving. Payment for stipends, repairs and supplies.*

[f. 25v] xvij die Martii. It is agreed by Mr Dean and the chapter that Mr Doctor Perkyns, tresaurer, shall bestowe in almesse the summe of xx li. after his discretion amonges the pore people here about Westm', havyng with hym assistent sum of the cumpanye and also ij or iij honeste persons to bere recorde, and that the said Mr Perkyns of this distribution shall make a bill to be brought in whan he makes his acoumpte.[79] Item decreed that Johan Multon shal delyver to Mr Doctor Perkyns for[a] payment of the stipendes[b] of the prebendaryes and mynisters, also for reparations, oyle, waxe and wyne, foure hundreth poundes.

Signed: Benson, Leighton, H. Perkyns, Redman, Britten, Elfred, E. Weston, Reynolds.

[a] Repl. 'money'.   [b] Repl. 'wa[ges]'.

41. *April 29. Larger endowment sought.*

[f. 26] 29 Aprilis. It is agreed by Mr Dean and the chapter that Mr Bretayn and Redmayn shall prosecute forthwith[a] the mater for the encrease of landes to Mr Chancelor of the augmentation, and that Mr Weston shall helpe at siche tyme as aether of the tother shall be letted. And[b] this to do to the uttermost of ther power to the fynyshyng therof, if hit maye be.[80]

Signed: Benson, Redman, Leighton, Britten, Elfred, Carleton, E. Weston, Reynolds.

[a] Word inserted.   [b] Repl. illegible word and 'Item'.

42. *May 22. Survey of estates. Jurisdiction.*

[f. 26v] 22 Maii. It is decreed by Mr Dean and the chapter that Johan Multon shall this somer at his going down into the cuntre see what reparations is to be doone and apoint[a] where as decays be to be repayred acordyngly, namely at[b] Hyncley the mylles[c] sich reparations to be made as shall be necessarrye. Item concernyng jurisdiction at Malden and otherwhere, that Mr Bellysis, Bretayn and Weston shall see the grauntes and so than further an offycer to be appointed.

[a] Repl. 'see'.   [b] Repl. 'to be'.   [c] Repl. 'wynd'.

---

[79] £100 was allowed in the erection book for alms: WAM 6478, f. 4v.

[80] The dean and chapter felt they had been cheated in the recent surrender (cf. nn. 72, 78 above), although the discrepancy was modest (£1 5s 7½d). They also claimed £10 8s 4d for stipends paid out before they received letters of discharge: WAM 6482, 43933, 6483, 6481 (in order of composition). Other cathedrals were similarly discontented (Westminster acquired details: WAM 37064, f. 5) and in 1550 the chancellor of augmentations was ordered to compensate the new foundations in keeping with their original endowments; the only enrolled grant resulting was for Ely: PRO, SP 10/4, no. 48 (*CSPDEdVI*, 432). *CPR* 1549–51, pp. 214–16; *ibid.* 1550–3, p. 173. See further below, no. **64**.

43. *May 21. Rectory of Islip.*

21º Maii anno regni regis Henrici 8 37º. It is agreed and graunted that Mr Doctor Perkins shall have thadvoison of the parsoneige of Islype.[a][81]

Signed: Benson, Redman, Leighton, Britten, Elfred, E. Weston, H. Perkyns.

[a] Followed by several words deleted.

44. *June 27. Leases sealed.*

[f. 27] 27 of June. It is decreed bi Mr Deane and the chappiter that the leases ensuyng shold be sealed, and also were sealed on the xxvij dai of June, videlicet a presentation for the vicarege of Bassingburne,[82] the lease of the parsonage of Stanford in Barckshire,[83] the lease of Offorthclunie[84] in Huntingtonshire, the lease of[a] Longdon in Wicettershire.[85] Also hit was farther agreed that Margeri Barnerd, wido, farmer of the maner of Hardwicke in Glocettershire shold have hir lease renued with one of hir sonnes joned with hir in the same for thoes yeres which she hath yet remaining in hir lease, and to pai for a fine iiij markes.[86] Item hit was farther decreed that Gallawai the bocher the elder shal have a lease of the howse that he now dwelleth in[b] in Totell strete with a certaine shoppe in the great gate at the Kinges strete ende,[87] and also Maistres Harberde shall have a lease of the howse that she now dwelleth in,[88] and also a fletcher named [*blank*] to have likewise a lease of his howse.[89] Also that Mr Haryngtons[90] lease shal be renued under the former conditions makyng it up xxx^{ty} yeres.

---

[81] The right of next presentation had been granted to John Parkyns of London, Thomas Parkyns of Eynsham, Oxon., and another, on May 5. In 1549 William Haynes, B.D. was admitted on Thomas Parkyns's presentation by virtue of this grant. Humphrey Perkyns himself was admitted on the dean and chapter's presentation on 29 August 1550 *vice* Haynes: Bodl. MS Oxf. Dioc. Papers d. 105, pp. 128–9, 138. Knighton, 'Collegiate Foundations', 400, where 1550 date is incorrect. Perkyns was deprived in the church of All Saints, Oxford on 19 April 1554, for marriage: PRO, E 331/Oxf./1, m. 3.

[82] William Balford, M.A. Oxon., (Emden, 22) was admitted on the dean and chapter's presentation 10 July 1545: CUL, EDR G/1/7, f. 174. He was deprived by 13 July 1554, presumably for marriage: *Inst. Cant. sed. vac.*, 7.

[83] See above, no. **38** & n. 76.

[84] Not traced.

[85] Not traced. Shortly afterwards granted to Lord Seymour of Sudeley: cf. below, no. **72** & n. 118.

[86] Not traced. As n. 85.

[87] Not traced. Perhaps William Galaway who died 'myserablie and pore' in Tothill St in 1554: WAM 37555, f. 1v.

[88] Betresse *alias* Batryse Harbert, widow, granted a tenement with little backside in St Margaret's churchyard for 60 years from previous Lady Day at £2 rent 10 February 1547: WAM 36051; Reg. III, ff. 88–9.

[89] Robert Dawson, fletcher, granted a tenement or two cottages in Tothill St for 30 years from Michaelmas following at £1 12s rent 19 September 1544: WAM Reg. III, ff. 80–80v.

[90] Sir John Harrington, farmer of Brooke in the parish of Oakham, Rutland: WAM 37049, f. 10. For him see *Hist. Parl. 1509–1558*, ii, 298–300.

Signed: Benson, Redman, Leighton, H. Perkyns, Carleton, E. Weston, Bellasis.

^a Word inserted.   ^b Word inserted.

45.   *October 22. Ecclesiastical patronage. Gift to the attorney-general.*

[f. 27v] 22° die Octobris anno Henrici 8ⁱ 37°. It is agreyd by Mr Deane and the prebendaryes that Sir John Smyth shalhave the vycaredge of Chadleworth in the counte of Barkshere and hath his presentatyon in the presens of the sayd prebendarys sealyd.⁹¹ Item it is agreyd by the sayde deane and prebendaryes that Mr Carlton, vicar of Standforde in the counte of Barkshere upon the resignatyon of his said vycaredge shall nominate oon to be his successor, and hath his presentatyon the day above wrytten both grauntyd and sealyd.⁹² Item Mr Parkyns hath a votyon of the parsonadge of Islype⁹³ both grauntyd and sealyd the same tyme.ᵃ Item agreed that the kinges attorney⁹⁴ shall have twenty okes in Islype wodde of our geyfte.

Signed: Benson, Leighton, Britten, H. Perkyns, Elfred, Carleton, J. Pekyns.

^a Followed by deletion: 'and a lease of the tombe house for xxj yeares'.

46.   *December 15. Election of officers. Deanery and canons' houses.*

[f. 28] 15 Decembris. The fyftenth day of Decembre Mr Dean and the prebendaries being assembled acording to the statutes have elected officers, fyrstᵃ Mr Elfride to be vicedeane, Mr Doctor Brettayn receyver, Mr Doctor Perkyns tresourer, Sir John Horne sextayn, Richard Priest and Antony Nicols subsextayns, Sir Ellis⁹⁵ chaunter. Item agreed the same daye that Mr Dean and his successors shal have the misericorde, the greate kitchin, and all edifices betwixt his own house and the scoole, andᵇ the great garden with the ponde and trees which he hath now in possession. And it is agreed that Mr Haynes shall have pertaynyng to his house to hym and his successors all the garden enclosed in the stone wall

---

⁹¹ Despite this four days later John Cordewne was admitted to the living on the dean and chapter's presentation: WRO, Reg. Capon, f. 26v. But Smith was in possession by 1550, when a grant of the advowson (*sic*) was made to John Lathbury: below, no. **103**. Lathbury was admitted 9 April 1554 on his predecessor's death: Reg. Capon, f. 53v. This Smith cannot therefore have been the provost of Oriel and canon of Westminster (Emden 522–3), who in any case would have not been given the 'Sir' prefix of inferior clergy. The Chaddleworth incumbent may, however, have been the minor canon of Westminster Abbey who became precentor in 1548 (below, no. **84**) and who died in the autumn of 1553: PRO, PROB 11/37, ff. 9v–10.

⁹² Canon Gerard Carleton had held the living since 1537, being admitted on a *pro hac vice* grant from the then abbot and convent to John Carleton and another. His successor John Fawken was admitted 25 November 1545: WAM Reg. II, f. 292. WRO, Reg. Shaxton, f. 8v; Reg. Capon, f. 26v.

⁹³ See above, no. **43** & n. 81.

⁹⁴ Henry Bradshaw.

⁹⁵ Ellis Pecock: WAM 37043, f. 11.

with the old dovehouse and the house called Caunterburie, with the garden grounde from his house to Mr Deans garden.[96]

Signed: Benson, Haynes, Redman, Leighton, Britten, J. Pekyns, H. Perkyns, Carleton, E. Weston.

  a Repl. 'Mr Doctor Brettayn' with erasure over.   *b* Repl. 'where'.

47.   *1546. January 2. The receiver-general granted a manor.*

[f. 28v] 2° Januarii anno predicto. It is grauntyd by the dean and chapyter that John Multon shalhave the lease of the hole manor of Burton and Morton Henmarshe in the counte of Glocester for terme of his lyfe, and oon yere after, with all profyttes and comodytes belongyng to the same, provydyd that in the stede of his fyne he shall make a terrtory*a* of all the hole possessyons of this howse, and shall paye the yerly rent accordyng to a pere of indentures in that behalf.[97]

Signed: Benson, Elfred, Leighton, H. Perkyns, Britten, E. Weston, Carleton, Redman, J. Pekyns.

  a *Sic* for 'terrier'.

48.   *January 29. The precentor to report absentees to chapter. Order for future meetings. Verger appointed. Bailiffship shared at Islip.*

[f. 29] 29° Januarii anno predicto. Mr Deane and the chapter be agreed that tomorow, that is to say the Saterdaie the xxx^{ti} daie of Januari shalbe a chapter at viij of the clock in the morning, and the chauntor to bring in his bill of perditions tomorow for all tyme heretofore paste. And that tomorow fortenite according to the statutes shalbe an other chapter at the said hower, and so*a* furth from fortenite to fortenite as the statutes appointeth. And that every prebendari being within the citie of Westm' or*b* London nott*c* lefully lettid, and suche lett signefied to Mr Deane or in his absence to the subdeane, shalbe present at every such chapter upon pein to forfaite for every such default v s. Item that Gwye Gasquine shall have*d* thoffice of the cheiff virger during his lyeff by patentt under the chapiter seall withe the*e* fee apperteyning to the saide office. Item that Jhon Pilkynton of Islype and Thomas Perkins of Eynsham shall have thoffice of the bayliwike of Islype by patentt under the chapiter seall[98] during their lyves and the lengger lyver of them withe the*f* fee limetted in the boke of particulers, and a pair of indentuers of covenaunttes to be made betwen the deane and the chapiter and the forsaide*g* Jhon Pylkynton and Thomas Perkins, and an obligation to be made by them for the performaunce of the covenaunttes to be kepte of ther partye.*h*

---

[96] For location of these see Robinson, *Abbot's House*, 51–2, 54–8.
[97] Granted for 48 years from previous Michaelmas at £32 13s 5½d rent 10 October 1545: WAM Reg. III, ff. 71v–74.
[98] Granted (on a bond of £100) with fee of 5 marks 18 November 1545: *ibid.*, ff. 71–71v.

Signed: Benson, Leighton, J. Pekyns, E. Weston, Britten, Elfred, H. Perkyns.

ᵃ Word inserted. *ᵇ* Repl. 'and'. *ᶜ* Repl. 'being'. *ᵈ* Word inserted. *ᵉ* Word inserted. *ᶠ* Repl. 'thaccustomed fee'. *ᵍ* Repl. 'the'. *ʰ* Followed by deletion: 'and Pylkinton to surrender his patentt'.

49. *February 13. The minor canons' subsidy payment. Wood to be felled. Houses for the master of the choristers and one of the canons. A chapter office established.*

[f. 29v] 13º Februarii anno predicto. It is agreyd by Mr Deane and chapyter that Lytgold, Harforde, Hadgrave and Dyxon, petycannons, shall nat be chargyd with the antycypatyon dewe at Michelmas last in consyderatyon they payd it at*ᵃ* mydsomer befor ther admyssyon here, as yt apperyth by ther quittaunces in that behalf remainynge in the thresarers custodye.⁹⁹ It is also agreyd by the sayde deane and chapyter that Mr Parkyns, thresarer, shall go unto Benflette to see the hoole woode there, contenyng by estymatyon xij acres, to be felde, made and caryd hyther at the chirchis cost and equally to devyde yt amonge the prebendarys. It is also agreyde by the parties aforesayde that Foxe, master of the quiresters, shall dwell*ᵇ* in the allmys howse and Mr Leghton to have his howse, and the howse that he lyith in nowe to be a howse for the audytt and to kepe the evydences in [*Margin (later hand)*: A praebend. auditor.]¹⁰⁰

Signed: Benson, Haynes, Leighton, Elfred, H. Perkyns, Carleton, J. Pekyns, E. Weston.

ᵃ Word inserted. *ᵇ* Repl. 'lye'.

50. *March 20. Payment of the subsidy. The dean and canons to share out the nomination to all inferior offices. Charges on appointment to the same.*

[f. 30] 20 Martii anno predicto. It is agreed by the vyecedeane*ᵃ* and the chapiter that the*ᵇ* peticanons shall paye quarterly x s. of their stipende untyll the kinges subsidye be fully payed, and that the thesaurar shall paye of the commyn tresure the residue.¹⁰¹ Item that the chylder of the grammer schole, the x queresters, the fower bellringars and the twoe subsextens shalbe divided into xiiij equall partes by balles,¹⁰² and Mr Deane to have the nomination and appoyntmente of twoe partes and every prebendary of one parte. Provided that aswell the deane as

---

⁹⁹ Not extant. The subsidy payment referred to is not that most recently granted (in December 1545) but the third and final instalment of that of 1543, being 6s in the £ over three years: 34 & 35 Hen. VIII c. 28. Lehmberg, *Later Parliaments*, 179–80, 220. In June 1545 the privy council had directed bishops to the immediate collection (i.e. anticipation) of tenths and subsidies due at the following Christmas: *LP* Add. ii, 1702. *APC* i, 451, cited in F.M. Heal, 'Clerical tax collection under the Tudors,' in O'Day and Heal, *Continuity and Change*, 106, 266 n. 31. Cf. R.W. Hoyle, 'War and public finance', in *The reign of Henry VIII. Politics, policy and piety*, ed. D.N.J. MacCulloch (Basingstoke 1995), 94, 266 n. 65.

¹⁰⁰ A misunderstanding of the text.

¹⁰¹ See above, no. **49** & n. 99.

¹⁰² It is probable that actual balls were used: cf. *Wells Act Book*, pp. xxii & n. 4, 68 & n. 1.

every prebendary shall bring his childe and scholar att every vacation into the chapiter ther to be examined accordyng to the statutes. And furthermore that all benefices and other prefermentes within the churche as the nomination of the peticanons, clerkes, virgers, pisteler and gospeller shalbe lotted and appoynted after the same manner. Item that every peticanon att his fyrste entering into the commyns shall paye towarde thimplementes of the howse v s., and every clerke iij s. iiij d., the scholemaister of grammer schole*ᶜ* vj s. viij d., the isher iij s. iiij d., every scholar viij d. and every other commyn officer *ᵈ* and servauntt xij d.

Signed: Elfred, Haynes, Redman, Leighton, Britten, J. Pekyns, E. Weston, H. Perkyns, Reynolds.

ᵃ Repl. 'deane'.   ᵇ Word inserted.   ᶜ Three words inserted.   ᵈ Word inserted.

51.   *July 10. Canons' houses.*ᵃ

[f. 30v] Anno regni regis Henrici 8ⁱ 38. 10 Julii. Master Deane and the chapiter be agreyd that Mr Pekyns and Mr Raynoldes*ᵇ* shall have the leasses of Vaughanes house and Burbeges house to them duryng ther lyves and to ther successors prebendarys to come, and*ᶜ* further hyt ys agreade by the deane and the chappyter that mony *ᵈ* for the redemptyon of the above namyd howsys wyth there apertenauns schalbe dysbursyd by the colledge to the behove off the fore namyd Mr Pekyns and Mr Raynoldys, farder condycyonyd that yff Mayster Belysus wyll suryender hys howse that now [he] possessys unto*ᶜ* the churche, then the sayde Belysus schall have Vaughanys howse, and this to be don with such expeditions as maye be, and Maister Brytan or Maister Perkyns furthwyth to dysburse.*ᶠ* Item hyt ys farder agrede that the forsayde Mr Raynold and Maister Pekyns shall have a lease yn reversyon to them and there assygnys of Cowperys howse wyth*ᵍ* the aperteynans.¹⁰³

ᵃ Whole entry deleted.   ᵇ Repl. 'Vaughan'.   ᶜ Repl. 'provyded that yf Mr Belasses list to have the preferment the sayd Pekyns and Raynoldes ar contentyd that ther with'.   ᵈ Repl. 'the'.   ᵉ Repl. 'unto ether off the forenamyd parsons'.   ᶠ Three words inserted.   ᵍ Repl. 'and'.

52.   *July 13. The preceding entry revised.*

[f. 31] Anno regni regis Henrici 8ⁱ 38. 13 Julii. Master Deane and the chapiter be agreyd that Mr Raynoldes and Mr Pekyns shall have the leasses of Vaughan and Burbegis houses, to eche of them one, duryng ther lyves and to ther successors prebendarys to come, and further yt ys agreyd that the mony for the redemption of Vaughanis house shalbe debursyd owt of hand by the deane and chapiter to the use of the sayde Raynoldes and Pekyns,*ᵃ* and this to be with all expedytione. And further more that uppon communycation with Burbege yf his house maye be redemyd for a convenyent some, the mony like wyse to be debursyd by the deane and chapiter. And to geve towarde the redemption of theis ij sayd houses

---

¹⁰³ For the houses see above, nn. 37, 39. William Couper's house is listed next to Burbage's: WAM 37036, f. 1; 37041, f. 4.

to ecche of them xx li., and they to be at the rest of they*[b]* charges at ther awne proper costes.

Signed: Benson, Britten, J. Pekyns, H. Perkyns, E. Weston, Reynolds, Carleton, Redman, Leighton.

[a] Repl. 'chapiter'. *[b]* *Sic*.

53. *Undated. Day boys to contribute to commons.*

[f. 31v] Hit ys agreyd by Mr Deane and the chapiter that as many childer as by suyte of ther frindes and licence of Mr Deane optayn licens*[a]* to be bordyd at home with ther fryndys that they shall pay quarterly xvj d. wherof*[b]* x d. to goo to the commyns of ther fellowis and the other vj d. to goo towardes the charges of napery and other necessarys belongyng to ther commyns.

Signed: H. Perkyns, Reynolds, Carleton, E. Weston.

[a] Repl. 'favor' which was inserted then rejected without being deleted. *[b]* Repl. 'to the commyns'.

54. *Undated. Lead from the infirmary chapel.*[104]

[f. 32] It is agreed that where as *[a]* Mr Dean of Peterborough hath*[b]* takin down the lede of Saint Kateryns chapell, the said lede shall be wayed and the tone*[c]* half of the price theroff Mr Kareleton shall paye out of hand to the churche, and the said Mr Carlton agreeth to make uppe buylding and lodgyng through-out*[d]* the bodie of the chapell or elles to be bound to leve to the church if he departe afore the fynishing of the said building*[e]* as myche as the tother half of the price of the said lede cummyth to.

Signed: Benson, Redman, Leighton, J. Pekyns, H. Perkyns, Reynolds, Carleton.

[a] Two words inserted. *[b]* Repl. 'shall'. *[c]* *Sic*, for 'the one'. *[d]* Repl. 'for where the b[odie]'. *[e]* Ten words inserted.

55. *1547. January 19. Appointment of rent collector and exchequer attorney.*

[f. 32v] xix° Januarii anno regni regis Henrici viij xxxviij°. Yt was agreed by Mr Deane and the chapiter that Edmonde Lorde of Westm' shall have the collection of suche rentes and revenews as Mr Lyster late departed had during his lyff tyme, and that for the collection of the same he shall have*[a]* the somme of fower powndes by yere for his fee, he fyndyng sufficient surties for the same. Item yt was then agreed that James Lorde shalbe our attorney for suche busynes as we shall have yn thexchecquer, and that for his fee he shall have xiij s. iiij d. by yer.[105]

104 For which see Harvey, *Living and Dying*, 88–90.

105 Robert Lyster had been collector of the rents of the former monk chamberlain (the rents were still grouped according to the monastic obediences): WAM 37050, ff. 8–8v. James Lorde was an attorney in the exchequer; he and his brother Edmund were the sons of George, purveyor of the king's works: WAM 37376. Rosser, 388.

Signed: Benson, Haynes, Leighton, J. Pekyns, Sandiforth, E. Weston, Reynolds, Carleton.

a Word inserted.

56. *May 2. A canon fined.*

[f. 33] Secundo die Maii anno regni regis Edwardi vj*ᵃ* primo. Mr Doctor Breton, whose*ᵇ* course was to preache apon Sonday last past[106] and was nott keptt (as occasion then served) paid by his owne accorde and consent iij s. iiij d. for the defaultt, and also promessed to fulfill the rometh of preaching apon Sonday next commyng, and this was agred by the hole chapiter.

a Repl. 'primo'. *b* Repl. 'howse'.

57. *Same day. Lease agreed.*

[f. 33v] Secundo die Maii anno primo regni regis Edwardi sexti. Yt was agreed in the chapiter house that Elsebeathe Peyne, widow, of St Martens le Grant in London shall have severally all suche leasses wiche she now hathe*ᵃ* of the said deane and*ᵇ* chapiter of Westm' to her and her assignes frome the*ᶜ* feast of St Michaell the Archangell next ensuyng unto thende and terme of thyrtie yers, paying the olde and accustomed renttes, wiche leasses ar granted unto the said Mres Peyne frely withowt any fyne geving, savyng only for the ordynarye fees of sealles, provided alweys that the*ᵈ* said Mrs Peyne shall have those tenementes wiche she holdethe by Messengers lease only for terme of twentie*ᵉ* yers, so that the said Mrs Peyne doo so long leve.[107]

Signed: Benson, Redman, Bellasis, Britten, H. Perkyns, Carleton, Sandiforth.

a Repl. 'enjo[yeth]'. *b* Repl. 'of'. *c* Repl. 'this presentt day unto'. *d* Repl. 'that'. *e* Repl. 'xx'.

58. *May 13. Sir Wymond Carew appointed steward of Westminster courts.*

[f. 34] xiij° Maii anno regni regis Edwardi vj primo. Yt was agreede by Mr Deane and the chapiter that Sir *ᵃ* Wymonde Carew, knightt,*ᵇ* shall have thorder of the courttes for good*ᶜ* rule within the citie of Westm',[108] and to levye the

106 The previous day (3rd Sunday after Easter).
107 Granted: (1) a little shop within Pouchmakers' Court, St Martin-le-Grand at 8s rent; (2) 14 tenements in Foster Lane at £3 rent; (3) a tenement and shop in St Martin-le-Grand at £3 15s 4d rent; (4) a tenement called 'Martyn' shop with others there at £7 18s 8d rent; (5) four tenements and shops in the court of St Martin-le-Grand at £9 13s 4d rent; all for years stated from Michaelmas following, (1–4) 1 April 1547, (5) 10 July 1547: WAM Reg. III, ff. 84v–86, 87–8, 90–2; rent of (3) correct in Reg. text but wrongly (–13s–) marginated there (f. 90v).
108 Prominent west-country landowner and courtier; receiver-general to three of Henry VIII's queens: *Hist. Parl. 1509–1558*, i, 581–2. His elder son Roger was a Westminster exhibitioner at Cambridge (perhaps O.W. as was his brother Matthew) and subsequently

profittes and commodities of the same, as fynes and amarcementes, to the use and commodite of the said deane and chapiter, for the wiche his peynes yt ys agreed that the said Mr Wymonde Carew shall have the halff of the comodite and profittes of the said courttes, so that the said Mr Carew shall beare the halff charge of stockes, pillery, couking stooles and suche lyke as apperteynethe to the said courtte. The charges of the dyners for the stuarde and other officers one the courte litte*ᵈ* days to apperteyne to the [said]*ᵉ* Mr Deane and the chapiter.

Signed: Benson, H. Perkyns, Redman, Britten, J. Pekyns, E. Weston, Reynolds, Carleton, Sandiforth.

ᵃ Repl. 'Mr'. ᵇ Repl. 'esquyer'. ᶜ Word inserted. ᵈ Word inserted. ᵉ Ellipse in MS.

59. *Same day. Chapters to be held fortnightly. Appointment of chapter clerk.*

[f. 34v] Eodem die. Decreed by Mr Dean and the chapter that where by the statute the prebendaryes be bonde to kepe chapter singulis quindenis,[109] the day for the said ordynary chapters is apointed every fourtnyght to be upon the Saterdays incontinent after matens and to begyn the xiiij day of Maye, every man being within the precincte of London or Westm' to be present at the said chapters under payn of losyng v s. at every tyme.*ᵃ* Item that William Brown shall be the chapter clerke and receyve for his stipend xl s. by yere.

Signed: Benson, H. Perkyns, Redman, J. Pekyns, Sandiforth, E. Weston, Reynolds, Carleton.

ᵃ Three words inserted repl. 'acordyng to the decree before made and writin 3º die Februarii anno regni regis Henrici viij 36ᵗᵒ'.

60. *May 14. Absentees from chapter guilty of contempt.*

[f. 35] xiiij° Maii. Decreed by Mr Dean and the chapter that who soever doth absent hymself from any chapter aether ordynary, that is to saye which is kept onys in the fortnyght upon the Saterdayes as is apointed in the decree last above writin, or from any other chapter duely and lawfully callid and wherunto the prebendaries be monyshed to cum, that than every one of the prebendaries so absentyng hymself and not certifying before the end of the chapter than kept*ᵃ* the cumpany of his lawfull and reasonable excuse siche as the statute doth admytte for his absence from the said chapter shall be coumptid incurrere crimen contemptus*ᵇ* for the which, acordyng to the statute, he shall be mulcted v s. de corpore prebendae.

Signed: Benson, Redman, H. Perkyns, Sandiforth, E. Weston, Reynolds, Carleton.

ᵃ Eight words inserted. ᵇ These two words also marginated.

scholar-fellow of Trinity College: WAM 37044, f. 8v; 43048. Trinity College, Cambridge, Senior Bursar's Muniments, Box 29, C.II.a, f. 1v. *ROW*.
109 *Statutes (1)*, 101/119.

61. *May 28. Presence only recorded.*

[f. 35v] Anno Edwardi vj^ti primo.^a The xxviij daye of Maye was the daye fortnyght^b appoyntyd for the chapiter, at the whiche chapiter was present Mr Deane, Mr Vicedeane, Mr Pekyns, Mr Barnarde,[110] Mr Raynoldes; the reste were forthe atowne or occupid in the kynges besenes.

   ^a Page heading.   ^b Word inserted (but in wrong place).

62. *June 11. Presence only recorded.*

The xj^th day of June was the fortnyght^a capiter appoyntyd, at the whiche tyme were present Mr Deane, Mr Vicedeane, Mr Docter Brytten, Mr Barnard, Mr Raynoldes and Mr Weston. Mr Pekyns sent his exscuse and Mr Redman was at Cambrydge,[111] and the rest were absent and sent not theyr exscuse accordyng to the ordynaunces and statutes.

   ^a Word inserted (in wrong place), following 'day of' inserted then deleted.

63. *June 15. Protector Somerset presented with Caen stone.*

This daye the xv^th of June was a specyall chapiter apoyntyd for the awnswer of my lorde protectors graces request concernyng xx^ti tunne^a of Cane stone, whiche then was grauntyd frely to be gevyn unto his grace yf that ther myght be so myche sparyd.[112] And further that thos that were apoyntyd to offer^b this gyfte shulde^c also besyche his grace to be good and gracyous lord unto us for a recompence of our dekayd landes.

Signed: Benson, H. Perkyns, J. Pekyns, Carleton, Redman, Keble.

   ^a Repl. 'lades'.   ^b Repl. 'open'.   ^c Repl. 'myght'.

---

[110] Bernard Sandiforth.

[111] He was the first master of Trinity College, the foundation of which in 1546 owed much to his influence: A.B. Cobban, *The King's Hall within the University of Cambridge in the Later Middle Ages* (Cambridge 1969), 289–90.

[112] Caen stone had been used extensively in Henry III's church, and more recently in Henry V's chantry, the nave, and Henry VII's chapel: W.H. St John Hope, 'The funeral, monument and chantry chapel of King Henry the fifth', *Archaeologia* lxv (1913–14), 147–9. C. Allmand, *Henry V* (1992), 180. H.J. Dow, *The Sculptural Decoration of the Henry VII Chapel, Westminster Abbey* (Durham 1992), 3. T.W.T. Tatton-Brown, 'Westminster Abbey: archaeological recording at the west end of the church', *Antiquaries Journal* lxxv (1995), 177, 184–6. It has been supposed that Somerset's requirement was for his house in the Strand (although this was chiefly built of Wilton stone), and that he may have envisaged pulling down St Margaret's, the (present) Deanery or the Abbey itself: P. Heylin, *Ecclesia Restaurata*, ed. J.C. Robertson (Cambridge 1849), i, 124–7; quoted and discussed in *HK*, 115–16 (but Heylin's reference to the deanery is to the office not the residence, which Benson in any case did not occupy). See also Westlake, *St Margaret's*, 35–6 and Seymour, *Ordeal by Ambition*, 316–18.

64. *June 21. Negotiation with the chancellor of augmentations. John Thynne appointed steward in Gloucestershire.*

[f. 36] Anno Edwardi vj^{ti} primo*^a*. This daye the xxjth daye of June was a specyall chapiter apoyntyd at the whiche tyme were present Mr Deane, Mr Haynes, Mr Redman, Mr Weston, Mr Barnard, Mr Pekyns, Mr Carleton and Mr Keble and*^b* Mr Bretten was absent and made his exscuse, and Mr Perkyns also. Yt ys agrede by Mr Deane and the chapiter that Mr Weston and Mr Barnarde shall prosecute forthwythe the matter concernyng the recompence of our landes to be had at Mr Chancelars¹¹³ handes untyll*^c* the fynysshing of the same,*^d* and they to have for ther labours vj li. xiij s. iiij d. Item yt ys agrede that Master Thynne,¹¹⁴ stuard to my lord protectors grace*^e* shalle have the stuardshipe of the hundred callyd Westm' hundred in Glouc' shere with xxvj s. viij d. fee untyll suche tyme that by his furderaunce yt may be brought to passe that we maye attayne a juste recompence for suche dekeyde landes and other necessarie charges*^f* that we be in suet for, and than to have the hole fee of foure markes to be gevyn as an anuyte and not as a fee insydent to the offyce. [*Margin:* West' hundred in Glocester shire.]

Signed: Benson, Haynes, Redman, Keble, J. Pekyns, Sandiforth, Carleton, E. Weston.

^a Page heading. *^b* Word inserted. *^c* Repl. 'and to have'. *^d* Word inserted. *^e* Six words inserted. *^f* Word inserted.

65. *June 25. Presence only recorded.*

[f. 36v] The xxvth daye of June was the fortnyghtes daye appoyntyd for the chapiter, at the whiche daye was present Mr Deane, Mr*^a* Haynes, Mr Pekyns, Mr Weston, Mr Carleton, Mr Docter Barnard and Mr Keble, and Mr Redman was absent and made his exscuse. Mr Perkyns *^b* was sycke. Mr Bretten was also absent.

^a Repl. 'Mr Vyce Deane'. *^b* Repl. 'Vy[ce Deane]'.

66. *July 7. Nomination of choristers and scholars.*

Anno domini 1547°. This daye the vij daye of July was a specyall chapiter apoyntyd at the whiche chapiter was present Mr Vycedeane, Mr Haynes, Mr Keble, Mr Bretten*^a*, Mr Pekyns, Mr Weston, Mr Barnard and Mr Carleton*^b* and Mr Raynoldes.*^c* Yt ys agred by Mr Vycedeane and the chapiter with the consent of Mr Deane by reporte of Mr Keble, fyrst yt ys concludyd and decrede that Mr Deane shall have the nomynaton and puttyng in of all the querysters and of

113 Sir Edward North, chancellor of the court of augmentations: cf. above, n. 80.
114 John Thynne, knighted later in 1547. His fortunes rose with those of Somerset, his patron and west-country neighbour. He was the builder of Longleat and ancestor of the marquesses of Bath: *Hist. Parl. 1509–1558*, iii, 463–7. He had written to the dean and chapter asking for this stewardship, [blank] June [no year, but must be 1547]; with letter in support from Thomas Smith [Kt 1549], same day: WAM 32893.

foure chylderne in the grammer scole accordyng to a ball or lott wherin the namys of the seyd foure chylderne are conteynyd, and that every prebendarye shall have the nomination and puttyng in of thre chylderne in the grammer scole accordyng to a byll or lott callyd a ball wherin the names of the seyd childerne are wrytten, provydyd that the seyd deane and every prebendary shall bryng in ther childerne to be so nominat by every of theym before the deane or vyce deane and the chapter to be examyned by the deane or vicedeane and the scolemaister*d* accordyng to the statutes of this churche before they be admyttyd. [f. 37] And yf every childe so to be nomynatyd eyther by the deane or any prebendary shalbe fonde by thexaminaton aforesaid*e* to have the qualyties re-hersyd in the statutes,[115] that then every suche childe so nomynatyd and ex-amynde to be forthwythe admyttyd by*f* the deane or*g* vicedeane and scolemaistre.

> *a* Two words inserted.   *b* Repl. 'Mr Deane of Peterbo'; the first 'Mr' not deleted.
> *c* Three words inserted repl. 'Mr Bretten made his exscuse'.   *d* Eight words inserted.
> *e* Three words inserted.   *f* Word inserted repl. 'withowte any furder consent of'.   *g* Repl.
> 'and chapter'.

67. *Record of scholars admitted according to the above agreement on 1 February 1548.*ᵃ

1º Februarii anno domini 1547. Allocatur in forma predicta concordie causa. [*Signatures*] Antonius Cooke. John Godsalve. Christopher Nevynson. John Madew.[116]

> *a* This entry has been inserted in the space left for the dean's signature, and before the signatures of H. Perkyns, vice-dean, Haynes, Keble, Britten, J. Pekyns, Sandiforth, E. Weston, Carleton and Reynolds.

68. *July 7 continued. Dividend of rent wheat. Canons' houses. Lease of the church of St Martin-le-Grand.*

Also yt ys agrede the same day by the seyd chapiter that Mr Deane shall have yerely to his parte tenne quarters whete and every of the prebendaryes fyve quarters*a* withowte any thing paying*b* for theym, whiche amountythe in the hole to threscore and tenne quarters and the very somme of all the rente wheat. Also yt ys agrede and concludyd that Mr Heynes, Mr Keble and Mr Bretten shall have every of theym twenty poundes in consyderaton of theyr severall charges in buldyng and purchasyng of leases of theyr howses, to be payd unto theym before Myhelmas next, provydyd alwayes that Mr Keble shall bryng in the lease of Vaughans howse and Mr Bretten the lease of his howse before the feast of Seynt Michell [f. 37v] next cummyng. And also yt ys agrede that the seyd Mr Heynes

---

115 The choristers were to be 'tenere etatis et uocibus sonoris, et ad cantandum aptis' (young and well-voiced, and able to sing); the scholars 'pauperes . . . amicorum ope destituti . . . ad discendum aptis' (poor, friendless, able to learn): *Statutes (1)*, 91/113.

116 This is the only such entry; but other admissions of scholars occur below, no. **185.** For all individuals see *ROW*.

shall have suffycyent stone of the churche cost within the close for the byldyng of a walle where the pale of his gardeyn stondyth now yf he wyll bylde a walle there at his owne charges. Also yt ys agrede that Harry Keble of London shall have the bodye of Seynt Martyns churche wythe the quyre and ylys*c* (our Ladys chappell with the lytle ile joynyng to yt only reservyd to the deane and chapiter), reservyd also to the same deane and chapiter all the leade, the belles, stone, tymber, glasse and iron, to have the seyd syte of the bodye of the seyd churche with the quyre and ilys to the seyd Harry for the terme of fyfty yeres, paying for the yerely rent fyve markes at foure termes of the yere by evyn portions, provy-dyd always that the seyd Henry shall not medyll with the vawtes or sellars under the premysses dueryng the seyd terme.

Signed: H. Perkyns, vice-dean, Haynes, Keble, Britten, J. Pekyns, E. Weston, Sandiforth, Carleton.

a Word inserted.   *b* Repl. 'payd'.   *c* Repl. 'yll'.

69. *July 9. Admission of scholars. Suit to the protector for reform of statutes and better endowment. Temporary provisions for attendance. Communal buildings. Nomination to offices. Fees of chapter clerk.*

[f. 38] Anno domini 1547°. The ix*th* day of July was the fortnyghtes day apoyn-tyd for a chapiter, at the which day was present Mr Vycedeane, Mr Heynes, Mr Bretten, Mr Keble, Mr Barnard, Mr Weston and*a* Mr Carleton. The seyd daye Mr Perkyns, vice deane, presentyd and dyd nominat a chylde callyd Barnes for a chylde in the grammer scole, which than was admyttyd before the seyd chapiter after that the seyd childe was examenyd. The same daye Mr Pekyns presentyd and dyd nomynat a childe callyd Brydges for a chylde in the grammer scole, whiche than was admyttyd before the seyd chapiter after that the childe was examenyd. Also the seyd daye*b* and yere yt ys decrede that Mr Weston, Mr Barnard and Mr Keble shalbe suters to my lorde protectors grace for reformaton of our statutes, and for recompense of our landes that lacke of our dotatyon for performance of the kynges fondaton here. It ys concludyd and decrede that sewte shalbe made to my lord protectors grace and other of the kynges majesties honorable cowncell for reformatyon of our statutes in certeyn thynges wherof sume do seme to imploye contradicton and sum not to stande with equytie and reson, and forsomuche as at the fyrst communicaton of our statutes to be observyd yt was decrede that all the same statutes indyfferently shulde be putt in executyon, which decre and determynaton was never kepte, nor at this day ys yet kepte, therfore yt ys now agrede [f. 38v] and determenyd that no prebendary shall lose any parte of his cotidian dystrybutions or other profittes of his pre-bende here for the tyme that ys past nor for the tyme that ys to come untyll the statutes shalbe reformyd and delyveryd unto us by sum of the kynges honorable cowncell to be kept upon our othes for a perpetuall order in this churche, provydyd allwaye that every prebendarye shall in the meane season quarterly preche in this churche on sermon by hym selfe or hys deputye, upon payne to lose x s. for every default, and that every prebendary being in London or in Westm' shall dayly be present in the quyre at mattens, masse or evensong, except a leefull lett, upon payne to lose xij d. for every suche defaulte to be devydyd amonge the deane*c* and prebendaryes. Item the seyd day and yere yt ys concludyd and agred that the hall, buttrye and kychyn for the peticanons, clerkes and*d* scollers shalbe byldyd uppe this yere and the next with the resydue of the chambres necessarye for the quyre, and that the graner for wheat shalbe devydyd in vij partes, wherof Mr Deane shall have on parte seperate to hym selfe, and the xij prebendaryes the other vj partes, ij and ij, to have on parte to laye in theyr wheate; thes partitions to be made at the churche coste, with dores and lockes. Also yt ys decrede and agrede that the benyfyces and offyces in the churche and belongyng to the gyfte of the deane and chapiter shalbe distributid bytwyxt the deane and prebendaryes by lottes and balles, and every man to dyspose suche [f. 39] benyfyces or offycys as be in his lote by auctorytie of the deane and chapiter withowte any ferther theyr commen assent or electyon. Ferther yt*e* ys agrede that the plummerye and the waxchanderye with other howses of offyce there shalbe removyd from whense they now are unto the ferder ende of the vawtys undernethe Mr Deanes graner, and that the dore now openyng into the seyd plummerye owte of the churche shalbe muryd uppe, all at the churche cost. Item that the clarke of the chapiter*f* shall have for every payer of indentures wrytyng of the partyes syxe*g* shillinges, and at the entry of every deane vj s. viijd., and of every prebendarye iij s. iiij d., and at*h* the admyssyon of every pryst viij d.,*i* every clerke viij d., every offycer viij d.,*j* and of every chylde and almesman*k* iiij d.

Signed: H. Perkyns, vice-dean, Haynes, Keble, Britten, Sandiforth, E. Weston, Carleton, J. Pekyns.

a Word inserted. *b* Repl. 'deane'. *c* Repl. 'p[rebendaryes]'. *d* Two words inserted. *e* Repl. 'ys'. *f* These five words also marginated. *g* Altered from 'fyve'. *h* Repl. 'of'. *i* Repl. 'xij d.' *j* Repl. 'and almesman' (inserted then deleted). *k* Two words inserted.

70. *October 29. Appointment of proctor in convocation.*

[f. 39v] Anno domini 1547. This day the xxix[th] day of October was a specyall chapiter appoyntyd at the whiche chapiter was present Mr Deane, Mr Perkyns, vice, Mr Bretton, Mr Pekyns, Mr Keble, Mr Barnard and Mr Weston. Yt ys agreed by Mr Deane and the chapiter that*a* Master Pekyns shalbe on of the convocaton howse att Polles for the howse of Westm' for this present parlyament begonne the iiij[th] day of November in anno Edwardi sexti primo.[117]

a Word repeated in error.

[117] Edward VI's first parliament was preceded by the customary mass in the Abbey on November 4, when the preacher was Nicholas Ridley, bishop of Rochester and also canon of Westminster. For the first time the *Gloria, Credo, Sanctus, Benedictus* and *Agnus Dei* were sung in English, somewhat in anticipation of the business of convocation: Wriothesley, i, 187. Procter and Frere, 37. P.G. le Huray, *Music and the Reformation in England, 1549–1660* (2nd edn Cambridge 1978), 10, 177. Benson, as dean, and Pekyns, as proctor for the

71. *December 1. Presence only recorded.*[a]

Anno domini 1547. This daye the fyrst daye of December was a specyall chapiter appoyntyd at the whiche chapiter was present Mr Deane, Mr Perkyns, vice, Mr Haynes, Mr Bretton, Mr Pekyns, Mr Keble and Mr Docter Barnarde.

[a] Whole entry deleted.

72. *December 8. A lease to Lord Seymour for 80 years.*

[f. 40] Anno domini 1547. This daye the eyght daye of December was a specyall chapiter appoyntyd at[a] the whiche chapiter was present Mr Deane, Mr Perkyns, vice, Mr Redmayne, Mr Keble, Mr Pekyns, Mr Barnard, Mr Weston and Mr Carleton. Wherat yt[b] ys agreed that[c] the ryght honorable Lord Admerall Lord Sudeley shall have to fferm for the terme of lxxx yeres the manors of Durhurst, Layngley and Bouerton with theyr appertenance scituat and beyng within the countie of Gloucester, yeldyng and paying yerely suche yerely rentes as hertofore hath byn accostumyd for the same,[118] and besydes that yt ys furder grauntyd unto his lordshipe the stuwardshipe of the sayd lordshipys wythe suche fee as hertofore hathe byn grauntyd unto Sir John Thynne, kynght,[d] as yt apperythe in an acte hertofore in this boke conteyned.[119]

Signed: Benson, H. Perkyns, Redman, Keble, J. Pekyns, Sandiforth, E. Weston, Carleton, Bellasis, Reynolds.

[a] Repl. 'w[hiche]'.   [b] Repl. 'ys'.   [c] Repl. 'b[y]'.   [d] Sic.

73. *December 15. Materials from St Martin-le-Grand to be sold.*[a]

[f. 40v] xv die Decembris. Yt was decred by the deane and prebendaryes the daye above wrytten that Mr Pekyns, Mr Barnard and Mr Keble shall commune,[b] talke and conclude for the bargayne and sale of belles, leade, irene, tymber, with all other thynges insydent to the same pertaynyng[c] to the churche, quere and our Ladie chapell of Saint Martyns le Grand, and also talke for the lease of the soyle

chapter, were among the diocesan clergy whose membership of convocation was certified to the bishop by his vicar-general on November 2: Guildhall MS 9531/12, f. 268v.

[118] Lord Seymour of Sudeley wrote to the dean and chapter asking for a lease of their western manors for the years stated, and for the stewardship to be given to his friend John Thynne (see above, no. **64** & n. 114) 6 December [no year, but must be 1547]: WAM 32892. Duly granted the manors of Deerhurst, Hardwicke, Haydon, Haresfield, Apperley, Walton, Corse Lawn, Tirley, Longney, Cowley, Bourton-on-the-Hill, and Moreton-in-Marsh, Glos., and those of Longdon with Greyndour, Castlemorton with Greyndour and Chaceley with Greyndour, and the rectory of Longdon, Worcs., for years stated from the date of the indenture at £203 17s 7¼d rent 6 June 1548: WAM Reg. III, ff. 106v–108. Seymour, the lord protector's brother and the late queen's husband, was executed for treason in 1549. These estates were then forfeit to the crown: *Hist. Parl. 1509–1558*, iii, 297–301. *CPR* 1547–8, pp. 182–3.

[119] Above, no. **64** & n. 114.

of the same, and what that they shall doo in that behalf the chaptir to ratifie and allowe.

a Whole entry deleted.   *b* Word inserted repl. illegible word.   *c* Repl. illegible words.

74.   *Same day. Appointment of officers. Rehearsal of preceding order.*

Upon Thursday the xv^th daye of December in the fyrst yere of kyng Edward the syxte was the chapter daye uppoyntyd by statute, at the whiche chapter was present Mr Deane, Mr Haynes, Mr Redmayne, Mr Reynalles, Mr Pekyns, Mr Bretton, Mr Bellasys, Mr Keble, Mr Barnard, Mr Weston and Mr Carleton. Yt was decrede by Mr Deane and the chapiter that Mr Bretton shalbe vycedeane for this yere, Mr Pekyns receyvour and Mr Barnarde treasorer, Sir Pecocke chaunter and Sir Croham[120] sexten. Item yt ys also*a* decred by Mr Deane and the preben-dayres above wryttyn that Mr Pekyns, Mr Barnard and Mr Keble shall commen, talke and conclude for the bargayne and sale of belles, leade, ierne, tymber, wythe all other thinges insydent to the same pertaynyng to the churche, quyre and our Lady chappell of Seynt Marteyns le Graunde in London, and also to talke for the lease of the soyle of the same, and what that they shall doo in that behalfe the chapter to ratifye and alowe. [f. 41] Item yt ys agreed that William Brow[n]e,*b* the clarke of the chapter, shall have for his yerely fee foure markes by yere.

Signed: Benson, Britten, Redman, J. Pekyns, Sandiforth, E. Weston, Reynolds, Carleton, Keble.

a Word inserted.   *b* Two words also marginated.

75.   *December 26. Incomplete entry.*^a

[f. 41v] This daye the xxvj^th daye of December was a specyall chapiter appoyn-tyd at the whiche was present Mr Deane, Mr Bretton,*b* vicedeane, Mr Bellasis, Mr Raynoldes, Mr Perkyns, Mr Pekyns, Mr Keble, Mr Barnard and Mr Weston. At the whiche chapiter yt was decrede [*entry abandoned*].

a Whole entry deleted.   *b* Repl. 'K[eble]'.

76.   *1548. January 14. A lease for the lord protector for 99 years.*

Anno*a* Edwardi sexti primo. This day the xiiij^th daye of January was a specyall chapiter appoyntyd at the whiche chapiter was present Mr Deane, Mr Bretton, Mr Bellasis, Mr Pekyns, Mr Keble, Mr Perkyns,*b* Mr Barnard, Mr Weston and Mr Carleton. Yt ys agrede by Mr Deane and the chapiter that my lorde protec-tors grace shall have in*c* lease the hole lordshipe of Islype for the terme of foure score xix yeres upon resonable covenauntes.[121]

Signed: Benson, Keble,*d* Sandiforth.

120 Robert Crome: WAM 37045, f. 1.
121 Grant for years stated from previous Michaelmas at £54 19s 4d rent, reserving the

a Repl. 'This day the xiiij^th daye of December was.'   *b* Two words inserted.   *c* Repl. 'to'.
d Partially erased.

[f. 42 *excised*]

77. *May 18. Leases granted.*

[f. 43] Upon Fryday the xviij^th daye of Maye anno ij^do regni regis Edwardi vj^ti ys
decrede by Mr Vycedeane and the chapiter that Rychard Neste, farmour of the
scyte of the manor of Chatesley in the countie of Worcester shalle^a have wythe
his yeres that he now hathe from Myhelmas next cummyng twentye on yeres of ^b
the same farme wythe thappertenaunce, paying for a fyne vj li. xiij s. iiij d.^122
Item that Robert Smythe, fermor of the scyte of ^c the manor of Pensham
besydes Parshore in the said countie of Worcester shalle lyke wise have wythe
the yeres that he now hathe from Myhelmas next cummyng twenty on yeres of
the same farme with thappertenaunces, paying for a fyne viij li.^123 Item that
Robert Symons, fermor of certen portion of tythes in Parshore, Byrlyngham,
Pynfyn, Pensham, Wyke and other shalle have from Myhelmas next cummyng
twenty on yeres of the seyd tythes with his olde yeres, payng for a fyne vj li. xiij s.
iiij d.^124 Item that John^d Redman of Westm' shall have a tenement wherin he
now dwellith, standyng wythein the Greate Sentuarye, for the terme of threescore yeres from the feast of thannuncyaton of our Lady next cummyng after the
date hereof.^125 [f. 43v] [*Margin*: In comitatu Essex.] Item it is agreed that John
Broke,^e farmor of the parsonage of Cressalle, in consyderaton of the charges and
costes whiche he hathe allredy bestowyd upon the sayd parsonage, amountyng^f
to the somme of twenty poundes shalle^g have a lease of the seyd parsonage for^h
lxx yeres from Myhelmas next cummyng, and^i frome hence forthe the said Jhon
Broke to beare all thacking, splenting and dawbing, the charges of the great
tymber only to aperteyne to the deane and chapiter.^126 Item it is agredd that
Rycharde Pryste shalle have the revertion of a tenement lying in Tothill strete
now in the holdyng of Harry Goodwyn for the terme of lx yeres next ensuyng
after the determinaton and ende of the lease whiche the sayd Goodwyn now
hathe and late on Lawrence helde, yeldyng the olde rente.^127 [*Margin*: Memoran-

advowson to the dean and chapter, with bond of £200 by Richard Taverner (February 5)
28 January 1548: WAM Reg. III, ff. 97v–99. Taverner was a distinguished humanist
scholar and man of business for the Seymour brothers: Emden, 557–8. *Hist. Parl.
1509–1558*, iii, 424–5.

122 Nest's rent for Chaceley was £4 6s 8d: WAM 37061A, f. 8v.

123 Smythe's rent for Pensham by Pershore was £8: *ibid.*, f. 3v.

124 Symons was bailiff of Pershore and paid £8 6s 8d rent for the tithes: *ibid.*, f. 5; 37141.

125 Redman, scrivener (presumably a relative of the canon his namesake) granted the premises for years stated at £2 6s 8d rent 1 March 1548: WAM Reg. III, ff. 120v–121v.

126 Broke, gent., granted the premises for years stated at £16 rent 18 June 1548: *ibid.*, ff.
119v–120v. A repair bill for Cressall parsonage Midsummer 1548 and 1549 amounted to
only 15s 10d: WAM 37263.

127 Richard Prest, yeoman, granted tenement and brewhouse, with equipment for the same,

dum that Mr Boughe dothe tender his lease for to be renuyde.][128] Item it ys agreed that John Tylar, collector of the rentes in Westm', shalle have the reverton of the Whyte Horsse in Longe dyche, and if he refuse this and can espye any fytter howse for his purpose, it is agreed that he shall have the lease therof for the terme of threscore yeres.[129] Item it is agred that John Clarke of Stanes shall have the revertyon of Henburyes howses in Tothill strete for lx yeres.[130] Item it is agred that John Penycote shalle have a lease of the howse callid the Ankers howse wythe thappertenaunce, payng yerely for the same vj s. viij d. for the terme of lx*j* yeres, or if yt can not be sparyd, to have the Talbot, wherin Hughe Byll dwellith, for terme of lx yeres for the olde*k* [rent].[131]

Signed: Britten, Haynes, Redman, H. Perkyns, Keble,*l* J. Pekyns, Sandiforth, Carleton, E. Weston, Bellasis.

a Repl. 'have'.   *b* Repl. 'Item t[hat]'.   *c* Two words inserted using 'the' twice.   *d* Repl. 'William'.   *e* Repl. 'Boke'.   *f* Repl. 'w[hiche]'.   *g* Repl. 'and from hensforthe to bere the reparations of the said parsonage at his owne costes and charges'.   *h* Seven words inserted.   *i* 'and . . . chapiter' marginated repl. 'wythe lyke covenauntes as are conteyned in his olde lease'.   *j* Repl. 't'.   *k* Words from 'or' inserted in margin.   *l* Written and deleted in one place, then written again above the rest.

78.   *June 9. Lease to Lord Seymour for 80 years.*

[f. 44] Upon Saterday the ix^th daye of June in the seconde yere of the reygne of King Edward the vj by the grace of God &c. yt was decrede by Mr Deane and the chapiter whos namys herafter are subscrybyd that my lorde admeralles lordeshipe shall have a lease of the manors of Derehurst with Hardwick, Heydone, Harfeld,*a* Aplarley, Waltone, Corselande and Turley, with also Longne, Cowley, Burtone, Murtone Henmarshe in the countie of Glouceter, and *b* also the manor of Longdon with the parsonage of the same, the manor of Murtone

for years stated from Michaelmas 1556 at £2 rent 2 November 1549: WAM Reg. III, ff. 124–5.

[128] See above, no. **5** & n. 16.

[129] He did spy fitter. Grant to him of several tenements under one roof and garden adjacent called 'Overyes' in St Martin-in-the-Fields from the end of existing interests for 60 years at 10s rent 23 January 1550: WAM Reg. III, ff. 141v–142.

[130] Clarke, yeoman, and Anne his wife, granted three tenements held by John Henbury and two osier grounds for 70 years from previous Michaelmas at £1 14s 4d rent 14 December 1549: *ibid.*, ff. 148–148v. For Henbury, see Rosser, 346, 347.

[131] Penycote (for whom see above, no. **30**) and Maryan his wife granted the Talbot in St Margaret's churchyard for years stated from Lady Day following at 13s 4d rent: WAM Reg. III, ff. 127v–129. The anchorite's house was on the south side of St Margaret's church, and was normally leased to the curate: WAM 36057. Westlake, *St Margaret's*, 18–21 and plate III facing p. 20. Rosser, 201 & nn. 143, 144. This was distinct from the monastic anchorage, the location of which was discovered by L.E. Tanner: his *Recollections of a Westminster Antiquary* (1969), 93–5. The two cells are confused by R.M. Clay, *The Hermits and Anchorites of England* (1914), 81, 126 and Stanley, 350 & n. 2, 361, 383, 384, who also (p. 398) assumes that Penycote was provided for according to the first option in this act.

Castell and Greyndour and the manor of Chadisley alias Chatley in the countie of Worcester for fourescore yeres.[132]

Signed: Benson, Redman, Keble, J. Pekyns, H. Perkyns, Sandiforth, Reynolds.

a Word inserted.   *b* Repl. 'w[ith]'.

79. *June 18. A lease granted at the request of the protector's wife.*

[f. 44v] Upon Monday the xviij daye of June in anno Edwardi vj[ti] ij[do] yt was de[c]rede by Mr Deane and the chapiter that John Bushe, at the instant request of my lady of Somersetes grace, shall have a lease of the parsonage of Godmanchester in the countie of Huntyngton, paying*a* no fine.[133]

Signed: Benson, Britten, Redman, Keble, J. Pekyns, H. Perkyns, Sandiforth, Reynolds.

a Repl. 'for terme of'.

80. *November 15. Grant of presentation* pro hac vice *to the duchess.*

[f. 45] Upon Thursday the xv[th] daye of November in anno Edwardi vj[ti] secundo yt is agreed by Mr Deane and the chapiter that my lady Somersettes grace shall have the nominaton and presentaton of a clarke to be preferredd unto the vyccarege of Godmanchester now presently voyde by the deathe of Mr Roukes,*a* late incumbente there, for this only tyme of this vacaton.[134]

Signed: Benson, Keble, Sandiforth, Britten, J. Pekyns, H. Perkyns, E. Weston.

a Repl. 'late'.

81. *December 5. A deputation to the bishop of Worcester.*[a]

Upon Wensdaye the v daye of December in anno*b* Edwardi vj[ti] ij [do] yt was decrede by Mr Deane and the chapiter that Mr Pekyns, Mr Barnard and Mr Multon shall repeyre to my lord byshope of Worcester.[135]

a Whole entry deleted.   *b* Word inserted.

---

132 See above, no. **72** & n. 118.

133 Bushe, gent., of London, granted the rectory for 21 years from expiry of existing lease from Merton priory at £50 rent, reserving the advowson of the vicarage to the dean and chapter, 20 December 1548: WAM Reg. III, ff. 129v–131. There are many testimonies to the interest taken by Duchess Anne in other people's affairs: Jordan, *Young King*, 496–7; cf. below, n. 296.

134 Seemingly ineffective, probably because of Somerset's fall from power in October 1549. Christopher Rookes, M.A., had been vicar since 1539; on 31 March 1550 William Samuel was admitted *vice* John (*sic*) Rokys, deceased, on the dean and chapter's presentation: LAO, Reg. XXVII, ff. 146v, 277v.

135 Nicholas Heath.

82. *December 8. Impropriation of a benefice in place of one surrendered.*

[f. 45v] Anno Edwardi vj^ti secundo. Upon Saterday^a the viij^th daye of December yt was agrede by Mr Deane and the chapiter there that Sir Anthonye Dennye, knyght, be forgevyn his dette whiche shalbe at Crystmas next xlvj li. xiij s. iiij d.^136 in consideraton that he hath procuryd the benyfice of Shoram in the countie of Kente of the yerely value of xxxiiij li. to be impropryd unto this howse in the discharge of xl^ti markes yerely for the benyfice of Chesthunte to him and^b his heyres surrendred for ever by the seid deane and chapiter.

Signed: Benson, Britten, J. Pekyns, Reynolds, Keble, Carleton, E. Weston, Redman, H. Perkyns.

  ^a Repl. 'Thursdaye'.   ^b Repl. 'surrendred'.

83. *December 10. Leases granted.*

[f. 46] Anno Edwardi vj^ti secundo. Upon Monday the xth day of December [yt]^a was agrede by Mr Deane and the chapiter that Robert Glover of Baxterley in the countie of Warwicke shalle have by lease all that^b theyr tythes of Wyckey^c other wise callyd Wekyng in the countie of Leycester for terme of xlj yeres, in as large and as^d ample maner as Robert Grene and John Rampton hertofore hylde.^137 [Also^e it is agrede that Thomas Hollande shall have a lease of a tenement^f wherin he dwellith with a garden plott lying in the Almery for terme of [*blank*] yeres.]^138

Signed: Benson, Redman, H. Perkyns, Sandiforth, Reynolds, E. Weston.

  ^a MS. 'is'.   ^b Word inserted.   ^c Repl. 'Wyckley'.   ^d Repl. 'ample'.   ^e Rest of entry deleted.   ^f Three words inserted.

84. *December 15. Election of officers.*

[f. 46v] Anno Edwardi vj^ti secundo.^a The xv^th day of December Mr Deane and the prebendaryes, beyng accordyng to the statutes assemblyd, have electyd officers for this yere folloyng, ffyrst Mr Redmayne vycedeane, Mr Haynes tresorer, Mr Raynoldes receyvour, and Sir Croham sexten, Sir John Smythe chanter.

  ^a Written and deleted as head to page, then repeated in margin: perhaps because it was anticipated that entries for 3 Edward VI (beginning January 28) would appear thereunder.

---

^136 This debt was more than twice the rent ($£26$ 13s 4d) and had accumulated over two years: WAM 37062, f. 11v; 37129. Cf. Knighton, 'Economics', 56.

^137 Not traced. Grant to others of these tithes as late held by Glover 1551: WAM 14472, 14475.

^138 Holland, cook, and Betres his wife granted two tenements in Love Lane in the Sanctuary and a garden plot in the Almonry for 60 years from Lady Day following at $£1$ 11s 4d rent 1 March 1550: WAM 36155; Reg. III, ff. 155–156v. He was the College under-cook: WAM 37064, f. 3v.

85. *1549. January 14. Leases granted. Lecterns, candlesticks and other metalwork sold as superstitious; proceeds to the library. Disorder in certain houses. Additions to the deanery and a canon's house.*

Upon Monday the xiiij[th] daie of January in anno predicto it is decrede by Mr Deane and the chapiter that William Grene shall have a new lease of the shoppe or howse in Seynt Marteyns in London wherof he is now tenaunte for the terme of threscore yeres, yeldyng the olde rente and paying vj li. xiij s. iiij d. for a fyne.[139] Also it is decrede that William Tylseworthe shall have Fourdove alley wythe the grete shoppe now in the tenure of William Sutton in Seynt Martens le Graunde for terme of threscore yeres, paying yerely xviij li. rent for the seyd alley and viij li. for the seyd grete shoppe, yf he wolle repayre theym at his owne charges and upholde theyme dueryng the terme.[140] Also it is decrede that Rychard Williames, ser[va]unte to my lady Frances, shall have a lease of syx tenementes lying[a] in Tothill strete whiche late were in the holdyng of wydowe Clowdisley, for terme of threscore and tenne yeres, the seyd Richard Williames to bere all maner of reparations in the discharge of the church, yeldyng and paying yerely the rent of fourty syxe shillinges [b] viij d. by yere.[141] [f. 47 *excised*][c] [f. 48] Also it is decrede that George Vaughan, farmer[d] of Kynsebarne, shall have to the yeres that he hathe allredy in his olde lease xxj[ti] yeres more, standyng to all the charges of reparations and paying tenne poundes for a fyne.[142] Also it is agrede that Gilliam Pulleyn shall have ij tenementes in Seynt Martens le Grande in on of the whiche tenementes the seyd William now dwellithe, and in the other tenement dwellyth on Anthony Campyon, for terme of threscore and x yeres, for the rente accustomed, and the seyd Gyllome to bere at his costes and charges all maner of reparatons dueryng the seyd terme.[143]

Also yt is lykwyse[e] determened that the tow lecternes of latten[144] and candel-

---

139 Grene, citizen and merchant tailor of London, granted the premises for years stated from Lady Day following at £4 rent 20 December 1548: WAM Reg. III, ff. 114v–115v.

140 See below, no. **100** & n. 184.

141 Williams, servant to Frances, marchioness of Dorset [the king's niece], granted the premises for years stated from Lady Day following at rent stated *vice* Joan Clowdisley 22 January 1549: WAM Reg. III, ff. 108–9. Lease to Clowdisley of same dated 1 June 1548 marked as vacated: *ibid.*, f. 103.

142 Vaughan, gent., and Joan his wife granted 36 years from Michaelmas following at £14 rent 14 January 1549: *ibid.*, ff. 113–114v.

143 Pollyn *alias* Polline (Heal, *Goldsmiths*, 228, 'Pullyn') granted the premises for 60 years from Christmas following at £4 rent 20 December 1548: WAM Reg. III, ff. 101v–102.

144 For these see Perkins, *Worship and Ornaments*, iii, 45–7, where it is noted that only one is mentioned in the suppression inventory: Walcott, 'Inventories', 350. Perkins raised the possibility that one of the Abbey lecterns had survived in the possession of an Italian noble family, whose ancestor Jean-Joachim de Passano was believed to have been given choir books from Westminster Abbey by Henry VIII. A bronze lectern was in the ownership of the same family, and for this a like provenance was conjectured. The matter was put to L.E. Tanner in 1929, but he could find no reason to suppose the lectern in Italy had once been in the Abbey: WAM 64264. It is obvious that Henry VIII could not have

styckes of latten wythe angelles of copper and gylte, and all other brasse, latten, belle mettell and brasse, shalbe solde by Mr Heynes, treasourer, by *f* cause they be monymentes of idolatre and superstityon,[145] and the monye therof cummyng to be receyvyd by the sayd treasaurer for makyng of the lybrary and bying of bookes for the same. And it is also agreed that Mr Pekyns and Mr Keble shall see the weyght of all the sayd metalle, and that the lybrary *g* shalbe fynisshed in the northe parte of the cloyster as sone as the money can be made of the premisses.

Also yt is decreed that Mr Wyllyamson, makyng a lease of his tenementes lying within this close for a c yeres savyng on, shall have a lyke lease of this churche of tenementes [f. 48v] of lyke yerely rente lying wytheowte the close in recompense for avoydyng of the evyll rule that is nowe kepte in the seyd Master Wyllyamsons howses.[146] Also it is agreed that it shalbe lefull for Mr Deane to take downe the tymber and tylles of two broken chambres standyng besydes the scole howse, and also that he shall have the grounde of the frayter with the stone walles *h* to the agmentaton of his gardeyn, and also that his gardeyne in the farmery,*i* and also the chambers joynyng to his howse of the dorter syd unto the abbottes*j* lodgyng, and that Mr Heynes shall have immediatly the howse with the gardeyne and douffe howse hertofore grauntid hyme.[147]

Signed: Benson, Haynes, Keble, J. Pekyns, Redman, Britten, Sandiforth, E. Weston, Carleton.

a Repl. 'liing'. *b* Word inserted repl. illegible word. *c* Foliation originally ignored the excision and ff. 48, 49 also numbered 47, 48. *d* Repl. 'shall have'. *e* Repl. 'de[terme-ned]'. *f* Repl. 'and'. *g* Repl. 'lybraye'. *h* Four words inserted. *i* Eight words inserted, corrected from 'and also the farmery gardeyne'. *j* Repl. 'walle'.

86. *February 19. Leases granted.*

[f. 49] xix*no* die Februarii anno tertio*a* dicti regis. Thes leases folloyng were sealyd in the presense of Mr Deane and the chapiter. Fyrst ij leases of Thomas Massey to be renewid*b* for the Swan in the Kinges streate and ij tenementes beside nexte adjoynyng for xxx*ty* yeares eyther of theym.[148] Item John Guy and hir *c* son for ij

bestowed what remained in the Abbey to be sold by the dean and chapter in 1549. A photograph of the marchese da Passano's lectern (WAM 64267) shows this to be markedly dissimilar to that visible in the only contemporary representation of the Abbey interior immediately before the dissolution, the funeral roll of Abbot Islip (d. 1532): WA Library; reproduced in Perkins, *op. cit.*, i, facing p. 50. The lectern was put for sale in 1931 following the marchese's death: J.D. C[arleton] to Tanner (WAM 64269).

[145] The removal of all images from churches was ordered by the privy council on 11 February 1548. Many London churches had already been spoiled: Jordan, *Young King*, 149–51, 165, 183–7. 'Monuments of idolatry and superstition' is a phrase widely found, e.g. in article 28 of the 1547 injunctions: *Vis. Art.*, ii, 126.

[146] Not traced.

[147] See Robinson, *Abbot's House*, 51–2.

[148] Massey, gent., granted the Swan for years stated from previous Lady Day at £4 rent, the other two for same term at £2 13s 4d, both dated 10 April 1548: WAM Reg. III, ff. 117–19. The property was opposite the Wool Staple: Rosser, 381.

leasis renewid of ij tenementes in Langdiche.[149] Item Annes Molde one lease renued.[150] Item a lease of William Grene for a house in Saynte Martens for threscore yeares.[151] Item a lease to be renued to Mr Bethell and Kent.[152] Item a lease renued to George Vaughan.[153] Item a new [d] lease to Thomas Hollande of ij tenementes in Love lane for lx yeares.[154] Item a new lease to John Tyler of ij cotages in Tutehill streate [for][e] lx yeares.[155] Item a newe lease to John Redmayn for lx yeares.[156] Item Richard Will[ia]ms,[157] a new lease for lxx yeares. Item a new lease to Guye Gascoyne of vj[f] small tenementes and a gardeyn for lxx yearis.[158] Item iij[g] leases, one[h] to Edward Rysson, another to John Lens and another to William Cowbrige for iij tenementes for xl yeares a piece.[159] Item Guyllam Pullyn at my lord Edward Semers suete, a lease of ij litil tenementes in St Martens for lx[i] yeris.[160] Item a lease to Robert Smythe for the ferme of Pensam for[j] xxj yeares.[161] Item a lease for the ferme of Charsley[k] renued to Richard Neste for xxj yeres.[162] Item a lease renuyd to John Broke for the ferme of Cressall for lxx yeres.[163]

---

[149] Joan Gye, widow, granted the premises for 55 years from Midsummer following at £1 10s rent 1 June 1548: WAM Reg. III, ff. 105–106v.

[150] Agnes Mowlde of London, widow, granted divers tenements in Gutter Lane called King's Alley for 73 years from previous Christmas at £4 16s 8d rent 10 February 1548: *ibid.*, ff. 109v–110v.

[151] See above, no. **85** & n. 139.

[152] Richard Bethell, a groom of the king's wardrobe of the beds, and Thomas Kente, a page of the chamber, granted the tenement they shared in St Margaret's churchyard for 59 years from Michaelmas following at £2 rent 18 June 1548: WAM Reg. III, ff. 102–102v. Richard Bethell, page and naval officer, is distinguished in *Hist. Parl. 1509–1558*, i, 428 from M.P. of the same name there noticed. The naval R.B. was captain of the king's ship *Hart* in 1549: *CSPDEdVI*, 221.

[153] See above, no. **85** & n. 142.

[154] See above, no. **83** & n. 138.

[155] See above, no. **77** & n. 129.

[156] See above, no. **77** & n. 125.

[157] See above, no. **85** & n. 141.

[158] Gascoyne, carpenter, and his son Edward granted the premises with four other tenements in Sayes Alley for years stated from date of indenture at £6 10s rent 1 October 1548: WAM Reg. III, f. 115v–116v.

[159] All three shoemakers of St Martin-le-Grand, granted the premises for years stated from Michaelmas following at £3 6s 8d (Cowbridge, Lense) and £2 13s 4d (Rysson) rent 20 September 1548: *ibid.*, ff. 103–4, 110v–113. The second name sometimes transcribed as 'Leuse' in WAM index and description slips, but 'Lens' clear in signature to original lease of above date: WAM 13050; cf. also bond for same, WAM 32141.

[160] See above, no. **85** & n. 143. This Edward was the duke of Somerset's second son by his first wife; his heir (by his second wife), also Edward, was only 9 years old, and in any case styled earl of Hertford. Lord Edward's line nevertheless eventually succeeded to the dukedom: Seymour, *Ordeal by Ambition*, 117, 371. Cf. *CSPDEdVI*, 590.

[161] See above, no. **77** & n. 123.

[162] See above, no. **77** & n. 122.

[163] See above, no. **77** & n. 126.

a Repl. 'secundo'. *b* Three words inserted. *c* Sic. *d* Word inserted. *e* MS. 'yeres'.
f Repl. 'iiij'. *g* Repl. 'a'. *h* Word inserted. *i* Repl. illegible figure. *j* Repl. 'yeares'
not deleted. *k* Five words inserted.

87. *February 19. Refusal to lease a canon's house.*

[f. 49v] xix° Februarii anno iij° Edwardi vj. Yt was agreed by Mr Deane and the
chapiter that in consyderation Vaghhans house*a* ys withein the close of the
cathedrall churche of Westm' and appoynted by*b* the deane and chapiter to be a
prebendares house, therfor by the order of the statutes of the churche we can
nott lett the*c* said Vaghans howse by lease, nor any other prebendares howse.*d*
And that Mr Keble, Mr Pekyns, Mr Carleton and Mr Barnarde ar *e* authorised to
make thawnsser unto my lord protectors grace as before.[164]

Signed: Benson, Haynes, Keble, J. Pekyns, H. Perkyns, Sandiforth, E. Weston,
Redman, Carleton.*f*

a Word inserted. *b* Repl. 'to'. *c* Repl. 'hitt' *d* Followed by deleted signatures of Benson, Haynes, Keble and Britten; i.e. what follows is postscript. *e* Repl. 'sha[ll]'. *f* The
last signature repeated, the repetition then deleted.

88. *June 24. Discharge of prisoners. Jurisdiction in St Martin's. Leases granted. Hoods to
be worn. Plate to be sold. Receipts. Commons.*

[f. 50] Anno tertio Edwardi sexti xxiiij*to* Junii. It is determenyd by Mr Deane and
the chapiter that a mane shalbe hyryd to bere a letter unto John Multon to
discharge theym whiche be in pryson for the pretensid*a* commyn of Orwell wood
upon condempnaton, yf any suche be, wyth all spede.[165] It ys determined that a
commyssyon shalbe sealyd for the exercysyng of the jurisdiction in Seynt Martens le Graunde to Mr Bellasis, Mr Bretton, Mr Sandiforde, Mr Weston, Docter
Croke, Docter Fullar and Mr Warmyngton,[166] to be exercysid by theym all or by

---

[164] The new foundation statutes did not specifically prohibit the leasing of canons' houses,
but this could be considered implicit in the requirement that the canons should all have
conveniently located residences: *Statutes (1),* 82–3/108–9.

[165] Once part of the royal forest (disafforested in the 13th century) covering much of southern Worcestershire, where the Abbey's greatest concentration of estates lay: R. Grant, *The
Royal Forests of England* (Stroud 1991), 144, 151. Disputes frequently arose over rights to
timber. There was litigation in king's bench and common pleas in 1547: WAM 37121.
Moulton was two days at Worcester assizes in February 1548, plying justices and jury with
food, wine and rewards. Specific complaint was made against the men of Rupple. Moulton also rode to the lord chancellor's house in Essex to stop an injunction brought by an
inheritor: WAM 37128, 37136, 37137. The recurrent references to Horwell wood relate to
a variety of trespasses.

[166] Three canons, with John Croke, D.C.L., chancellor of the diocese of London, John Fuller,
D.C.L., lately fellow of All Souls and afterwards master of Jesus College, Cambridge, and
Robert (or more likely Thomas) Warmyngton, B.C.L.: Emden, 151, 221–2, 607. This is
the first indication that the cathedral had resumed the peculiar jurisdiction of the dissolved abbey. Their acts begin 25 February 1550: WCA, Reg. Wyks, f. 163. See Introduction, p. xix.

thre or ij of theym at the least. Also this day is sealyd the confirmaton of thre leasys of certen tenementes belongyng to the parishe of Seynt Butholfe besydes Aldersgat.[167] [*Margin*: To paie for every seale x s.]

Also that Mr Deane and the prebendaryes shall use after Myhelmas next hoddes accordyng*b* to the order taken by the parlement, and that every of theym shall provyde his hodd convenyaunt before the seid day accordyng to his degree.[168] Also that certen plates of latten shalbe solde by the treausorer this yere. Also it is determened that Mr Heynes shall receyve all maner oblatyons, tythes, rentes, emolumentes and profittes of the parsonage of Shorham and Otford from the feast of the annunciaton last past unto the same feast next cummyng, and shall yelde accompt therof to the deane and chapiter, he havyng for his costes and charges resonably, and lyke wise shall take accompt of Mr Keble for thinges by him recevyd syns Crystmas last past hetherto. [f. 50v] Also the said daie and yere it is determyned that every chi[l]de of the grammer scole shall paie from hensforthe only*c* viij d. every quarter, wherof vj d. shalbe devydyd amonge the childerne that are in commyns, and ij d. quarterly of every childe beyng so*d* owte of commens to be devydyd emonge the peticanons and other commyners. Also it is decreede that it shalbe lefull for any servaunt of Mr Deane or any prebendary or chapiter clarke*e* in their absenses to goo to comens wythe the peticanons, their masters to see their commens paid for, and moreover that it shall not be lefull to the seid peticanons to putt any*f* man owte of commens that is assigned by the statutes or this decree to be in commyns, upon payne to be discommynyd them selfes.

Signed: Benson, Haynes, Bellasis, Sandiforth, Carleton, H. Perkyns 'to all, hoddes exept', Reynolds.

a Word inserted. *b* Repl. 'of'. *c* Word inserted. *d* Repl. 'ow[te]'. *e* Three words inserted. *f* Repl. 'owte'

89. *July 2. Leases in St Martin-le-Grand to be made to natives or denizened aliens. Minor canons allowed to opt out of commons. Proceeds of Shoreham rectory.*

[f. 51] Upon Tuysday the seconde day of July in anno Edwardi vj*ti* tertio it was decrede by Mr Deane and the chapiter that Mr Raynoldes shall sett and lett nine parcelles or *a* tenementes lying in Saint Martens le Graunde with all reparations, the tenauntes fydyng sufficient suertyes wythin the cytie of London or Westm' to buylde and repare theyr howses and paye ther rentes, so they be Englishe men or strayngers that be denesyns, which ix parcelles aperythe by a byll subscrybyd with the handes of Mr Deane and the prebendaryes. Also because ther is

---

167 The dean and chapter were the rectors. For more detailed instances of such confirmation see below, nos **387** and **429**.

168 Hoods for graduates were mandatory in cathedrals and colleges by virtue of the 'Certayne Notes' appended to the first Edwardine Prayer Book (and so authorized by 2 and 3 Edw. VI c. 1) which had come into force on Whit Sunday, June 19: Procter and Frere, 49, 55, 360. The Michaelmas deadline is therefore a local order.

contentyon rysen emonge the peticanons abowght their beyng in commyns, yt is decred that it shalbe free for every peticanon to be owte of commyns at his plesure, whether he be maryd or unmaryde, paying contrybutions ij d. wyckley. This decre to endure untyll Alhalowtid next. Also Mr Heynes have dischargid him selfe from medelyng any more with the parsonage of Shorham and Otford, and that Mr Multon[b] shall take order for the frutes therof.

Signed: Benson, Haynes, H. Perkyns, Sandiforth, E. Weston, Reynolds, Carleton.

[a] Three words inserted repl. 'certen'.   [b] Repl. 'Rainoldes and'.

90.   *July 27. Assertion of rights in Horwell Wood.*

[f. 51v] xxvij° die Julii anno iij° regni regis Edwardi vj. Yt was agreed by the deane and those whose names ar subscribed and condescended and agreed that Mr Deane and Mr Pekins shall make awnsser unto my lord protector his grace concerning Horwell Wood after this sorte.[169] That consydering the kinges majesties lawes hathe determined the right of Horwell Wood to apperteyne to the deane and chapiter of Westm' with the great [a] trees ther (the commen[b] of grase and pasture and hedgeboutt to thinhabitans ther about reserved) to requyre my said lordes grace to permitt the[c] said deane and chapiter to enjoy the profitt of the said wood according to the kinges majesties lawes, by the wiche lawes also the v li. wiche ys requyred to be restored was adjudgid unto the said deane and chapiter, whearfore they requyre that they may not be dreven to restore yt ageyne. And seing the law alredye hathe proceded on the behalff of the said deane and chapiter, they think yt not meete nor raisonnable[d] to put the matter ageyn in commission. [*Margin*: For Horwell wode.]

Signed: Benson, Keble, Britten, J. Pekyns, H. Perkyns, Sandiforth.

[a] Repl. 'woodes the'.   [b] Repl. 'commens'.   [c] Repl. 'us'.   [d] Two words inserted.

91.   *July 28. Deputation to examine the people of Horwell.*

[f. 52] xxviij^{vo} die Julii anno iij° regni regis Edwardi vj. Yt was agreed by the[a] deane and those whose names are subscribid that Mr Docter Heynes [b] and Mr Raynoldes shall take their jorney in to Worcester shere and there to sytt commyssioners with ij [c] other gentyllmen of the same shere to here and take the examynaton and depositions of the commyners of Horrewell Wood, and[d] of the same to make relasion unto my lord protectors councell with that expedition that convenyently may be had, as commawndement is gevyn[e] unto Mr Deane and Mr Pekyns by the said cowncell to see namyd therunto.

[169] Cf. above, n. 165. Further expenses this year were incurred in trips to Worcestershire, and Moulton and Carleton visiting the lord protector at Richmond: WAM 37243*, f. 7; 37271, 37281. On 1 September 1549 the protector wrote to the dean and chapter requiring their attention in a related matter: WAM 22689.

Unsigned.

^a Repl. 'those'. ^b Repl. 'Bretten'. ^c Number inserted. ^d Repl. 'in the shere aforeseyd'.
^e Repl. 'had'.

92. [*1551. August 6. Dismissal of a lay vicar.*^a

Die Jovis sexto die Augusti anno domini 1551. The deane in the presens of Mr Perkyns and the hole company of the quyer have dyschargid John Markcant of his rome of a syngyngman wythin this churche because he hathe usyd hym selfe byseley, raylyngly^b and sedytyously by castyng of bylles agaynst Scorsse^c and slanderyng of Roche.]

^a Whole entry deleted. Repeated in correct chronological position (f. 69: no. **115** below).
^b Repl. 'and'. ^c Repl. 'Roche'.

[f. 52v *blank*]

93. *October 22. Richard Cox installed as dean.*¹⁷⁰

[f. 53] xxij° Octobris anno tertio Edwardi vj^{ti}.^a Mr Richarde Coxe, doctor of divinite and highe almoner to the kinges majestie tooke possession of the deanery of Westm' and was installed in the same, and placed in the chapiter house there with all other rites^b and usages to the same apperteyning the xxij day of October the thirde yer of the reigne of the most noble prince Edwarde the vjth of Englande, France and Irlande, king, defendor of the faithe, and of^c the churches of England and Irland in^d earthe the supreme head, in the presence of theis prebendares whose names ar hier subscribed.
Signed: J. Pekyns, Sandiforth, E. Weston, Eyre.

^a Repl. 'tertii'. ^b Repl. 'thin[ges]'. ^c Repl. 'oth'. ^d Repl. 'th/under g[od]'.

[f. 53v] iiij^{to} Novembris anno Edwardi vj^{ti} tertio [*rest blank*].
[ff. 54, 55: *numbers dropped*]

94. *November 16. Sermons in St Botolph, Aldersgate. Attendance at services. Sermons. Residence. Chapters. Precentor to report absentees. Frequency for receiving communion. Canons' houses. Duties of vergers and granary keeper.*

[f. 56] Sabato xvj° Novembris anno tertio regni regis Edwardi vj^{ti}. Yt is agrede by Mr Deane and the chapiter that there shalbe every quarter on sermon made in Seynt Butollfes withowte Aldersgate in London by on of the prebendaries of this churche in course, that is to saye the junior to begynne and so upwardes; the precher to have v s. for his labour, to preache by hym self or elles by his deputie. [Also^a it is agreed that the deane of this churche and every prebendary therof beyng in Westm' or London shalbe dayly present from hensforthe at mattens in the quyar or communion tyme or at evynsong in thir surplesis and hodis lynyd

<hr>

¹⁷⁰ Dean Benson died between 10 and 23 September 1549: PRO, PROB 11/32, ff. 290–291v.

with sylke, upon paine to forfett every prebendary for any suche default xij d. and the deane ij s., to be applide to the dyvydent at the yeres ende emonge the deane and prebendaryes resident in this churche, except any man be sicke or be lettyd by the kynges commaundement or his honorable counsell or elles be occupyd in the churche*b* busines. Also it is agreed that the deane and every prebendarye shall preache in this churche upon som Sonday or holyday before none every quarter on sermon by hym selfe or by sum lerned man of this churche, upon payne to forfett xx s. for every suche default, to be imployed as before is sayd to the dividint of the residensaries.

Also it is agreed that the deane and every prebendarye of this churche which is or shalbe exceptid[171] resident in the same shall ons every yere kepe xxj*ti* dayes together hospitalitie in his owne howse and be present at divine service as above is rehersid, and in*c* every other quarter the deane and every prebendarye shall kepe xij daies at the least together or at severall tymes howsholde within the close of this churche in his owne house, and be present at som parte of divine service as before is expressid, upon payne to lose for every suche quarter wherin he is not so resident xij d. for every day, and the deane ij s., and likewise all that*d* portion of every mans severall dividint the same quarter. Providid alwayes that if the deane or any*e* prebendary do preche or ys sicke*f* or have any other necessarye busines to be allegyd in the chapter house dueryng the tyme of his said residence of x[x]*ti g* [f. 56v] dayes together, that then he may be absent from divine service wytheowte any losse or perditon if his famely be here in his howse, and shalbe countid as resident every suche daie, providid alwaies that the deane and every prebendary whiche hathe kepte house xij daies or shall kepe house xij daies before Cristmas next shalbe acceptid resident for this quarter.]

[*Margin*: Ordre for sealing of leases.] Also it is agreed that from hensforthe every Saterdaie in the yere the deane and every prebendarie of this churche beyng in Westm' shall assemble in the chaptre howse immediatly after mattens, whiche shalbegynne dayly at viij of the clocke, to common and determyne thinges for the profit and quietnes of this house, upon payne every of theym beyng at home for lackyng there to forfett xij d., to be imploidd to the common dividint (except he be lawfully letted). And upon the last Saterday of every quarter in the yere the deane and other officers whiche kepithe keyes of the commen seale or their deputes shall assemble in the chapiter house to seale all leases grauntid the quarter before, so that they be fyrst redd and examened in the chapiter. Also the chaunter yerely, when he is chosen, shall take an othe to marke bothe the absence of syngyngmen from the quyer and also of the deane and every prebendarye, and further to note the dayes of their residence truly

---

[171] I.e. accepted. These provisions attempt to clarify the statutes, which require the canons to reside (in the general sense) throughout the year (with allowed absences), but permit only those who had £40 a year from other sources to perform residence (in the technical cathedral sense) of 21 days: *Statutes (1)*, 82–5 / 108–10.

withowte partyallite, and present the defautes at every wekys ende in the chapiter howse, accordyng to this order taken.

[*Margin*: Ordre for the communion.] Also every prebendary beyng at home and not sicke nor otherwise lawfully lettid shall receyve every Sonday or ons every weke the holy communyon, and every peticanon likewise; and every clarke in the quyer and other officer of this churche shall receve it ons in a monethe.

Also it is agreed that every prebendary whiche hathe recevyd xx li. for pur-chasyng the lease of his house shall bryng in the lease of his house before Crystmas next, or elles then to restore the money to the churche wytheowte delay. [*Margin*: It was never observed but only by Mr Perkins, who brough in the lese of tombe house.[172]]

[f. 57] [*Margin*: The vergeres.] Also it is agreed that the vergires shall gyve dayly attendaunce in the quyer as prestes and clarkes doo to kepe owte straungers that occupie the deane and prebendaries placis, and to see good order kepte at the communyon tyme and other divine service; and also on of the vergires shall evermore goo before the precher to the pulpit and bryng hym agayne to his place in the quyer when semon is don, and to goo before the prest to the communyon.

Also it is agreed that the graner keper shall receve all the wheate indyfferently for the deane and prebendaryes and shall delyver yerely unto every of theym beyng resident his owne portyon and no more, that is to saye to the deane beyng resydent ten quarters and to every prebendary resident fyve quarters, the yere to begynne yerly for newe wheate at Crystmas, and the portions of theym that are not resident shalbe devydyd yerly among theym that are resident.

Signed: Cox, Keble, J. Pekyns, H. Perkyns, Sandiforth, E. Weston, Eyre, Haynes, Redman.

a Remainder of entry on f. 56 and part of the verso deleted. *b* Repl. 'kynges'. *c* Word inserted. *d* Or 'the'. *e* Two words inserted repl. 'and eny'. *f* Three words inserted. *g* MS. torn.

95. *November 23. Housing arrangements.*

[f. 57v] Upon Saterday the xxiij[th] daye of November in anno Edwardi sexti tertio at a chapiter then kept,*a* Mr Deane beyng present and sevyn more of the prebendaries, on Rychard Elyot, syngyngman, was *b* contentyd that Mr Keble shall have his house scituat within the scircutt*c* of the close, Mr Keble*d* payng for the repares of the seid*e* house don by the seyd Ellyott accordyng to the judgement of iiij men endyfferyntly chosen by the seid*f* partyes, whos names herafter folloythe: the seid Elyot hathe chosen Percyvall Joyner and Stocdale the barber,

---

172 *Sic*, from MS. 'tube' (with abbreviation over) in no. **112** below; in fact 'tub' house, otherwise known as the Long House or Calbege – containing a tub for cooling in the cellarage: Stanley, 361. Robinson (*Abbot's House*, 26) identified 'Calbege' with 'Cawagium'. The latter term principally meant to describe a division of the refectory, but was also applied to a chamber in the bakery: Harvey, *Living and Dying*, 41 & n. 21.

and Mr Keble hathe chosen Rychard Sherrard and John Wolman.[173] And the
forseyd Edward Keble and Rychard Elyot do bynde them selfes to abyde the
awarde of the iiij persons before namyd, upon payne to forfet theyr severall
interest and ryght in the forseyd house.[g]

Signed: Keble, Elyot.

[a] Word inserted. [b] Repl. 'is'. [c] Repl. 'scircuet'. [d] Repl. 'Kep'. [e] Word inserted.
[f] Word inserted. [g] Followed by 'and the' deleted.

96. *November 30. Leases granted.*

[f. 58] Sabato xxx^mo Novembris anno regni regis Edwardi vj tertio. [It^a is agreed
by Mr Deane and the chapiter that he that dwellythe in the greet shoppe of
Seynt Martyns le Grande shall have a lease therof, paying a fyne as an^b other
man will geve, whiche is x li.[174]] Also it is agreed that Smalbone the fermer of
Styvynton shall have the revertyon of the parsonage there, payng a fyne as any
other man will geve.[175]

Signed: Cox, Haynes, Redman, Keble, Bellasis, J. Pekyns, H. Perkyns, Sandiforth, E. Weston, Eyre.

[a] Entry deleted. [b] Word inserted.

97. *December 7. The audit and accounts. No canon to be receiver during John Moulton's
tenure.*

[f. 58v] Sabato vij° die Decembris anno regni regis Edwardi vj^ti tertio. [*Margin*:
For the audet.] It was decreed by Mr Deane and the^a chapiter that the Monday
next after Alhalowes^b day the awdett shall from hensforthe ever begynne, and
that the officers from hensforthe evermore shalbe chosen the next daye after the
cownte ys fynysshid. Also it is agreed that the accompte of all revennewes of this
churche shall goo from Myhelmas to Myhelmas, the first halfe yere to begynne at
Myhelmas, the last halfe yere at thannunciaton of our Lady, so as the receyvor
may be redy at Myhelmas evermore to make his accompte, and lykwyse the
treasorer this yere and yerly from hesforthe shalbe redy with^c his accompte by
the seyd feast of Saynt Mychell, and the new treasorer to paye this yere and so
yerly from hensforthe the stypendes of Mr Deane, the prebendaryes, and of all

[173] Grant to Harry Keble, yeoman, of the tenement where Edward Keble, canon, dwells, on
the highway towards Lady Margaret's rents, for 90 years from Lady Day following at 5
marks rent 1 January 1550: WAM Reg. III, f. 143v. In 1565 Keble, yeoman of Everdon,
Northants., assigned to another of that county his lease of a property held for these years
(but at 10 marks rent and dated 1 February 1549): WAM 39076. For Lady Margaret
Beaufort's buildings see Stanley, 353; Jones and Underwood, *King's Mother*, 233 & n. 6.

[174] Robert Mason of London, leather-seller, granted the premises for 50 years from Lady Day
following at £8 rent 16 January 1550: WAM Reg. III, f. 148.

[175] Thomas Smalbone, gent., of Steventon granted the parsonage for 50 years from the
expiry of the interest of William Mylward (to whom Henry VIII through the court of
augmentations granted 21 years from Michaelmas then following 18 March 1541) at £20
10s 6d rent 25 January 1550: *ibid.*, ff. 142–142v.

mynystres dwe at Crystmas.[176] Also it is agreed that none of the prebendaryes shalbe chosen receyvor this yere nor any yere from hensforthe dueryng the patent of John Molton, but yt is agreed that Mr Weston shalbe surveyour of all the tenementes in Westm' and London and of the leases of theym, and he to have v li. for his labour.

Signed: Cox, Haynes, Redman, Keble, Britten, J. Pekyns, H. Perkyns, Sandiforth, E. Weston, Eyre.

  a Repl. 'that'. *b* Repl. 'Alhalowne'. *c* Two words inserted repl. illegible word.

98. *December 14. Notice to be given for renewal of leases. A house appointed for the under master.*

[f. 59] Sabato xiiij die Decembris anno regni regis Edwardi vj tertio. It is agred by Mr Deane and the chapiter that warnyng shalbe gevyn by the curat of Saynt Margarettes[177] openly in the churche that every man whiche hathe any lease with clause of renovaton holden of the deane and chapiter shall bryng in their leases to be renewyd immedyatly upon payne*a* of forfayture. Also it is agreed that the howse wherin Roo[178] dwelte shall pertayne evermore to the ussher of the grammer scole.

Signed: Cox, Haynes, J. Pekyns, Keble, H. Perkyns, Reynolds, Eyre.

  a Word inserted.

99. *December 28. Canons to nominate tenants. Other leases.*

[f. 59v] Sabato xxviij^vo die Decembris anno Edwardi vj^ti tertio. It is agreede by Mr Deane and the chapiter that Mr Barnard shall name one who shall have a lease of a barne withe a garden plott therunto annexid for the terme of fourescore and xix*a* yeres, yeldyng yerely for the rente vj s.*b* and to stande to the reparations.[179] Also it is agreed that Mr Pekyns shall name on who shall have a lease of two cottages, two garden plottes and a lytle close, beyng scytuat at the furder parte of all Petifraunce*c* at the turnyng of the parke walle, wyth like yeres as before, paiing the accustomable rente.[180] Also that George Pervys, servaunt to Mr Deane, shall have a lease of a tenement in the Greate Saynctuary latly in the

---

[176] Moulton's account for 1548/9 is WAM 37243*. Hitherto he had shared responsibility with a canon receiver; that post now became redundant: Knighton, 'Collegiate Foundations', 60–5; *idem*, 'Economics', 48. But cf. below, nos **212** & n. 101, **215** & n. 110 for canons acting for the receiver.

[177] Henry Mote: Westlake, *St Margaret's*, 232. Rosser, 336, 339–40 (n. 34).

[178] Thomas Rowe *alias* Roo, sometime lay vicar: WAM 37045, ff. 2v, 8; 37112, f. 5.

[179] Thomas and Ralph Sandeforthe *alias* Sandford (doubtless relatives of Canon Bernard Sandiforth) granted the premises, in Petty France, for *89* years from Michaelmas 1556 at rent stated 16 January 1550: WAM Reg. III, f. 149v.

[180] Rachell Pekyns, maid (likewise presumably a relative of the nominating canon) granted the premises for 99 years from previous Christmas at 12s rent 3 January 1550: *ibid.*, ff. 143v–144; years correct in Reg. text but wrongly (89) marginated there (f. 144).

tenure of Agnes Swallowe, for terme of threscore and tenne yeres, payng the customable rent, and to stande to the reparations, the howse fyrst made tenentable to his hande.[181] Also that Anthony the sexten shall have a lease of a tenement in Pety France wherin on William Marche dwellithe, with a barne*d* tylyd, and the voyde grounde betwene the said tenement and the parke walle, for terme of threscore yeres, paying the yerely [rent] of [xiij s. iiij d.]*e* and he to stande to the*f* reparations.[182] Also it is agreed that Robert Mason, letherseller, shall have a lease of the greate shope in Saynt Martens le Graunde in as ample maner as before tyme it hath byn lett, for terme of fourty yeres, yeldyng*g* the olde rente.[183]

Signed: Cox, J. Pekyns,*h* H. Perkyns, Sandiforth, E. Weston, Reynolds, Keble, Eyre.

a Repl. 'tenne'. *b* Repl. 'x s.' *c* Repl. 'Tothill strete callyd'. *d* Repl. 'tythe'. *e* Ellipse in MS and sum deleted. *f* Word inserted. *g* Repl. illegible word. *h* Deleted then repeated.

100. *1550. January 11. The audit. Leases granted.*

[f. 60] Sabato xj^mo die Januarii anno regni regis Edwardi vj^ti tertio. Iyt is agrede by Mr Deane and the chapiter that Mr Keble and Mr Weston shall contynually assiste Mr Deane in heryng of the awdyt, and they to have for theyr paynes vj s. viij d. apece. Also that Mr Tylsworthe shall have Fourdove alley, yeldyng xvj li. by the yere for terme of $\overset{xx}{iiij}$ x yeres, beryng all maner of reparations.[184] Also that James Weston shall have a lease of a howse in the cloyster of Saynt Martens le Graunde which*a* Maisteres Payne holdythe for terme of her lyf, for the terme of lx yeres.[185] Also that Anthony shall have a lease of thre cotages with a barne*b* lying in Petifraunce, beyng in the occupying of on Lewys Lawrence, for the terme of lx yeres.[186]

Signed: Cox, H. Perkyns, Keble, Britten, J. Pekyns, Sandiforth, Reynolds, E. Weston.

a Repl. 'of a tenement'. *b* Three words inserted.

[181] Not traced. For Pervys see below, no. **102**.

[182] Anthony Nycholson, yeoman, granted (1) the tenement where Marche dwells in Petty France for years stated from Michaelmas 1556 at 10s rent, and (2) three tenements, a toft and stable there for 60 years from Lady Day following at 13s 4d rent; both 16 January 1550: WAM Reg. III, ff. 137v–140v. In the accounts he is named as bellringer rather than sexton: WAM 37044, f. 2v; 37387A, f. 4.

[183] See above, no. **96** & n. 174.

[184] Tyllesworth (*q.v.* above, n. 8) granted the premises with three other tenements at £16 rent, with three more at £4 2s 4d, all for 98 years from Lady Day following, with scouring the jakes, 4 March 1550: WAM Reg. III, ff. 162–162v.

[185] *Robert* Weston, gent., granted four tenements in the court of St Martin-le-Grand, and five other shops, previously granted to Elizabeth Payne 10 July 1547 [with others; cf. n. 107 above] for 70 years from the expiry of the existing lease at £21 rent; with later note that the lease was commenced at Michaelmas 1577: WAM Reg. III, ff. 304v–305.

[186] See above, no. **99** & n. 182.

101. *January 18. Leases granted.*

[f. 60v] Sabato xviij die Januarii anno Edwardi vj^{ti} tertio. It is decrede by Mr Deane and the chapiter that*a* Thomas Smalbone shall have a lease in revertion of the parsonage of Stevynton for the terme of fourty yeres,[187] yeldyng the custumable rent and to stande to the repartons, paying for a fyne xiij li. vj s. viij d.*b* Also*c* it is agrede that Mr Keble shall have a lease of the howse that he now dwellithe in, and also the lytle howse that Ellyott had, paying*d* the olde rente, for terme of threscore yeres.[188]

Signed: Cox, Haynes, Keble, H. Perkyns, J. Pekyns, Reynolds, Eyre, Sandiforth.

a Word inserted. *b* Repl. 'xx' then 'xiiij'. *c* Repl. 'Also that Mr Pekyns and Mr Keble'. *d* Repl. 'w[ith]'.

102. *January 25. Leases granted. Collector of Westminster rents appointed.*

[f. 61] Sabato xxv die Januarii anno Edwardi vj tertio. Iit is agrede by Mr Deane and the chapiter that Mr Pekyns shall have the ferme*a* of the portyon of tythes in the townes of Parshore, Wyke, Byrlingham and Penseham in the countie of Worcestre callyd the farmary tythe for the terme of lxxx yeres, paying the olde rente.[189] Also it is agreed that wheras Mr Heynes hathe the graunte of the ferme of Tyddysley parke in the countie of Worcestre, that he relinquisshing his interrest in the said Tyddesley parke shall have the lease and ferme of the manor of Mathon and the parsonage*b* to hys assignes from the feast of the annunciaton next cummyng unto the ende and terme of*c* lxxxx yeres from thens next followyng, paying the olde rente, the churche to be bounde to reparations and the fermer to be bayly there and to have the accustomed fee therof if the fermer will have the collection of the rentes there, reservyd always to the deane and chapiter all fynes and perquysites of courtes and tymber growyng upon the premisses if the fermer were not wounte to have theym as parcell of the rente, and it is agreed that John Multon shall have commawndement to bryng in the olde lease immediatly, and the rerage to be called for.[190] Also it is agreed that John Tylar shall have the lease of foure tenementes together under on rouffe with the garden plottes to theym belongyng now in the tenure of William

---

187 See above, no. **96** & n. 175 [*50* years].
188 See above, no. **95** & n. 173.
189 Henry Pekyns, citizen and draper of London, granted the premises from the expiry of existing interest for 87 years at £8 6s 8d rent 23 January 1550: WAM Reg. III, f. 143; duplicated f. 149. Cf. Harvey, *Estates*, 389 (no. 13).
190 Tiddesley had been granted to George Wyllughby of Netherton, Worcs., and John Carlton of Brightwell, Oxon., esquires, for 81 years on 24 November 1549. The manor and rectory of Mathon were granted to William son of John Mason of Mildenhall, Suffolk [Canon Haynes's assign] for the years stated from Michaelmas following at £40 13s 8d rent 6 February 1550: *ibid.*, ff. 134–5, 166–7.

Henbery, chandeler, paying the olde rente.[191] Also it is agreed that on William Coxe shall have the revertion of the Whyte Horsse in Longedytche wyth an ortchard and garden therunto belongyng for terme of lx yeres, paying the rente accustomed, and to fynde reparations.[192]

Also it is agreed that George Pervys shall have the office of the collectorsshipe of the rentes in Westm' and elleswhere whiche John Tylar now occupithe, wythe the accustamed fee, he fyndyng sufficient suerties for the payment of the rente.

Signed: Cox, Haynes, Redman, H. Perkyns, Keble 'ys content for all thyngkes afore sayd only excepteyd[d] Tyler office off recethe', Sandiforth, Eyre.

[a] Repl. 'p[ortyon]'.   [b] Eight words inserted.   [c] Word repeated then deleted.   [d] Repl. 'excepteyd the baylewyke'.

[f. 61v *blank*]

103.   *February 1. Benefice and leases granted.*

[f. 62] Anno quarto regni regis Edwardi sexti.[a] Sabato primo die Februarii anno regni regis Edwardi vj quarto. It is agreede by Mr Deane and the chapiter that Sir John Lathbury shall have the advouson of the vicarege of Chatysley wyche Sir John Smythe now hathe.[193]

Also it is agrede that Mr Perkyns shall have for his assignes the howse that Elyzabethe Clarke, wydowe, dwellythe in after [b] her yeres expyryd, for the terme of lx yeres. Also that [Thomas][c] Mountford, shomaker, shall have the revertyon of a tenement now in the tenure of Elyzabeth Clarke, whiche tenement Wylson, the kynges ser[va]unt dwellythe [in],[d] for the terme of lx yeres.[194] Also it is agrede that yong Pychyn shall have the lease of the manor of Sowthe Benflet from this day unto the ende and terme of xxj yeres, paying xx li. for a fyne and the olde rente.[195]

[191] Untraced. John Dymmock, yeoman, of St Martin-in-the-Fields, granted three tenements there in tenure of Henbury 10 February 1550: *ibid*., ff. 153–153v.

[192] Coxe, of London, gent., granted the premises for years stated from end of lease to William Gye [12 years from Christmas 1548: *ibid*., ff. 104–5], including scouring the jakes, at £1 13s 4d rent 12 March 1549: *ibid*., f. 148v. For the property see Rosser, 76 & n. 165. Cf. below, n. 296.

[193] See above, no. **45** & n. 91. Lathbury, a former monk of Westminster, was admitted on 9 April 1554 on the presentation of William and Robert Lathbury, patrons *pro hac vice*. He resigned by 20 March 1557: WRO, Reg. Capon, f. 53v. WAM Reg. IV, f. 8v. Pearce, *Monks*, 191 (incorrectly identifying the living). Although, as Pearce noted, he had been nominated as a Westminster university exhibitioner, his place was taken by another before the foundation: WAM 6478, f. 3v. He was a witness to Dean Benson's will: PRO, PROB 11/32, f. 191v.

[194] Munford and Elizabeth his wife granted a tenement in Tothill St for years stated from end of Clarke's lease at 16s rent 13 February 1550: WAM Reg. III, ff. 153v–154.

[195] John Pynchyn, gent., of Writtle, Essex, granted the manor and rectory of South Benfleet, reserving the advowson to the dean and chapter, for years stated from Michaelmas following at £20 rent 8 February 1550: *ibid*., ff. 152v–153. This man's or his father's will

Signed: Cox, Haynes, Keble, H. Perkyns, J. Pekyns, E. Weston, Sandiforth, Eyre.

^a Head to page. ^b Repl. 'f[or]'. ^c MS. blank. ^d Ellipse in MS.

104. *March 19. Lease granted.*

[f. 62v] Anno regni regis Edwardi vj^{ti} quarto.^a xix° Martii anno iiij° Edwardi vj. [Yt^b ys agreed by the deane and chapiter of Westm'^c that Mr Doctor Coxe, deane ther, shall have the nominaton of hym to whome a lease shalbe grantend ^d and by theis presentes ys ^e granted of the ferme or manor^f of Achelenche in the cowntie of Wigorn',^g to have and hold to him whome the said Mr Doctor Coxe shall nominate for the terme of lxxx yers, paying the olde rent, withe all commodites and profittes belonging to the same.]

xix° Martii anno iiij° regni regis Edwardi vj. Yt ys agreed by the deane and chapiter that Thomas Hobbey shall have the lease of the manor and ferme of Achelenche yn the cowntie of Wigorne for the terme of lxxx yers, paying the old rent, and the said Thomas to have hit with all commodites and profittes belonging to the same.¹⁹⁶

Signed: Cox, Keble, J. Pekyns, H. Perkyns, Sandiforth, Eyre, E. Weston.

^a Head to page. ^b Whole first version deleted. ^c Two words inserted. ^d *Sic.* ^e Repl. 'ar'. ^f Two words inserted. ^g Three words inserted.

105. *March 20. Leases granted.*

[f. 63] xx^{mo} Martii anno iiij° Edwardi vj. It is agrede by Mr Deane and chapiter that they whose names ensue shall have leases of suche howses as herafter ensuythe; fyrst, that Masteres Pekyns shall have a howse in Tothill strete;¹⁹⁷ Samson Lever, Margarett Vyolett, Harry Clocker, for the [houses]^a that they dwell in, in Seynct Martens le Graunde;¹⁹⁸ Frauncys Catcott for the revertyon of the howse that he dwellith in;¹⁹⁹ Thomas Massey to have the howse next unto^b that Harry Flemmying, shomaker the howse that he^c dwellyth in;²⁰⁰ John

---

printed in *Elizabethan Life: Wills of Essex gentry and merchants proved in the Prerogative Court of Canterbury*, ed. F.G. Emmison (Chelmsford 1978), 239–40.

¹⁹⁶ Hobbey, yeoman, of Middlesex, granted the manor, reserving feudal dues, fishings etc. to the dean and chapter, for *81* years from previous Michaelmas at £9 15s 2d rent 12 March 1549: WAM Reg. III, f. 149.

¹⁹⁷ Untraced. But cf. above, n. 180.

¹⁹⁸ Grants to: Lever, for 80 years from Lady Day following at 4 marks rent 20 April 1550: WAM Reg. III, ff. 157–157v; Vyolat, widow, for 60 years from Midsummer following at £3 rent 10 March 1550: *ibid.*, f. 151v; Clocker, goldsmith, for 60 years from previous Lady Day at £3 6s 8d rent 29 March 1550: *ibid.*, ff. 161v–162.

¹⁹⁹ Catcotte, tailor, granted the tenement, in King St, from expiry of Nicholas Gravener's lease for 60 years at £1 0s 10d rent 12 February 1550: *ibid.*, f. 163v.

²⁰⁰ Massey, yeoman, chandler, granted a tenement in King St where Clement Joyner then dwelt, for 60 years from expiry of lease of Nicholas Gravener, glover, at 17s 10d rent 12 February 1550: *ibid.*, f. 150.

Campe, for the howse that he dwellyth in;[201] William Whitworth[d] and Rychard Sawford[e] for ij howses in Tothill strete;[202] and that Mr Perkyns shall have a lease for his frende[f] whom he shall name of Churche Honyborne in Worstester shere.[203]

Signed: Cox, Keble, J. Pekyns, H. Perkyns, Sandiforth, E. Weston, Eyre.

[a] MS. 'leases'. [b] Two words inserted. [c] Four words inserted. [d] Repl. 'Wilson'. [e] Three further words inserted. [f] Word inserted.

106. *May 6. Lease to the duke of Somerset's secretary.*

[f. 63v] vj[to] die Maii anno Edwardi vj[ti] quarto. [It[a] is agreed by Mr Deane and the chapiter that Mr Fyssher, servaunte to my lord of Somersettes grace, shall have a lease of the parsonage of Shorham and Otford for terme of lxxxix yeres, the lease to begynne at the feast of thannunciation of owre Lady next cummyng after the date herof, paying the accustomyd rente.]

It is decrede by Mr Deane and the chapiter that Mr Thomas Fyssher, servaunte to my lord of Somersettes grace, shall have a lease of the parsonage of Shorham[b] and Otford for terme of lxxxxix yeres, the lease to begynne at the feast of the annunciatyon of our Lady next cummyng after the date herof, paying the accustomyd rente and beryng all reparations.[204]

Signed: Cox, Haynes, Keble, J. Pekyns, H. Perkyns, Sandiforth, Eyre.

[a] Whole first version deleted. [b] Repl. 'Otford'.

107. *May 31. Benefice for a canon.*

[f. 64] 31 die Maii anno regni regis Edwardi vj[ti] 4°. It is decrede by Mr Deane and the chapiter that Mr Docter Perkyns shall have the next avoydance of the parsonage of Islype.[205]

108. *June 14. Leases granted.*

xiiij[mo] die Junii anno regni regis Edwardi vj[ti] iiij[to]. It is agreede by Mr Deane and the chapiter that Harry Porter of Hynckley shall have a mease with thappertenaunces callyd the priorye, which he now dwellyth in, for terme of xl yeres

[201] *Hugh* Campe, tailor, granted tenement in King St where he dwelt, for 70 years from previous Michaelmas at £1 10s rent 20 March 1550: *ibid.*, f. 154v.

[202] Grants to: Whytworthe, yeoman, for 60 years from Michaelmas following at 13s 4d rent 10 March 1550; Sawford, yeoman, for 60 years from Lady Day following at £1 rent 10 November 1550: *ibid.*, ff. 158, 170–170v.

[203] Grant to Brian Morehouse, yeoman, of Eynsham, Oxon., of the manor for 80 years from previous Michaelmas at £10 9s 4d rent 26 November 1550: *ibid.*, f. 174v.

[204] No grant to Fisher registered. He was imprisoned in February 1550 as a consequence of his master's fall: *Hist. Parl. 1509–1558*, ii, 137–8. He was nevertheless granted a reversion of the receivership on November 20 (WAM Reg. III, ff. 159v–160v), to which he eventually succeeded but never exercised: see below, no. **212** & n. 101. Shoreham and Otford were leased to Edward Bashe: see below, n. 237.

[205] See above, no. **43** & n. 81.

with lyke covenauntes as is in his indenture, payng yerely iij li. xij s., a cottage there of iij s. by yere, another cottage of v s. by yere, another cottage of vj s. viij d. by the yere, a lytlye close of viij s. by the yere, and a tenement or*a* cottage of viij s. by the yere, and he to be at coste and charges of reparations, savyng great tymber if it can be had or founde uppon the premisses, and he to geve for a fyne xl s.[206] Item William Seale, tenaunte at will of a tenement there of viij s. by the yere to*b* have lyke lease and lyke terme, he beryng all charges and reparatyons. [207] Item that Ro. Robynson,*c* Mr Deanes porter, to have a lease of the spitle howse at Knyghtes brydge of iiij s. rente for terme of l yeres, he beryng the charges of reparatyons.[208]

Signed: Cox, Keble, Britten, J. Pekyns, Sandiforth, H. Perkyns, E. Weston, Reynolds.

a Repl. 'of v[iij s.]'.   *b* Word inserted.   *c* Repl. '[*blank*] Hunte'.

109. *November 8. Restatement of orders for residence. Dividend of wheat. Appointment of legal counsel and officers. Plate to be sold to pay for building work.*

[f. 64v] Decres and orders made by the deane and chapiter of this churche for good order to be had and contynewed wythin the same untyll a fynall ordre by statutes be taken by the kynges majesties auctorite herafter.

viij*vo* die Novembris anno 4° regni regis Edwardi vj*ti*. Fyrst it is agreid that the deane of this churche shalbe bounde to preche yerly in this churche iiij sermondes by hym selfe or sum other prebendary therof, that is to saye upon Crystmas day, Ester day, thascension daie, and the day of all sayntes, upon payne to forfait for every suche defaulte and sermon omittid xx s., to be employed to the commen divident at the yeres ende. Also it is agreid that every prebendary of this churche resident or not resident shall every quarter of the yere preche on sermon by hym self or by some other prebendary of this churche wythin the same, upon payne to forfait for every suche sermon omittid xx s., to be imploied to the

---

206 Grant to Porter, yeoman, for years stated from previous Michaelmas, including one further cottage (at 6s 8d) at £5 2s 8d rent 10 November 1550: WAM Reg. III, f. 151. St Peter's, Hinckley, Leics., had been subject to the abbey of Lire in Normandy: D.J.A. Matthew, *The Norman Monasteries and their English possessions* (Oxford 1962), 52. Like many of the other alien priories, it had subsequently belonged to the Carthusians; in this case Mount Grace, Yorks. Granted to the dean and chapter as part of the 1542 endowment: WAM 6478, f. 12v. *LP* xvii, 714(5); said in Nichols, *Hist. county of Leicester*, iv, 681–2 to have been in exchange for land taken by Henry VIII for the creation of St James's Park, but this would appear to be a confusion with the grant of *Hurley* in 1536 (cf. *LP* xi, 202(4). Harvey, *Estates*, 337–8).

207 William Seell of Hinckley, baker, and Richard his son granted a tenement in Hinckley for 40 years from previous Michaelmas at rent stated 6 December 1550: WAM Reg. III, f. 171v.

208 For St Mary's hospital, Knightsbridge see M.B. Honeybourne, 'The leper hospitals of the London area', *TLMAS*, 2nd ser. xxi (1963–4), 38–43.

commen divident. Also it is agreid that the deane and every prebendary of this churche which is or shalbe acceptid as resident in the same shall kepe yerly xxj days together hospitalite in his owne howse betwyxt the fyrst daie of October and the first daie of Aprill, and shalbe present at some parte of divine service daily dueryng the said xxj daies, that is to saie eyther at mattens, or *a* at the communion, or elles at evensonge, and in every other quarter of the yere besides the quarter wherin the said deane and every prebendary shall kepe their severall residence of xxj daies, the deane and every prebendary of this churche shalbe bounde to kepe hospitalitie xij daies together or at severall tymes in his howse wythin the close of this churche, and to be present at some parte of divine service as before is mentioned, upon payne to lose all the profittes of his hole yeres residence for lacke of keping of his xxj dais hospitalitie, and for not beyng present at divine service as is before specifid, and to forfait all other severall profittes of their quarters divident for every quarter wherin any of the said deane and prebendaries shall omitt to kepe hospitalite in their severall howses or omitt to be present at divine service in maner and forme above specifid. [f. 65] Providyd alwaye that if the said deane or any prebendary do preche a sermon in any place, or is syke, or have any other necessary busynes to be alleged in the chapiter howse, or signefied to the chaunter for the tyme beyng, dueryng the tyme of his said xxj daies residence together, or dueryng*b* his other residence of xij daies in any other quarter, that then he may be absent from divine service wythowte any losse or perdition, so that his family be here in his*c* howse that day, and the deane and every prebendary in suche cases and every of theym shalbe acceptid as resident that daie. And to the entent the deane and every prebendary of this churche may be the more encoragyd to kepe hospitalitie here in this churche in maner and forme above specified, it is agreed that the deane of this churche, keping residense and hospitalitie in his howse and beyng present at divine service as is before specified, in the first quarter of the yere, that is to say betwyxt the feast of Saynct Mikaell tharchangell and the feast of Crystes nativi-tie, shall receve of the commen landes and provysion of this church twenty busshelles of wheat. And every prebendary of this churche, kepyng hospitalite in his owne howse here and beyng present at divine service as before is specifid, in the fyrst quarter of the yere above mentioned, shall receve lyke wise of the commen landes and provision of this churche tenne busshelles of wheat, and so forth for every other quarter of the yere wherin the said deane and prebendaryes shall kepe hospitalite and be resident accordyng to the forme before specifid and not other wise. And moreover the deane and every prebendary of this churche whiche shall kepe hospitalite in his owne howse and be resident accordyng to the forme prescribyd shall receve proportionably their severall dividentes of the fynes, seales and other casuall profittes after the rate, maner and forme of the last yeres dyvydent made at the feast of Saynct Mikaell tharchangell and not otherwyse. [f. 65v] Also it is agreed that the portyon of wheat of the deane and every prebendarie not keping hospitalite and not beyng resident accordyng to the forme before prescribid shalbe devydyd proportionably betwene theim that be residensaries every quarter, secludyng all theim that be not resident from the divident of wheat, lyke as from all other dividentes and portyons due to theim that shalbe resident.

Also it is agreed that Mr Weston and Mr Stapleton shalbe of cowncell of this churche for matters in the law, and eyther of theym shall have xl s. fee yerly.[209]

Also Mr Bretten is chosen vycedeane, Mr Pekens treausorer and Mr Weston surveyor.

Signed: Cox, Haynes, Redman, Nowell, Britten, J. Pekyns, H. Perkyns, Bricket, Sandiforth, Keble, E. Weston.

Also the said day yt was decreed that certeyne plate remaynyng in the vestre shall be solde by Mr Deane, Mr Heynes and Mr Pekyns for to bear the charges of the alteration and removing the queer, and for the alteration of the dark entre and the college great gate.

Signed: Cox, Haynes, Redman, Keble, Britten, J. Pekyns, H. Perkyns, Sandiforth, Eyre, E. Weston.

a Repl. 'communion'.   *b* Repl. 'if'.   *c* Word inserted.

110.   *November 15. Benefice for a canon. Leases granted.*

[f. 66] 15° die Novembris anno Edwardi vj^{ti} 4°. It is decreed by Mr Deane and the chapiter that Mr Bryckett shall have the vicarege of Saynct Brydes at the resingnation of Mr Cardemaker,[210] and that Bryan Sherington, Walter Davys, [Thomas]*a* Stockedale, Mother Cryspe, Kynver and Sampson Awdeley shall have their howses by lease, and also that Thomas Halle shall have a lease of a voyde grounde lyng in the parishe of all sayntes Barkyng.[211]

Signed: Cox, Haynes, Redman, Keble, H. Perkyns, J. Pekyns, Eyre, E. Weston.

a MS. blank.

---

209 Richard Weston of Middle Temple and Anthony Stapleton of the Inner Temple: *Hist. Parl. 1509–1558*, iii, 374–5, 588–90. WAM 37404 is Stapleton's receipt.

210 Thomas Birkhed [*alias* Bricket], vicar of Christ Church, Newgate, had written to William Cecil on 9 September 1550 (the month that Cecil became one of the principal secretaries) asking for another living, near London, such as the next vacancy at Westminster or Windsor: PRO, SP 10/10, no. 26 (*CSPDEdVI*, 461). In the following May he obtained a grant of precisely that option, subsequently converted into a Westminster canonry: Le Neve, 82. There is no record of his being admitted to St Bride's. For Cardmaker see above, n. 25.

211 Grants to: Sheryngton, carpenter, and Alice his wife, two tenements in Tothill St for 80 years from Lady Day following at £1 16s rent 3 November 1550: WAM Reg. III, f. 173; Davys, citizen of London, one tenement in St Alphege within Cripplegate for 80 years from Lady Day following at £1 6s 8d rent 6 December 1550: *ibid.*, f. 172; Stockdale, barber, one tenement where he dwelt in the Sanctuary for 60 years from previous Midsummer at £4 rent 7 November 1551: *ibid.*, f. 177v; Alys Crypps, widow, three tenements in the Sanctuary for 70 years from Lady Day following at £3 5s rent 10 November 1550: *ibid.*, f. 169; John Kynver, surgeon, and Bryde his wife, one tenement in St Margaret's churchyard for 40 years from previous Lady Day, with scouring the jakes, at £2 rent

111. *November 22. Lease granted.*

[f. 66v] xxij die Novembris anno regni regis Edwardi vj^ti 4°. It is agreed by Mr Deane and the chapter that Mr Heyre shall have in reversion the greate howse in Tothill strete now in the tenure of Mr Shelley, and before in the holdyng of John James, and also the voyde grounde that lyethe betwyxt Mr Perses Mr Redmaynes extendyng to the said Mr Heyres stable.[212] Also it is agreede that John Moulton shall have l yeres of the late priorye of Saynct Bartelmewes next Sudbury, which he bowght of Sir William Buttes, knyght.[213]

Signed: Cox, Redman, J. Pekyns, H. Perkyns, E. Weston, Eyre.

112. *December 6. Leases granted (one to William Cecil). Work on canons' houses.*

[f. 67] Die Sabato vj^to die Decembris anno Edwardi vj^ti 4°. It is agreed by Mr Deane and the chapiter that Thomas Worlyche, fermer of the parsonage of Awconbury Weston, shall have a lease of the same parsonage for terme of lxxx yers.[214] Item yt ys agreed that William Seale of Hynkeley to have by lease the house he dwellithe yn for terme of lx yers.[215] Item that William Elles shall have the reversion of thre tenementes in Theving^a lane wiche now ar in the tenure of Edmonde Lorde, for terme of lx^b yers.[216] Item that Tymwell thonger of the garde shall have his lease renewed for terme of ffiffty^c yers.[217] Item that^d Jhon

---

20 November 1550: *ibid.*, f. 172v; Awdeley, gent., one tenement with shops in St Margaret's churchyard for 60 years from previous Michaelmas at 4 marks rent 15 November 1550: *ibid.*, f. 173; grant to Hall not traced. Kynver, *alias* Kynnard, owned A. Carpenter, *Destructorium Viciorum* (Paris 1497), now WA Library shelfmark CC. 31, inscribed by the owner as resident in Little Sanctuary 1543: Rosser, 211 & n. 191. Audeley was the under–sexton: WAM 37387A, f. 3.

212 No grant to [Canon] Eyre traced. Grant to Richard Shelley of Hampstead, alebrewer, Agnes his wife and John James her son, of a tenement and three cottages in Tothill St for 99 years from Christmas following at £1 10s rent, and a piece of void ground in the Sanctuary by the convicts' house with three tenements for 99 years from Christmas following at £1 rent, (the premises having been granted in 1515 and 1529 to John and Margaret Jamys), 10 November 1551: WAM Reg. III, ff. 176v–177. For the elder John James, a lay servant of the abbey and farmer of Hampstead manor, see Rosser, 382–3; after Margaret he had married Agnes, presumably herself subsequently married to Shelley.

213 Grant to Moulton for years stated from previous Michaelmas at £10 rent 22 November 1550: WAM Reg. III, ff. 167v–168v. Butts (d. 1545) had been physician to Henry VIII: *DNB*. Sudbury priory, Suffolk, was given to Westminster by Henry I: *Charters of St Bartholomew's Priory, Sudbury*, ed. R. Mortimer (Suffolk Records Soc., Suffolk Charters vi, 1996), no. 1.

214 Worliche *alias* Woorlyche, gent., granted the premises for years stated at £24 rent 1 November 1550: WAM 14087.

215 See above, no. **108** & n. 207.

216 *Nicholas* Ellys, the king's mason, granted the premises, then in the tenure of Edmund Lorde, from the end of Lorde's lease for *80* years at 15s rent 6 December 1550: WAM Reg. III, ff. 164–164v.

217 Edmund Tymwell, yeoman of the chamber, granted a tenement in the Sanctuary next to

Baughe shall have the ballywyk of Pynfon, Comerton,*e* Brightlaunton and Elmeley for terme of lyff.[218] Item that Mr Doctor Raynold shall have the reversion of the ferme of Westburye in the countie of Wilteshire to bestoe wheare he shall appoynt, for terme of lx yers.[219] Item yt ys agreed that Mr Cecill, on of the secretares to the kinges majestie, shall have a lease of the house wherin Mr Piersee now dwellethe, for terme of threscore yers, so that he shall use the howse him selff and nott lease yt owt during his [f. 67v] owne lyff*f* to any other.[220]

Item [it] ys agreed that Mr Weston, surveyor, shall*g* at the coste of the howse cause a wall and a paire*h* of gates and a dore*i* to be made betwyxt Mr Bernardes house and his stable, withe all*j* the charges therunto apperteyning, and also a wall withe a dore to*k* the churche at the commen charges of the said howse. Item that Mr Pekins shall have annexed to his house the hall whearin the tube ys,[221] withe the yerde, the keching, stables, with all other edifices that somtyme apperteyned to the monk ballyes office.

Signed: Cox, J. Pekyns, H. Perkyns, Reynolds, Sandiforth, E. Weston.

a Repl. 'S'.   *b* Repl. 'ffyfty yers'.   *c* Repl. 'fiffty'.   *d* Repl. 'Mr'.   *e* Repl. 'In Wosester shire'.   *f* Two words pre-guided.   *g* Repl. 'of'.   *h* Repl. 'strong'.   *i* Three words inserted.   *j* Word inserted.   *k* Following several words heavily deleted.

113. *1551. January 9. Building work. Lease granted.*

[f. 68] 9° die Januarii anno iiij*to* regni regis Edwardi vj*ti*. It is concludyd and agreed by Mr Deane and the chapiter that a new waye shalbe made owte of the darke entry in to the courte, and that apece of the pryvey dorter shalbe pullyd downe, so moche as shalbe necessary for that purpose. And lyke wise all the house callyd Patches house,[222] and that*a* so moche of Mr Deanes house which

---

[Canons] Reynolds and Britten for 50 years from Christmas following at 13s 4d rent 6 December 1550: *ibid.*, ff. 171–171v.

[218] With fees of £1 (Pinvin) and £1 6s 0¾d (Comberton, Bricklehampton, Elmley), all Worcs.: WAM 37381, f. 3v; 37386, m. 2.

[219] Jerome Raynoldes (presumably a relative of the nominating canon) granted the premises for years stated from Michaelmas 1562 at £10 rent 6 December 1550: WAM Reg. III, ff. 175–175v.

[220] William Cecil granted the tenement called Little St Albans in the Sanctuary, where Thomas Perssey, gent., then dwelt, the premises enclosed by a brick wall with the old palace to the south-east, for 60 years from Christmas following at 10s rent, with condition that if Cecil and his wife do not reside, the rent to be £1 6s 8d, 10 November 1550: *ibid.*, ff. 169–70. In fact Cecil did not live here, but bought property in Cannon Row at about the same time: PRO, SP 10/10, nos 36, 44 (*CSPDEdVI*, 471, 479). Read, *Cecil*, 67. Little St Albans was soon found another tenant: below, no. **129** & n. 249. For the property see WAM 67171 (notes by L.E. Tanner). Cecil became tenant again in 1588: below, no. **407**.

[221] See above, no. **94** & n. 172.

[222] Cf. 'Patchys chamber' in the dissolution inventories, which is identified with John and his son Richard Pache, successive Abbey carpenters in the 15th century: Robinson, *Abbot's House*, 40 & n. 1, 41. This house in the cloister must be distinguished from the larger property in Goose Mead at the west end of the Almonry, leased to John Pacche, esq., in

shalbe harmyd and hurte by the new makyng of the waye shalbe made agayne of the churches charge. Also it is agreed that Mr *b* Bellasis shall have a newe chamber and a parler sett uppe in his gardeyn at the commen charge of the churche. Also it is agreed that the college gate by*c* Mr Pekyns house shalbe enlargyd so as a carte may cum in to the courte before Mr Deanes dore and to the new waye in to the cloyster.

Also it is agreed that Johane Chauncy, wydowe, and Harry her sonne, shall have a new lease of fourty yeres more then she hathe in the parsonage of Sabrygeworthe, paying for a fynne xl markes.[223]

Signed: Cox, Haynes, Keble, H. Perkyns, Sandiforth, E. Weston.

   a Word inserted.   *b* Repl. 'the d'.   *c* Repl. 'shalbe enlargyd'.

114. *February 21. Leases granted. Appointment of constable.*

[f. 68v] xxj^{mo} die Februarii anno regni regis Edwardi sexti 5°. It is agreed by Mr Deane and the chapiter that Mr Barnard Sandiford shall have a lease of thos tenementes whiche some tyme Mr Cowper helde by lease, and nowe are enjoyde by Mr Daye for lxxxxix*a* yeres.[224] Also it is agreed that Mr Pekyns shall have a lease in revertion of thre cottages in Tothill strete, wherof John James hathe now a lease for lxxxxix yeres.[225] Also that Robert Weston shall have the*b* revertion of all suche leases as Elsabethe Payne holdythe of the deane and chapiter, for lxx yeres.[226] Also that Robert*c* Bothe shall have a lease of the corner house at Creple gate for lx yeres.[227] Also Wyllyam Browne shall have a*d* lease in revertion of thre cottages in Longdytche, now in the tenure of Harry Bayle, for terme of lx yeres.[228] Also John Greete shall have a lease of a house next Sent Margaretes

1477: WAM 17831. Rosser, 86. A suggested association with Wolsey's fool Patch [*alias* Sexton] made by Stanley (p. 395 n. 3) may be discounted.

[223] Grant of the rectory, with barns lately built by Henry Chauncy, reserving the advowson to the dean and chapter, for *60* years from previous Michaelmas at £12 13s 4d rent 10 December 1550: WAM Reg. III, ff. 167–167v.

[224] Thomas and Ralph Sandyforthe (presumably relatives and assigns of the nominating canon) granted one tenement lately occupied by William Cowper, six of nine tenements lately called the bishop of Salisbury's rents, and one tenement lately occupied by Richard Cowper, all in Tothill St, for 99 years from Michaelmas following at £1 13s 4d rent 1 February 1550 [*sic*, 4 Edw. VI; ? *recte* 5, i.e. 1551]: *ibid.*, ff. 174v–175. The Salisbury or Sarum rents had sustained the anniversary of Bishop John de Waltham (d. 1395): Rosser, 61 n. 88.

[225] Not traced. For James see above, n. 212.

[226] Not traced. For Payne see above, no. **57** & n. 107.

[227] Bouthe, joiner, granted the premises for years stated from Lady Day following at £1 9s 4d rent 21 February 1551: WAM Reg. III, f. 173v, where lease said (in error) to be from dean only.

[228] Browne, gent., granted one tenement there (held by Cecill Bromley, widow, Harry Baylye of London, mercer and Agnes his wife, and Joan the daughter of Agnes) for years stated from Lady Day 1554 at 13s 4d rent 10 December 1550: *ibid.*, f. 172v, where whole entry is deleted.

churcheyarde for[e] lx yeres.[229] Also Rychard Roche shall have the lease of the house that[f] he now dwellyth in for [*blank*] yeres.[230] Also that Thomas Corryng-don of Poughley shall have his lease renewyd for xl yeres.[231] Also that John Kenver shall have his lease renewyd for fourtye yeres.[232] Also that Horne the chaunter[233] shall have a lease of the corner house in the Almery for fyftie yeres. Also that Gale shall[g] have the constableship of Seynt Mertens le Graunde. Also that the lease of the manor of Belsis to be renewyd to Mr Goodrycke.[234]

Signed: Cox, Britten, J. Pekyns, H. Perkyns, Redman, Sandiforth, E. Weston.

   [a] Altered from 'lxxxix'.   [b] Repl. 'a lease'.   [c] Repl. 'Thomas'.   [d] Repl. 'the r[evertion]'.   [e] Repl. 'of'.   [f] 'þt' repl. 'that'.   [g] Repl. 'the const[ableship]'.

115.   *August 6. Dismissal of a lay vicar.*

[f. 69] Die Jovis 6to die Augusti anno Edwardi sexti 5. The deane, in the presens of Mr Perkyns and the hole companye of the quyer have dyschargid John Markcant of his rome of a syngyngman within this churche by cause he hathe usid him selfe buseley, raylyngly and seditiously by castyng of bylles agaynst Scorse and slanderyng of Roche.[235]

116.   *September 19. A canon's absence permitted.*

xix[no] die Septembris anno 5[to] Edwardi 6. Where as Mr Keble, on of the preben-daries of this churche, for dyvers busynes assigned him, as well by the councell as for that his wyff lyethe sycke at Sarysbury[236] in parrell of deathe, cannot per-forme his residence at Westm' for the quarter of mydsomer endyng at Myhel-mas next ensuying; in consideraton of the premissez Mr Deane and the chapiter ar content that the said Mr Keble be accomptid here resident and to receyve and

229 Greete, yeoman, granted a tenement in the Sanctuary for years stated from Lady Day following at £3 rent 21 February 1551: *ibid.*, f. 174v.
230 Roche, cobbler, granted a tenement in Tothill St for 50 years from Lady Day following at £1 rent 10 February 1551: *ibid.*, f. 171v.
231 Coryngdon, yeoman, granted the manor of Poughley, Berks., for *43* years from previous Michaelmas at £5 rent (also the rectory of Chaddleworth for same term at £8 rent) 20 November 1550: *ibid.*, f. 174.
232 See above, n. 211.
233 John Horne *alias* Wheathampstead, B.D. Oxon., former monk of Westminster: Pearce, *Monks*, 186–7. Emden, 620 (where called Thomas). Lease not traced.
234 Probably Richard Goodrich, attorney of the court of augmentations: *Hist. Parl. 1509–1558*, ii, 231–3. Belsize manor was, however, retained as a perquisite for Dean Cox as it had been to his predecessor: WAM 33185, m. 8d; 37373.
235 A repetition of f. 52 (no. **92** above). Marcant(e) was admitted a minor canon on 16 November 1549 and replaced on 22 October 1551: below, no. **185** (ff. 279, 279v). Richard Scorse and Christopher Roche were also priest vicars (minor canons): WAM 37664, f. 3. Guildhall MS 9531/12, f. 256v.
236 Keble was also canon of Salisbury and prebendary of Torleton in Salisbury Cathedral; he had been admitted residentiary there on the previous June 18: Le Neve, vi, 78, 94.

take all maner of profittes and commodities of his prebend here for this quarter only as though he had byn present.

Signed: Cox, H. Perkyns, J. Pekyns, Bricket, Keble.

[f. 69v *blank*]

117. *October 19. Lease to the lord president.*

[f. 70] 19 die Octobris anno Edwardi sexti quinto. It is decred by Mr Deane and the chapiter that Bashes leas of Shorham and Otford shalbe renewyd to the use of the ryght honorable John*ᵃ* therle of Warwyck &c., wythe lyke yeres and condytions as the said Bayshe helde the same.[237]

Signed: Cox, Britten, J. Pekyns, H. Perkyns, Reynolds.

ᵃ Repl. 'lord'.

118. *October 31. Appointment of officers.*

Upon*ᵃ* Saterday the last day of October in anno Edwardi sexti quinto Mr Deane, wyth dyvers other prebendaryes whos names herafter are subscrybyd, hyld a chapiter at the whiche were chosen certen officers for that yere followyng, that is to sey Mr Pekens to be subdeane, Mr Bretten treausorer, Mr Parkyns surveyour, Sir Croham sexten and Sir Markham chaunter.[238]

Signed: Cox, J. Pekyns, Britten, Sandiforth, H. Perkyns, Bricket.

ᵃ Word repeated after false start.

119. *December 5. Bailiff appointed. Presentation to benefices.*

[f. 70v] Anno 5° Edwardi 6.*ᵃ* Quinto Decembris anno Edwardi sexti quinto. It is decrede by Mr Deane and the chapiter that Cresse[239] shall have a patent of the baylywyke of Whethamsted for terme of his lyf.

[Also*ᵇ* that Sir Thomas Warter, curat of Saynt Brydys, shall forthewythe have a presentaton for to be vyccar of the same.] Also that John Hurleton, clerke, shal have the presentation of the vicarage of Sainct Briget.[240]

ᵃ Head to page.   *ᵇ* Entry deleted.

---

[237] Edward Bashe (or Baeshe) granted the rectory of Shoreham and Otford, Kent, for 99 years from Lady Day 1551, reserving the advowson to the dean and chapter, at £55 rent 18 January 1551: WAM Reg. III, ff. 168v–169. He was surveyor-general of victualling for the navy: *Hist. Parl. 1509–1558*, i, 388–9. D.M. Loades, *The Tudor Navy* (Aldershot 1992), 150, 203–7. Warwick (head of the government, and advanced to the dukedom of Northumberland eight days before this act was made) had acquired the manor of Otford earlier in 1551: B. Beer, *Northumberland. The political career of John Dudley, Earl of Warwick and Duke of Northumberland* (Kent [Ohio] 1973), 119, 188. No lease to Northumberland is registered. See further below, no. **135** & n. 256, no. **137** & n. 262.

[238] Robert Crome and Henry Markham: WAM 37387A, f. 4.

[239] William Cressey: cf. no. **134** below.

[240] Hurleton, B.D. Cologne and Oxon., compounded for first fruits 12 February 1552,

120. *1552. January 30. Constable of St Martin's reappointed. Lease granted.*[a]

Upon Saterday the thirty daye of January in anno Edwardi sexti sexto[b] it was decreed by Mr Deane and the chapiter that Wyllyam Cox shulde contynewe in the office of the constableshipe of Seynt Mertens le Graunde.

Also that John Parker shall have a[c] revertyon of the parsonage of Bassingbourne for the terme of foursescore yeres.[241]

Signed: Cox, J. Pekyns, H. Perkyns, Bricket, Sandiforth, E. Weston, Nowell, Haynes.

   [a] Entries follow directly on the preceding.   [b] Repl. 'quinto'.   [c] Repl. 'the'.

121. *February 3. A house assigned to the former bishop.*[242]

[f. 71] 3° die Februarii anno regni regis Edwardi sexti sexto. It is agreede by the deane and chapiter that my lord bysshope of Norwyche shall have and enjoye the mancyon howse[a] with the garden wythin the close of Westm' latly in the tenure of George Vaughan, for the terme of twenty and on yeres, with certen conditions referryd to a lease to be expressid [b] in that behalfe.

Signed: Cox, Haynes, J. Pekyns, H. Perkyns, Nowell, Britten, Bricket, Sandiforth.

   [a] Word inserted.   [b] Three words inserted repl. 'made'.

122. *February 13. Leases granted.*

13 die Februarii anno Edwardi vj[ti] sexto. It is agreed by Mr Deane and the chapiter that James Rychardes shall have a lease of fyve[a] parcelles of medowe grounde lying in Offyngton and Sparsholde in the countie of Bark' and certen areble grounde lying in Uplytcombe alias Lytcombe Basset, for terme of twenty and on yeres besides[b] thos yeres[c] he hathe alredy, paying for a fyne xl s.[243] Also

admitted February 14; deprived for marriage 1554: PRO, E 334/4, f. 12. Guildhall MS 9531/12, ff. 313v, 453v. Emden, 306 (Hurleston).

[241] Parker, yeoman of Kingston, Cambs., granted the rectory, with the advowson reserved to the dean and chapter, for years stated from Lady Day 1570 at £50 rent 10 August 1551: WAM Reg. III, ff. 200v–201v.

[242] No lease registered. Bishop Thirlby had resigned the see of Westminster on 30 March 1550 and been translated to Norwich: Le Neve, 69; ratification of surrender by dean and chapter March 31: WAM Reg. III, f. 129. The diocese of Westminster had been dissolved by the patent which translated Ridley to London (*CPR* 1549–51, pp. 171–2), and although it required an act of parliament (5 & 6 Edw. VI c. 36; WAM 6490) to establish that the church was thereby the second cathedral of the bishop of London, he had not been thought in need of the bishop of Westminster's former palace, which on 30 May 1550 had been granted to Lord Wentworth, in whose and whose son's hands it remained until the restoration of the abbacy: Robinson, *Abbot's House*, 13–14. Shirley, *Thirlby*, 105–6.

[243] Richardes, yeoman, of Farnborough, Berks., granted these premises in Uffington and Sparsholt for 40 years from previous Michaelmas at 5s rent 10 May 1554: WAM Reg. III, ff. 242v–243.

that Mr Morgan shall have a lease of Ekynton tythe lying within the countie of Worcester, for terme of threscore*ᵈ* yeres.²⁴⁴

Signed: Cox, J. Pekyns, Britten, H. Perkyns, Nowell, Sandiforth, E. Weston.

   ᵃ Repl. 'certen'. *ᵇ* Repl. 'w[ith]'. *ᶜ* Word inserted. *ᵈ* Repl. 'fyftye yeres'.

123. *February 20. Lease granted.*

[f. 71v] 20 die Februarii anno Edwardi 6 sexto. It is decreed by Mr Deane and the chapiter that Mr [Gedeon]*ᵃ* Pekyns shall have Atkyns alley with all edifices and grounde lying within the same, beyng within the Grete Saynctuary, to alter and amende the same at his will and plesure, and the same to have in lease for lxxxix yeres, paying yerely therfore tenne shillinges, and in the last yere of the seid tyme to paye xxvj s. viij d.*ᵇ* [*Margin*: The indentures in the register are to Johon Pekyns and to Gedeon Perkyns.]²⁴⁵

Signed: Cox, J. Pekyns, Britten, H. Perkyns, Bricket, E. Weston, Sandiforth.

   ᵃ Word inserted in margin. *ᵇ* Repl. 'xl s.' and 'and the tombe house with the garden and the orchard for xxj yeares paying xxvj s. viij d.'

124. *March 12. All future leases to prohibit sub-leasing.*

12 die Martii anno Edwardi sexti sexto. It is agreed by Mr Deane and the chapiter that after this present day no lease nor leases other than be hertofore grantyd shalbe made of any office, fferme, tenement or any other thing apper-taynyng to the churche of Westm' to eny person or persons but that in the said lease so made it shalbe expressid that the partie to whome and in whose name the said lease shalbe made shall for his owne use occupye the said office or ferme or tenement, and by no meanes to overlett it to any other under ffermoure or under tenaunt, upon payne of forfayture of the said lease and clause of reentre in to the seid office, ferme or tenement as though the said lease had never ben made.

Signed: Cox, J. Pekyns, H. Perkyns, Sandiforth, E. Weston, Bricket.

125. *March 19. Debasement of coinage compels sale of plate and stuff to pay current expenses.*

[f. 72] xix° die Martii anno vj Edwardi vj. Forasmiche as the cathedrall churche of Westm' hathe had suche losse by the late fall of the monye²⁴⁶ that at this

²⁴⁴ Edward Morgan, gent., of Comberton, granted the premises for years stated from May 10 following at £2 13s 4d rent 13 February 1552: *ibid.*, ff. 177v–178.

²⁴⁵ Pekyns (Peakins), canon, and Gedeon his son granted the premises for *99* years from previous Michaelmas at 10s rent (£1 6s 8d in the final year) 20 February 1552; Gedeon alone granted a cellar with loft over in the same alley for 99 years from Michaelmas following at 6s 8d rent 26 August 1553: *ibid.*, ff. 183–183v, 196v–197.

²⁴⁶ During 1551 the silver currency had been decried, the testoon of 12d to 9d then 6d, the groat from 4d to 3d. There was widespread anticipation of further debasement: C.E.

present ther ys not mony ynough in the treasorers handes to pay the charges of this next*ª* our Ladye day quarter, yt ys therfore decreed by Mr Deane and the chapiter that certeyn plate and stuff shalbe furthewithe sold to mak monye whearwithe to pay the ministers and other officers wages and other charges now presently to be borne.

Signed: Cox, J. Pekyns, H. Perkyns, Sandiforth, E. Weston, Bricket.

ª Repl. 'our'.

126. *April 8. Lease granted. Collector of Westminster rents appointed.*

viijᵒ die Aprilis anno vj regni regis Edwardi vj. Itt ys decreed by Mr Deane and the chapiter that Mr Ashton shall have the revertion of the*ª* ferme of Lidcome Regis in Berkshire after Dances yers exspired, for terme of xxxᵗⁱ yers,²⁴⁷ so that the said Mr Ashton*ᵇ* shall not let yt over to any other under fermor.*ᶜ*

Yt ys farther decrede by Mr Deane and the chapiter that Herry Perves shall have the collection of the rentes in Westm' by patent during his lyff, so that he continew in service with Mr Deane wiche now ys*ᵈ* so long as he ys hier deane, with the fee appoynted.

Signed: Cox, Haynes, H. Perkyns, J. Pekyns, Britten, Sandiforth, Bricket.

ª Repl. 'manor'. *ᵇ* Repl. 'Fermor'. *ᶜ* Followed by illegible word. *ᵈ* Three words inserted.

127. *Same day. Dean and canons not to profit from nomination of scholars.*

[f. 72v] viijᵒ die Aprilis anno vj regni regis Edwardi vj. Yt ys decreed by Mr Deane and the chapiter that yf at *ª* any tyme hierafter the deane or any of the prebendaries shall be proved to receyve any kynd of *ᵇ* rewarde for the nomination of any scoler to be admitted in to the scoole, that then he shall loose the nomination of his scolershipes for ever.

Signed: Cox, J. Pekyns, Britten, H. Perkyns, Sandiforth, Nowell, Bricket, E. Weston.

ª Repl. 'any of the'. *ᵇ* Two words inserted.

128. *Undated. Revision of rules for residence.*

[Where*ª* as the eyght daye of November in the fourth yere of owre soveraygn lord kyng Edward the sixt there was an ordre or decre made by the deane and chapyter for theyr severall resydense to be kept in thys churche,²⁴⁸ ffor as moche as thes wordes (upon payne to lose all the profytes of hys hole yeres resydense) be

Challis, *The Tudor Coinage* (Manchester 1978), 105–7. Money collected as rent therefore lost value before it could be used to pay wages or buy goods.

²⁴⁷ No lease to Ashton traced. Grant to Nicholas Weston in succession to William Daunce (who himself had a reversionary grant in 1524) 8 March 1554: WAM Reg. III, ff. 225–6. See below, no. **148** & n. 277.

²⁴⁸ Above, no. **109**.

ambyguose and doubtefull, and also the tyme of residense therin prescribyd ys so
lytle that the churche is ofttymes destytute of prebendaryes to furnyshe the
churche and to make answere to suettes occurraunt; we thefore, to make clere the
sayd clause do declare owre understandyng and decree that under the name of
all the profytes of hys hole yeres resydense shalbe comprisid and understand his
hole cotydyan dystrybutions of xij d. by the daye dewe for the hole yere, and the
dyvydent of seales and fynes, wheate and wood dew*b* to residensiaries that yere.
And also we take ordere and decree that nother the deane nor ony prebendary of
thys churche whiche shalbe acceptyd and taken for resydent here in every other
quarter of the yere (except only the quarter wherin he kepith hys xxj dayes),
before he*c* hathe kepte hospytalytie wythin hys owne howse by the space of
twenty dayes together or at severall tymes, upon payne to loose for every quarter
wherin ony of theym shall omytt to kepe suche resydense all hys and their
cotydyan dystributions and other profittes of theyr resydense aforsayde.]

 a Whole entry deleted.   *b* Repl. 'dwe'.   *c* Word repeated then deleted.

129.   *July 5. Lease granted.*

[f. 73] Quinto die Julii anno regni regis Edwardi vj sexto. Yt ys agreed by Mr
Deane and the capiter that Mr Richard Shelley, at the sute of Sir Jhon Gattes,
vicechamberlaine to the kinges majestie, shall have a lease of the howse called St
Albons, late in the tenure of Mr Cicell, withe the garden plott and vacant
grownd betwixt that howse and Mr Noweles wall, for the terme of *a* lx yers. The
said Mr Shelley to stand to all the reparations and to pay yerly for the rent therof
xiij s. iiij d.[249]
  Signed: Cox, J. Pekyns, Bricket, Sandiforth, H. Perkyns, Britten, Bellasis 'unto
the last graunt in v*to* Julii anno predicto'.

 a Three words repeated and deleted.

130.   *November 11. Appointment of officers. Lease granted. Deductions from a canon's
stipend to pay his debt.*

[f. 73v] xj° Novembris anno regni regis Edwardi vj. Yt was then agreed by Mr
Deane and the chapiter and*a* by ther hole consent have elected and chosen Mr
Birkett to be subdeane for this yere following. Farther they have elected Mr
Pekyns to be treasorer for this yere followyng. Also yt ys decreed that Markham
and Crome shall remayne for this yere in ther offices of the sextonship and the
chantership.
  Item yt ys agreed that Mr Todd shall have a lease of the howse he now

[249] Shelley, esq., of Sussex, granted the premises for *99* years from Lady Day following at 13s
  4d rent (or £1 3s 4d if not resident), with right to bring water by lead pipe from [Canon]
  Bricket's cistern, 15 February 1553: WAM Reg. III, ff. 189–189v. Shelley was a courtier
  and diplomat: *Hist. Parl. 1509–1558*, iii, 308–10. Gates (*ibid.*, ii, 198–9) was also the dean
  and chapter's tenant, but a bad one: WAM 37388.

dwelleth yn for terme of xl*ᵇ* yers, so that he doo not alienate yt withowt the consend of the deane and chapiter.²⁵⁰

Farther yt ys agreed betwixt Mr Deane, the chapiter and Mr Keble that owt of Mr Kebles quarter payment the treasorer for the tyme being shall reteyne in his handes quarterly to the use of one Thomas Norton the somme of l s., and to the use of the house xv s. quarterly, untyll the some of xij li. be fully paid.

Signed: Cox, Bricket, H. Perkyns, J. Pekyns, Keble, Sandiforth, Nowell.

ᵃ Repl. 'th[at]'.   *ᵇ* Repl. 'ffiffty'.

131.   *December 3. A house for the under master.*

[f. 74] 3° die Decembris anno regni regis Edwardi vj sexto. Yt was than agreed by Mr Deane and the chaptre that Edward Cratford, husher of the gramer schole,²⁵¹ shall have for his lodginge and dwelling howse that chamber or chambers adjoininge to the howse wich laite was Mr Belosses, commenlie called Patches howse, untyll sotche tyme as the said Edward Cratford shall be otherwyse well provided for.

Signed: Cox, Bricket, Sandiforth, E. Weston, J. Pekyns, H. Perkyns, Nowell, Perne.

132.   *1553. February 5. Leases granted.*

[f. 74v] The vᵗʰ day of February anno vij° regni regis Edwardi vj. Yt was then agreed by Mr Deane and the chapiter that Robert Hobbey shall have the reversion of the tenement*ᵃ* in Westm' called the thre townnes for terme of fowerscore yers.²⁵² Item yt was then agreed that Garret Clargyer of St Martens shall have the howse he now dwellethe yn by lease for terme of fortye yers, yelding for the fyne therof iij li. vj s. viij d.²⁵³

Signed: Cox, Bricket, J. Pekyns, H. Perkyns, Sandiforth, Keble, Grindal, Alvey.

ᵃ Repl. 'iij townnes'.

[ff. 75–7: *numbers dropped*]

---

250 William Todd, clerk, granted a tenement in the Great Sanctuary for years stated from Christmas following at £2 rent, with prohibition of sub-letting without licence [cf. this act and no. **124** above], 11 November 1552: WAM Reg. III, ff. 193v–195.

251 I.e. under or second master. He had been an Oxford exhibitioner on the foundation of Worcester Cathedral; student of Christ Church 1547 x 1554, with interval 1552–4 during his teaching at Westminster: Emden, 148. For Patche's house see above, n. 222.

252 Hobbye, yeoman, granted reversion of one tenement called the Long House or Long Story, in the Sanctuary, another called High Story, and a chamber lately belonging to the porter's office, for years stated from expiry of lease to John Grene at 5 marks rent 12 March 1553: WAM Reg. III, ff. 211v–212v.

253 Clargier, pouchmaker, of St Martin-le-Grand, granted a tenement there for years stated from previous Michaelmas at £3 18s rent 10 February 1553: *ibid.*, ff. 187–8.

133. *February 7. Leases granted and house improvements.*

[f. 78] The vij^th of Februarie anno vij° regni regis Edwardi vj^ti. Yt is decreed by the deane and chapter att the earneste sute of Sir Jhon Gates, knight, &c., that Mr Shelley[254] shall have the howse in lease called St Albanes with the garden lately in^a in the tenure of Mr Bernarde Sandiforthe, and with the stable apperteyninge to Mr Birckhed,^b so that Mr Birckheede shall in recompense therof within one yeare and a halfe nexte ensuyng shall make att his owne costes and charges the floure of a chamber, a new chimney and a studie of xviij foote long and tenn foote broode, and thatt Mr Shelley and his successours shall (for as moche as in them shall lye) be bownd to grawnte to the sayd Mr Birckheed and his successours free cowrse and passage of the sayd Birchedes sinke frome his kitchen as it doth now runne, with libertie att all tymes to view and to scowre the same. Ytt is also agreed that Jhon Moodie, Jhon Burrie, Garrett Clargie shall have the lease of Bell allye in St Martens le Graunde in London for the tearme of threescore and ten yeares.[255]

Signed: Cox, J. Pekyns, H. Perkyns, E. Weston, Keble, Grindal, Alvey, Bricket.

^a Repl. 'cal[led]'. ^b Altered from 'Ba-'.

134. *March 11. Appointment of bailiff.*

[f. 78v] The xj daye of March anno vij regni regis Edwardi vj. Hit ys agreed by Mr Deane and the chapiter that John Pekyns shall have the revertyon of the offyce of the baylywyke of there lordship and manor of Whethamsted and Harpenden in the countie of Herford after the decease^a or forfeture of William Cressey now bayle there.

Signed: Cox, H. Perkyns, E. Weston, J. Pekyns, Keble, Alvey, Grindal.

^a Repl. 'dysse[se]'.

135. *July 26. Distraint on the rectory of Shoreham. The former bishop surrenders his house. House for a canon. Appointment of rent collector.*

[f. 79] Anno 1mo Marie regine xxvj^to die Julii.^a Iit is decreed by Mr Deane and chapiter that Mr Alexander Nowell shall have a letter of attorney to reentre^b in to the parsonage of Otford and Shorham in the countie of Kente, in^c the name of the said deane and chapiter, and there to strayne and staye all maner of haye, corne and all other frutes rysyng and cummyng of the said parsonage to the use of the said deane and chapiter, or to compounde with any convenyaunt person or persons by a certen pryce for the same upon theyr sufficient bonde in wrytyng for one hole yere.[256]

---

254 See above, n. 249.

255 Moody, citizen and grocer of London, (alone) granted several tenements and yards comprising the said alley for years stated from Lady Day following at £4 8s 8d rent, and to purge the jakes, 15 February 1553: WAM Reg. III, ff. 195–6.

256 The tenant, the duke of Northumberland, was the day before taken to the Tower, follow-

It is decreed by Mr Deane and the chaptre that wheras my lord of Norwiche hathe by his lettre declared that he hathe surrendred to Sir Richard Cotton, knight, all sotche intereste in the reversion of the howse now in Mr Vaghans tenure within the cloose of Westminster as the said deane and chaptre had granted to hym for xxj yeres,[d] the said Sir Richard Cotton shall have the reversion of the said howse by lease with this condition, that he shall kepe it in his owne possession and not alienat it to enie other person[e] without the consent of the said deane and chaptre.[257] [f. 79v] Also it is furder decreed by Mr Deane and the[f] chapiter that Mr Byrkhedd shall have a lease of the smythes house in the Saynctuary and the tenement joynyng[g] to the same on the west syde for lxxxj yeres, paying therfor yerly dueryng the said terme xlvj s. viij d., excepte the last yere, for the which he must paye fyve markes, with this condition, that the smythe now dwellyng there be not expellyd tyll he woll wyllyngly departe.[258]

Also it is decreede that William Cox shall have the collection in London whiche he hathe nowe for terme of his lyf, so that he put in sufficient suerties for the same.

Signed: Cox, Bricket, E. Weston, J. Pekyns, Nowell, Perne, Alvey, Griffith, Keble, Grindal.

[a] This and all entries from the accession of Mary to the last act of Cox's decanate (f. 81v) deleted. [b] Repl. 'strayne, collecte and staye'. [c] Repl. 'and'. [d] 'for . . . yeres' inserted. [e] Word inserted. [f] Word inserted. [g] Repl. 'of the weste'.

136. *July 30. Assignment of tithes. Appointment of cater. A lease extended.*

[f. 80] 30 die Julii anno primo regni regine Marie. Itt is decrede by Mr Deane and the chapiter that Thomas Rogers, clarke, viccar of Hincley in the countie of Leycestre, shall enjoye and have the tythe of Stocle, parcell of the parsonage of the said Hincley, the said Thomas paying therfor to the said deane and chapiter the somme of six shillinges eight pense yerly, moreover fyndyng of the proper costes of the said Thomas on sufficient curat at the chapell of the seid Stokley as other havyng the said tythe before have done, so to contynewe dueryng his beyng viccar there.[259]

It is also furder decrede by Mr Deane and chapiter that[a] William Browne shall

ing his unsuccessful attempt to make his daughter-in-law Lady Guildford Dudley queen upon the death of Edward VI on July 6: D.M. Loades, *John Dudley, Duke of Northumberland* (Oxford 1996), 266. See further below, no. **137** & n. 262.

257 Lease not registered. For the bishop of Norwich see above, no. **121** & n. 242. Cotton was comptroller of the household at Edward VI's death, and involved in Northumberland's plot; but he defected to Mary at the last minute: *Hist. Parl. 1509–1558*, i, 711–12.

258 Robert Byrkhedd (presumably a relative of Canon Thomas Bricket) granted a tenement and backside in the Great Sanctuary for years stated from Michaelmas following at £2 6s 8d rent 26 July 1553: WAM Reg. III, ff. 199–200.

259 Cf. Nichols, *Hist. county of Leicester*, iv, 684.

have the office of *b* the catershipe whiche*c* he nowe enjoyithe, for terme of his lif, beyng of the foundation wythin the cathedrall churche of Westm'.[260]

Also it is furder decrede that Richard Worley, serjeant at armes, shall have added unto the yeres whiche he hathe by vertue of a lease of certen tenementes in Seynt Martens in the feldes to make uppe an hundrethe savyng on yere, paying the accustomable rente.[261]

Signed: Cox, E. Weston, J. Pekyns, Keble, Grindal, Perne, Alvey, Griffith.

a Word inserted. *b* Repl. 'of the office'. *c* Repl. 'belong[ing]'.

137. *August 4. Arrangements for Shoreham parsonage.*

[f. 80v] 4º Augusti anno regni regine Marie primo. It is agreed by the deane and chapter that Mr Alexander Nowell shall enjoye and have the parsonage of Hotforde and Shoram in the cowntie of Kente, the sayd Mr Nowell yearelye payenge to the sayd deane and chapter the accustomed rente, provided that if the qwenes majestie doo make juste title to it, or thatt anie other man will paye for the preferrmente of the sayd lease, the arrerages of a cth x li. now beinge*a* behinde, thatt in these cases the sayd Mr Nowell shall surcease frome his title of the sayd lease.[262]

Signed: Cox, Bricket, E. Weston, J. Pekyns, Grindal, Perne, Alvey, Keble, Griffith.

a Word inserted.

138. *August 26. Payments to canons. House for a canon's servant. Appointment of collector and verger. Houses for canons.*

[f. 81] xxvj[to] die Augusti anno regni*a* regine Marie primo. It is decrede by Mr Deane and the chapiter that the somme of tenne poundes and fyve shillinges shalbe repaide to Edward Keble, prebendary of the same churche, for the suppliment of xx[ti] poundes, in consideration that the said Edward shall recover the lease of Vaughans house and*b* the same to the deane and chapiter delyver accordyng to the tonure of a former decre made in that behalfe to Mr Heynes, Mr Bretten, and to the said Mr Keble.[263] Also it is decred that Mr Gryffith shall have his whole quarter stipent from our Lady daye untill mydsomer last past.[264]

---

[260] Grant for life of the offices of chapter clerk and cater with fees of 4 marks and £6 13s 4d respectively 24 August 1554: *ibid*., ff. 223v–224.

[261] Worley and Isabell (or Elizabeth) [? his wife] granted nine tenements in Charing Cross St for 99 years from previous Christmas at £2 13s 4d rent 20 March 1553: *ibid*., ff. 214–15.

[262] Northumberland was awaiting trial for treason (August 18); upon condemnation his goods would be forfeit to the crown, an outcome which the chapter act envisages. After the duke's execution the dean and chapter continued to press for the £110 arrears, which represented the full rent payable during the duke's two-year tenancy: WAM 18518; 37388. No grant to Canon Nowell is registered. The property was next leased in March 1555: below, no. **167** & n. 321.

[263] Above, no. **68**.

[264] There must have been uncertainty who was entitled to the stipend for the March–June

Also that Richard Johnson, servaunt to Mr Gryndall, shall have a lease for xxj^ti yeres of a house and a garden in the Brode Saynctuary nowe in the tenure of on Cowleys wiff.[265]

Also that John Marsshall of Westm' shall have the hole office of the collector-shipe of Westm' and Knyghtes bridge with the accustomed fee appertaynyng to the same, the said John fyndyng sufficient suerties to the deane and the chappiter for the discharge of the said office.^c Provydyd allwayes that if Harry Pervyce wylle^d comme and serve him selfe in the said office, observyng all covenauntes to him belongyng to be performed with the paiment of arrerages upon his hedd remaynyng, that than the said John shall surcease and surrendre the occupiing of the said office with the fee to the same belongyng. Also that Robert Hobbey shall have and enjoye the revertion of the vergershipe which nowe Gye Gascon hathe, with the fee to the same belongyng, in the which office the said Robert hathe nowe this xij monethes allredy servyd.

Also that Mr Pekyns shall have a lease of a lofte with a celler under the same, which he now occupithe with his haye and strawe^e and lyethe within the yarde where he hathe nowe buyldyd, for terme of suche yeres as he hathe the reste, paying yerly for the same vj s. viij d. [f. 81v] Also that Alexander Nowell, prebendarye of the same howse, shall have paid unto him yerly the somme of fyve poundes dueryng the terme of foure yeres, to be employd upon the reparations of the howse belongyng to his prebende, beyng in utter ruyn and dekeye.

Signed: Cox, Bricket, subdean, J. Pekyns, Keble, Nowell, Grindal, Griffith.

^a Repl. 'regni regis'. ^b Repl. illegible word. ^c Repl. 'rente'. ^d Repl. 'offer'. ^e Altered from 'straye'.

[ff. 82, 82v *blank*]

139. *September 18. Installation of Dean Weston.*[266]

[f. 83] Decimo octavo die Septembris anno regni regine Marie primo. Master Hughe Weston, docter of divinitie and chapleyn unto the quenes highnes, toke possession of the deanrye of Westm' and was installyd in the same and plasyd in

quarter. Canon Hugh Griffith had been appointed *vice* Nicholas Ridley in 1550. Ridley, however, had licence to hold his canonry *in commendam* until Midsummer 1553, but he resigned it in advance of this and (in his capacity as bishop of London) instituted Griffith on March 6, with mandate to induct of same date: WAM Reg. III, f. 179v. Le Neve, 78–9. Griffith was installed on July 4: below, no. **184** (f. 273); the appointment was the only one to a canonry while Westminster stood within the diocese of London.

265 Untraced. Edmund Grindal, later archbishop of Canterbury, was no longer in immediate prospect of promotion, but unmolested in his Westminster canonry for the first months of Mary's reign: Collinson, *Grindal*, 65, 71–2.

266 Dean Cox had been imprisoned in the Marshalsea on August 5; he was released on August 19 and ordered to keep to his house at Westminster: *APC* iv, 427. Garrett, *Marian Exiles*, 134. His signature to the preceding act is his last known function before vacating the deanery. Weston was appointed by Queen Mary's patent on September 14: Le Neve, 69.

the chapter howse there, wyth all other ryghtes and usages to the same apper-taynyng, the xviij^th daye of September in the fyrst yere of the reygne of owre soveraygn lady Mary, by the grace of God quene of England, Fraunce and Ireland, defendour of the feyth, and in earth of the churche of England and also of Ireland the supreme hedd, in the presence of thies prebendaries whos names are here subscribid.^a

  ^a Presumably after the following entry.

140. *September 19. A canon admitted to sanctuary.*

19° die Septembris anno regni regine Marie primo. [*Margin*: Priviledg of sanctu-ary.] It is decreed by Mr Docter Weston, deane of the cathedrall churche of Westm' and the chapiter of the same that Mr Edward Keble, clarke, shall enjoye all kynde of priveleges and lyberties within the close of the said churche and every parte and parcell therof concernyng saynctuary men tochyng hym for any kynde of depte, demaunde, action, querrell, suetes and prosses^a that myght molest or vex his person, or by seasonyng upon any parte of his goodes, cattalles or moveables; we beyng movyd and provokyd to have this consideration for the diligent service that he hath donne in the kynges affayres, together with the pyttye and compassion whiche he had uppon others, becummyng suertye for theym so endettyng him selfe, by the meanes wherof of late [he]^b hathe cum to troble. Further the said deane and chapiter, at the request of the bayly of the greate saynctuary and all other the lybertyes of Westm', dothe admitt the name of the said Edward to be registred to thenjoying of the owteward and forren liberties of the greate saynctuary of Westm' as far forthe as the lawes of this realme dothe permitt to the privelege of the saynctuary of Westm' or hereafter shall do.^267

  Signed: H. Weston, Bricket, J. Pekyns, Perne, Griffith, Keble, Sandiforth, [H. Perkyns],^c Alvey.

  ^a Repl. 'proce[ss]'. ^b Ellipse in MS. ^c Deleted.

---

^267 Keble, who had been chaplain to Protector Somerset (WAM 9418), had been involved in disputes over canonries here and at Salisbury: above, n. 63. Le Neve, vi, 78. He was later in arrears of rent for the Porch house in the close: WAM 37555, f. 4. In November 1557 he was pardoned for debts of £30 in London, Wiltshire and Essex: *CPR* 1557–8, p. 347. Stanley was wrong in assuming (p. 352) that the sanctuary disappeared with the dissolu-tion of the abbey. The residual ecclesiastical sanctuaries were abolished by 32 Hen. VIII c. 12, which became law in the summer of 1540 (before Westminster Abbey fell). Eight new civil sanctuaries were then created, of which Westminster was one. The Henrician act was repealed by legislation of James I, but vestigial elements of the institution remained until the 18th century: I.D. Thornley, 'The destruction of sanctuary', in *Tudor Studies presented . . . to A.F. Pollard*, ed. R.W. Seton-Watson (1924), 203–4 & n. 116. Elton, *Reform and Renewal*, 137–8. Lehmberg, *Later Parliaments*, 100, 102. See also J.R. Hertzler, 'The abuse and outlawing of sanctuary for debt in seventeenth century England', *HJ* xiv (1971), 467–77.

141. *September 23. Plumbing arrangements.*

[f. 83v] Anno primo regni regine Marie. Upon Saterday the xxiij day of September it was decreede by Mr Deane and the chapter that Mr Keble shall*ᵃ* have the waste water*ᵇ* from Mr Raynoldes cesterne with the pyps and his cesterne of his condet for the leade only*ᶜ* at the howses coste so longe as he hath the use of the howse in whiche he nowe dwellith, provydyd that at what tyme he lettith his house to any of his assigns or otherwise levyth it, that then the pyps and leade shall retorne to the howse use frome whens it came.

Signed: H. Weston, Bricket, J. Pekyns, Reynolds, Keble, Sandiforth, Nowell, Griffith.

ᵃ Repl. 'sholde'. *ᵇ* Repl. 'wast' repeated. *ᶜ* Word inserted.

142. *Undated. Canons' installation fee.*

[It*ᵃ* ys decreed by the deane and chapiter that every prebendary before*ᵇ* his enstallyng shall paye to the chapiter for a dyvydent to be dyvydyd amongste the deane and the prebendaryes than beyng [*four lines illegible*].

Signed: Perne, Griffith, Bricket.]

ᵃ Whole entry heavily deleted. Repeated at f. 85 (no. **146** below). *ᵇ* Repl. 'at'.

143. *October 24. Canons' houses. Appointment of collectors.*

[f. 84] xxiiij*ᵗᵒ* die Octobris anno regni regine Marie primo. It is decreed by Mr Deane and the chapter that Mr Bryched shall have a lease of the smythes house in the Saynctuary and the tenement of the west part joynyng to the same for lxxxj yeres, paying therfore*ᵃ* yerly dueryng the said terme xlvj s. viij d., except the last yere, in the whiche he must paye fyve markes, with this condition, that the smythe now dwelling there be not expellyd tyll he will wyllyngly departe.²⁶⁸

Also it is decreed that [William]*ᵇ* Rossat shall have and enjoye the office of the*ᶜ* collectorshipe of Westm' and Knyghtes brydge with the accustomed fee apertaynyng to the same, the said [William]*ᵈ* Rossat fyndyng sufficient suerties to the deane and chapter for the dyscharge of the said office.²⁶⁹ Also*ᵉ* that*ᶠ* William Weston shall have the office of the*ᵍ* collectorshipe and the collection in London whiche William Cox nowe hath,*ʰ* so*ⁱ* that he put in sufficient suerties for the same.²⁷⁰

---

²⁶⁸ See above, no. **135** & n. 258.

²⁶⁹ *Alias* Rossey, also keeper of the Star Chamber, who in 1556 became involved in the so-called Dudley conspiracy to steal the queen's silver and thereby finance her overthrow: Loades, *Conspiracies*, 191, 218, 231. See particularly *CSPDM*, 352, 361–4, 393–4, 398, 401, 431–4. For the mounting arrears of his collection, see WAM 37555, 37560, 37663, 37664. It is unclear whether his financial troubles were the cause or effect of his treasonable activities. See further below, no. **176** & n. 364, no. **181**.

²⁷⁰ William Weston was the dean's kinsman and subsequent executor: PRO, PROB 11/42B, ff. 56–56v.

Item it is decreed that Mr Pekyns shall have a lease of a lofte with a celler under*ʲ* the same which he nowe occupithe*ᵏ* with his haye and strawe, and lyeth within the yarde where he hathe nowe buyldyd, for terme of suche yeres as he hathe the rest, paying yerly for the same vj s. viij d. Item it is decreed by Mr Deane and the chapiter that the somme of v li.*ˡ* v s. shalbe repayd to Mr Keble, prebendary of the same churche, for the suppliment of xx li., in consideration that the said Mr Keble shall recover the lease of Vaughans house, and the same to the deane and chapiter delyver*ᵐ* accordyng to the tenure of a former decree made in that behalfe to Mr Haynes, Mr Bretten and to the said Mr Keble.²⁷¹ [f. 84v] Item it*ⁿ* is decreed by Mr Deane and the chapiter that Alexander Nowell shall receve of the tresorer of the churche fyve poundes yerly dueryng the terme of foure yeres, to be imployd upon the reparations of his prebendaryes house, beyng in utter ruyne and dekaye.

Signed: H. Weston, Bricket, Reynolds, J. Pekyns, Alvey (*bis*), Keble, Perne, Nowell, Griffith.

ᵃ Repl. 'therof'. *ᵇ* MS. blank. *ᶜ* Three words inserted. *ᵈ* MS. blank. *ᵉ* Repl. 'It'. *ᶠ* Repl. 'decreed'. *ᵍ* Three words inserted. *ʰ* Two words inserted repl. 'latly hadd'. *ⁱ* Repl. 'for terme of his lyff'. *ʲ* Repl. 'of the [*illegible word*] same'. *ᵏ* Repl. 'dwellithe'. *ˡ* Repl. 'x li'. *ᵐ* Repl. 'reco[ver]'. *ⁿ* Altered from 'is'.

144. *Undated. House for a canon. Appointment of chapter clerk and cater.*

It is decreid that Mr Parkynes shal have the revertion*ᵃ* of Clementes Crikedot widowe howse by lease for the*ᵇ* tearme of xlj yers, so that he or his assines shall beare and susteyne all the reparationes of the sayd house*ᶜ* and so leave it at the ende of the terme of xlj yer.²⁷²

Item it is agreid that William Browne shall have his officis of the clarkeshipe of the chapiter and the catershipe for the tearme of his lyve, exercisinge the sayde officis him selve except in tyme of his sikenes, and than his depute to be allowid by Mr Deane, and his wagys lyke wyse to be apoyntyd by hym.²⁷³

Signed: H. Weston, Bricket, J. Pekyns, H. Perkyns, E. Weston, Perne, Alvey, Griffith.

ᵃ Two words inserted repl. 'a lease'. *ᵇ* Word repeated. *ᶜ* Four words inserted.

145. *November 25. Appointment of officers.*

[f. 85] xxv° Novembris anno regni regine Marie primo. Yt ys then agreed by Mr Deane and the chapiter that Mr Birkett shall be subdeane within this churche for this yere following, with the fee of sixe powndes. Item then was Mr Raynols

---

²⁷¹ See above, nos **68** and **138**.
²⁷² Not traced. She was allowed 2s deduction from her rent this year because of the decay of the property: WAM 37555, f. 2v.
²⁷³ See above, n. 260. An acquittance of his for the scholars' commons due Midsummer 1554 shows continuing uncertainty over their designation ('quenes' replacing 'kynges'): WAM 37587.

chosen to be surveaor, he to have yf he do ryde about x li., yf not v li. Item then was chosen Mr Bernard to be treasorer, with the fee of vj li. xiij s. iiij d.

Signed: H. Weston, Bricket, J. Pekyns, Alvey, H. Perkyns, E. Weston, Keble, Perne, Sandiforth, Griffith.

146. *Undated. Canons' installation fees.*

It is decreed by Mr Deane and the chapiter that every prebendary before his installation shall paye to the chapiter for a dyvydent to be devydyd amongst the deane and the prebendaryes then beyng [resident]*a* twenty shillinges and a pounde of pepper; to the chapiter clarke – v s., to the chaunter vj s. viiij d., and to every of the two vergers – iij s. iiij d.

Signed: H. Weston, Griffith, Perne, H. Perkyns, Alvey.

a Ellipse in MS.

147. *1554. March 3. Lease granted. Assignment of tithes. Advowson for the dean.*

[f. 85v] 3° die Martii anno regni regine Marie primo. It is decreede by Mr Deane and the chapiter that John Harrys of London, [*blank*], shall have a lease of a tenement at Broken Wharffe callyd the Haye house for lxx yeres, paying the accustomid rente, so that he newe*a* buylde or sufficiently repayre the said house and so sufficiently repayryd*b* do leve the same at the ende of the said terme.[274]

It is decreed by Mr Deane and the chapiter the same day that Davy Polhyll and John Hodshole of the parisshes of Shorham and Otford in the countie of Kente, yemen, shall have the tythe with all thappertenaunces*c* belongyng to the parsonages of the said Shorham and Otford in the said countie for one hole yere next and immediatly after the date herof to be endyd and complet at the feast of thannunciation of our Lady which shalbe in the yere of our Lord a thowsande fyve hundred fyfty and fyve, payng therfore the accustomid rente.[275]

Item [it]*d* ys decred that Mr Doctor Weston, deane of Westm', shall have a vouson under chapiter seale of the parsonage of Islipp in the countie of Oxford for the first and next vacation.[276]

Signed: H. Weston, Bricket, H. Perkyns, J. Pekyns, E. Weston, Sandiforth, Nowell, Perne, Griffith.

a Repl. 'b[uylde]'.   *b* Repl. 'd[o]'.   *c* Three words inserted.   *d* Ellipse in MS.

---

[274] Harrys, 'straweman', granted the premises for years stated from Lady Day following at £1 10s rent 3 March 1554: WAM Reg. III, ff. 217–217v.

[275] Not traced. But cf. below, no. **167** & n. 321.

[276] Weston was admitted on 20 or 21 April 1554 on presentation *pro hac vice* by William Pye, dean of Chichester [who was himself appointed to a Westminster canonry nine days later]: PRO, E 331/Oxf./1, m. 3. Bodl. MS Oxf. Dioc. Papers d. 105, p. 151. Le Neve, 82. Vacant by Weston's death 15 December 1558: *Inst. Cant. sed. vac.*, 64 (which establishes date of Weston's death more precisely, i.e. November 26 x December 15, than Emden, 617).

148. *March 4. Leases granted. Advowson for a canon.*

[f. 86] iiij° die Martii anno primo regine Marie.*ᵃ* Yt was agreed by Mr Deane and the chapiter that Nicholas Weston shall have the reversion of Litcome Regis in the countie of Berkshire for the terme of lxx yers.[277] Item yt ys agreed that William Cottesford of Lurgeshall shall have the reversion of the wood called Hodford wood and Beachame grove*ᵇ* for lxx yers.[278] Item yt ys agreed that Jhon Leame shall have the reversion of Hame Marche for lxx yers.[279] Item that Jhon Dames shall have the reversion of the manor and parsonaige of South Benflett for lxx yers.[280] Item that George Carleton shall have the reversion of the ferme of Bynhome for lxx yers.[281] Item that Mr Hugh Griffeth shall have a presentation of the parsonage of St Leonardes Foster Lane in London.[282] Item that Clement Newese and Thomas Hunt shall have the reversion of the parsonaige of St Brides for the terme of lxx yers.[283] Item that Thomas Sandiforthe and Nicholase Brok shall have the reversion of the manor of Kennesbarne for lxx yers.[284]

Signed: H. Weston, Bricket, E. Weston, J. Pekyns, H. Perkyns, Sandiforth, Griffith, Perne.

ᵃ 'iiij°' in left margin, repeated with rest of date in the right.   *ᵇ* Three words inserted.

[277] Weston, of Carleton, Leics., granted the manor from the expiry of lease to William Daunce (1524) or of subsequent reversion to William's son John (1550), for years stated at £60 rent 8 March 1553: WAM Reg. III, ff. 225–6. Weston was the dean's brother: PRO, PROB 11/42B, f. 56.

[278] Cottesford (Cottiforde), yeoman, of Ludgershall, Bucks., granted the premises, with property in West Betterton, Berks., for years stated from the expiry of lease to John Collyns, at 5s rent for Hodford wood and 3s for Beacham grove, both in Hendon, Middlesex, 8 March 1554: WAM Reg. III, ff. 204v–205.

[279] Not traced. Probably the same as John Leime, yeoman, clerk in the Tower, who leased a tenement in Tothill St 6 November 1553: *ibid.*, ff. 220–220v.

[280] Dames, citizen and clothworker of London, granted the premises from the expiry of lease to Roger Appulton (1553) for years stated at £20 rent, reserving the advowson to the dean and chapter, 23 December 1553: *ibid.*, ff. 218–19.

[281] Carleton, of Walton-upon-Thames, Surrey, granted the manor of Binholme in Pershore for years stated from end of lease made to John (now deceased) and George Carleton (1534); with tithes of Birlingham for same years at rent totalling £19 6s 8d and £2 for the tithes 23 December 1553: *ibid.*, ff. 205–7. In fact Binholme and Pershore were coterminous: Harvey, *Estates*, 363 n. 2.

[282] Griffith (canon) admitted *vice* Robert Crome (minor canon), deprived for marriage 20 March 1554: Guildhall MS 9531/12, f. 449.

[283] Not traced. But for Newese see below, no. **150** & n. 290.

[284] Sandiforth and Brooke granted the premises from the expiry of lease to George and Joan Vaughan (above, n. 142) for years stated at £14 rent 23 December 1553: WAM Reg. III, ff. 203v–204v.

149. *March 10. Grant to Secretary Petre. Appointment of verger and treasurer. Extension of a canon's house. Lease granted. Tithes assigned to a canon.*

[f. 86v] x° die Martii anno primo regine Marie. Yt was then agreed by Mr Deane and the chapiter that Sir William Peter, knight, shall have the reversion of the weekes and marches at Southbenflett withe the fishing, foullyng and other the appurtenance, for the terme of xxxj yers.[285]

Item yt ys agreed that William Rosett[a] of Westm' shall have a patent in[b] reversion of the vergership after the deceasse of Guy Gascon.[286] Item yt ys agreed that Mr Doctor Perne shalbe[c] treasorer of this churche.[d]

Item yt ys agreed that Mr Perne shall have perteyning to his howse to him and his successors all the garden and buyldinges[e] enclosed within the stone walle withe the house called Canterbery.[287]

Item yt ys agreed that Jhon Heithe shall have in lease the wood in Woocestershere called Horwell wood, for the terme of lx yers, for the rent of xl s. by yere.[288]

Item that Mr Alvey shall have the tithe of Plesshey by lease for lxx yers.[289]

Signed: H. Weston, E. Weston, J. Pekyns, H. Perkyns, Sandiforth, Perne, Bricket, Griffith, Keble.

[a] Repl. 'Rossey'. [b] Three words inserted, repl. 'the'. [c] 'be' repeated. [d] Followed by several words deleted and illegible. [e] Two words inserted.

150. *March 17. Lease granted. Appointment of head verger, porter, cook, surveyor and carpenter. Advowson for a canon.*

[f. 87] xvij° Martii anno primo regine Marie. Yt was then agreed by Mr Deane and chapiter that Clement[a] Newes shall have tow tenementes with[b] a nother litell ferme of xxj s. viij d.[c] called[d] Stretley in Barkshere for terme of lxx yers.[290]

Item Mr Deane and chapiter is contented to accept the service of William

285 Petre granted the premises for *60* years from expiry of lease to William Dyx [for 21 years from Michaelmas 1546: *ibid*., ff. 74–5] at £18 6s 8d rent 13 March 1554: *ibid*., ff. 210v–211v; duplicated ff. 299–299v. The marshes were a principal source for the provisions of Petre's Essex houses: F.G. Emmison, *Tudor Secretary* (2nd edn 1970), 147.

286 *Alias* Rossey: see above, n. 269.

287 Canon Andrew Perne. Among items in Perne's library published abroad (and so perhaps acquired) when he resided here was the posthumous *De Justificatione* of a former canon of Westminster John Redman (Antwerp 1555): D.J. McKitterick, 'Andrew Perne and his books', in McKitterick, *Perne*, 51. Cf. MacCulloch, *Cranmer*, 343.

288 Hethe, esq., of London granted the premises for 60 years from Lady Day following at rent stated 8 March 1554; assigned by tenant to Sir John Bourne for remainder of term March 28 same year: WAM 22707.

289 See following note.

290 Clement Nuce, citizen and mercer of London, granted two tenements in Broad Sanctuary for 70 years from previous Christmas at £3 13s 4d rent; also land at Streatley, Berks., with tithes of the free chapel of Pleshey, [Essex], also for 70 years, from end of lease to John, Joyce and Anthony Carleton (1534) at £1 1s 8d rent 28 February 1554: WAM Reg. III, ff. 207–8. The chapel was given by Henry VII in 1503: Harvey, *Estates*, 409.

Rose[291] touching the highe vergership during the naturall lif of Guy Gascon, and the said Guy Gascon to give[e] the said Rose[f] for his paynes in that behalff vj s. viij d. quarterly during the liff of the said Guy. Item that Robert Medcalff shall have a patent in[g] reversion of the portership after the decease of Alexander Palmer.[292] Item that Richard Whit shall have a patent of one[h] of the cookship, the same to be delyvered to him at Mr Deanes pleasure.[i][293] Item that William Russell shall have a patent of the surveorship and carpentership.[294]

Item that Mr Perne shall have the vouson of the vicaraige of Godmanchester.[295]

Signed: H. Weston, Bricket, H. Perkyns, J. Pekyns, E. Weston, Perne, Sandiforth, Griffith, Keble.

[a] Repl. 'the'. [b] Repl. 'with a l[itell]'. [c] 'viij d.' inserted. [d] Repl. 'a yere'. [e] Word inserted. [f] Two words inserted. [g] Three words inserted repl. 'the'. [h] Repl. 'the'. [i] Eleven words inserted.

151. *March 22. Leases granted.*

[f. 87v] xxij° Martii anno primo regine Marie. Yt ys agreed by Mr Deane and chapiter that a terme of xxxj yers shalbe geven unto Jaques Wynkfeld and Thomas Maria Wingfeld of the parsonaige of Ottford and Shorham in the countie of Kentt, withe condition that Mr Deane and Mr Pekyns have the custodie of the lease therof sealled withe a blank untyll they have taken order betwyne the said Jaques and Thomas Maria[a] of [b] thone partie and Mr Nowell of thother partie.[296] Item yt ys agreed that Jhon Baughe shall have a revertion of the manor of Pennesham in the countie of Wygorn' for terme of xxxj yers, and he to pay for a fyne eight powndes.[297]

---

[291] *Alias* Rossey: see above, n. 269.
[292] Not traced.
[293] Not traced.
[294] Not traced.
[295] A blank deed of presentation dated 7 March 1554 survives, but although Perne retained his stall throughout 1554 it was the bishop of Lincoln who collated by lapse on November 26, appointing William Weston; vacant by his death 9 November 1557: LAO, PD 1554/2; Reg. XXVIII, f. 121. WAM Reg. IV, f. 22v. This William was the dean's brother: WAM 37687.
[296] Not registered. For next lease of Shoreham see below, no. **167** & n. 321. These Wingfields were brothers; Thomas Maria was, it seems, the godson of Mary Tudor, queen of France and duchess of Suffolk (Henry VIII's sister): *Hist. Parl. 1509–1558*, iii, 641–2, 645–6. The duchess of Somerset twice attempted to have Thomas Maria made collector of the Westminster rents: letter to the dean and chapter dated 15 March [no year; probably 1550 because referring to grant of reversion of White Horse (to William Coxe) when the reversion of the collectorship was otherwise bestowed (to George Pervys): see above, no. **102** & n. 192]: WAM 9753.
[297] Not registered. This manor with others granted to Secretary Bourne in 1555: WAM Reg. III, ff. 303v–304v.

Signed: H. Weston, Bricket, H. Perkyns, J. Pekyns, Sandiforth, Griffith, Keble, E. Weston, Perne.

a Word inserted.   *b* Repl. 'and'.

152.   *Undated. Lease granted to a canon's brother.*

[f. 88] It is decreed by Mr Deane and the chapter that Mr Keble shall have a lease of the Castell taverne for his brother Harry Keble, whiche lyithe in the Greate Saynctuary, for terme of lxx yeres, paying the accustomed rent in as large and ample maner as Kateryn Staffarton, wydowe, latly hylde and enjoyd the same. [And*a* also the revertyon of a*b* tenement callyd the Bell scituat in the Kynges strete of Westm' wherin on Edmunde Lord now dwellythe, for the terme of lxx yeres, paying the accustomed rente.]²⁹⁸

Signed: H. Weston, Bricket, J. Pekyns, Perne, Griffith, Keble, Sandiforth, H. Perkyns.

a Rest of entry deleted.   *b* Repl. 'the Bell'.

153.   *March 31. Appointment of sub-dean.²⁹⁹ Lease granted.*

Ultimo Martii anno regni regine Marie Primo. It ys decreed by Mr Deane and the chapiter that Mr Gryffith shalbe subdeane wythin this churche for this yere followyng, wyth the fee of six poundes. Item it is decreede that Raffe Petit shall have the house or tenement whiche Mr Sackfeld nowe holdithe in revertyon, for terme of fortye*a* yeres, paying the accustomed rente.³⁰⁰

Signed: H. Weston, Perne, Griffith, H. Perkyns.

a Repl. 'thyrtye'.

²⁹⁸ No lease for the Castle traced. Grant to Lord, gent., and Joan his wife of the Bell for 72 years from Lady Day following at £6 6s 8d rent, with in addition at Lady Day 1568 a fine of £3 6s 8d, 10 March 1555: *ibid.*, ff. 302v–303. For the Lorde family and this (the southern King St) Bell see Rosser, 388. For the later history of the tavern see Pepys, x, 418.

²⁹⁹ *Vice* Bricket, who had been elected in the previous November (above, no. **145**), being deprived along with others on March 30 (by virtue of a commission dated the previous day intended to remove married canons) by the lord chancellor, who came to the Abbey in person, and was entertained by the traitor Rossey for £6 16s 2½d: *CPR* 1553–4, pp. 261–2. WAM 37451. The others removed were H. Perkyns (although he signs to no. **153** of the following day), Alvey, Keble, Nowell, J. Pekyns, Sandiforth and E. Weston. Grindal (who was a bachelor) was presumably ejected at the same time, though he made a personal deed of resignation at Landbeach, Cambs., on May 10: CCC, MS 106, p. 512; cf. Collinson, *Grindal*, 72. Successors were appointed between April 5 and May 22: Le Neve, 72–7, 79–82.

³⁰⁰ Petit, yeoman, and Ellynor his wife, granted the King's Head in the Great Sanctuary, for 50 years from the end of the lease to William Sackvyle, gent., at £2 6s 8d rent 31 March 1554: WAM Reg. III, ff. 263v–264.

154. *May 13. Division of the great orchard.*

[f. 88v] 13ᵐᵒ die Maii anno domini 1554. It is decreede by Mr Deane and the chapiter that the greate orcharde latly belongyng to Mr Docter Perkyns shalbe equally devydyd betwene Mr Docter Cole, Mr Pye and Mr Alphansus.[301]

Signed: H. Weston, Griffith, Reynolds, Mallet, Cole, Pye, Ramridge, Richarde, Moreman, de Salinas.

155. *Undated. A letter from the queen.*

[f. 89] A coppey of the quenes graces letter sente to Mr Deane and the chapiter for thadmission of almesmen by senioritie of bylles.

Trusty and welbelovyd we grete you well. And for as moche as dyverse letters have byn directyd to yow by us for the preferment of certen poore men to the romes of bedmen or almesmen wythin owre cathedrall churche of Westm' according to your foundation, and that some of the same letters have byn wrytten in suche forme that the partie for whome they were wrytten shulde be plasid at the next avoydaunce of any of the said romes, so that suche poore men as by us since the begynnyng of owre raygne hadd former letters grauntyd to be preferred to any of the said romes shulde by that meanes be disapoyntyd, we therfore, desyring to see a good order taken and kepte in that behalfe, wyll and commawnde you that from hensforth all suche poore men as by our letters have byn or herafter shalbe appoyntyd to any of the said romes of bedmen or almesmen, in what forme or maner so ever they be wrytten, be plasyd in the said romes accordyng to the date of the same letters, to thentent that thos that have the fyrst graunte orderly may be fyrst preferryd, and those shalbe unto you at all tymes a sufficient warraunt and discharge in that behalfe.

156. *September 16. A letter from Lord Wentworth, lord deputy of Calais.*[302]

[f. 89v] A copey of my lord Wentfordes letter sent to Mr Deane concernyng the cloyster.

After my very hartye commendations. Where I understand that yow are desierous to have my parte of the cloyster at Westm', I therfore advertyse yow that I ame content yow shall have the same, so in exchaunge therof I may have from yow one parcell of the longe house adjoynyng to my towre there, so moche therof as this berer my surveyor and you can agree upon. So I byd you right hartely well to fare. From Calleice, the xvjᵗʰ of September 1554.

Your very lovyng frend, Johnᵃ Weyntworthe.

ᵃ *Recte* Thomas.

---

[301] Alphonso de Salinas, one of the newly appointed canons.

[302] The second Baron Wentworth of Nettlestead, who had succeeded his father to the title and to the possession of the former abbot's house in 1551. The tower was part of the then unfinished south-west tower of the church: Robinson, *Abbot's House*, 13–15.

157. *October 27. Grant of advowson.*

27 die Octobris anno domini 1554. It is decrede by Mr Deane and the chapiter that Mr John Cole this *ᵃ* daye shulde have the presentatyon of the vicarege of Shorham and Otford wythein the countie of Kente, and acording to the same decre the said presentatyon was sealyd this same day to his said use.³⁰³

Signed: H. Weston, Griffith, Reynolds, Baker, Pye, T. Wood, de Salinas.

ᵃ Repl. 'hathe'.

[ff. 90, 91 *excised*]

158. *November 17. Court perquisites granted to Sir John Bourne, principal secretary.*

[f. 92] xvij° die Novembris anno domini 1554. It is decred by Mr Deane and the chapter that Mr Secretory Bourne shall have the lawdaies and the manred of Redgreve courte and Calcrofte courtes for terme of his lyffe, in as ample wise as it is graunted to the said deane and chapter, reservynge all former grauntes hertofore made to any person, payenge by the yere xx s. above all other the said deane and chapter is chargid.³⁰⁴

159. *December 15. Appointment of officers. Dividend. The keepership of the gatehouse.*

xvᵗᵒ die Decembris anno 1554. It is decreed by Mr Deane and the chapter that Mr Gryffith shalbe subdeane this yere folowynge, and Mr Pye surveyor, and Mr Pearne treasorer. It is decreyd that suche profittes as shall come of ffynes, seales and wood sales to be devided betwixt the seid Mr Deane and the prebendaries, so the state of the churche be preservyd.

It is decreyd that Robert Medcalfe shall have a patent sealyd of the kepynge of the gatehouse, to remayne in Mr Deanes kepynge, so that if Ralfe Browne be provyded for with some other offyce of the churche to his contentation, or else the forseid Browne to have the kepynge of the said gatehouse by patent, and the forseid Robert to have some other house by lease of the churche, so that they bothe be stayed and delyveryd at Mr Deanes pleasure and not otherwise.³⁰⁵

---

³⁰³ John Coles, B.D., admitted on 31 October 1554; but another was admitted on the resignation of an un-named predecessor on 2 May 1555: *Inst. Cant. sed. vac.*, 116. Uncertainty about this appointment is reflected in the chapter's further resolution: no. **162** below, December 18. Coles appears to have secured possession, and the abbot and convent presented on his resignation 23 December 1557: WAM Reg. IV, f. 49.

³⁰⁴ Bourne granted the courts leet and views of frankpledge in numerous properties [*specified*] in South Worcs., for *80 years* from Lady Day following at 15s rent 1 January 1555: WAM Reg. III, ff. 288v–289. Bourne was probably born on the Abbey's manor of Wick, Worcs., and became a substantial landowner in the county during his brief term in government under Mary: *Hist. Parl. 1509–1558*, i, 466–9.

³⁰⁵ Probably Ralph Browne who by Michaelmas 1556 had been appointed one of five laymen to make up the number of (12) minor canons: WAM 37708, 37709.

160. *December 15. Lease granted.*

[f. 92v] Anno 1554 xv^{mo} die Decembris. It is decreid that John Hall have the revertion of the Cocke after the lease be expiryd, and the lyffe of hym that nowe occupieth it be endyd, so that if John Hall do not dwell in the forseid Cocke, that then his wife that nowe dwellith in hit shall have it before any other, agreynge with the seid John Hall after suche sorte as Mr Deane and Mr Pye shall thynke reasonable; and if the said John Hall do dwell in the Cocke aforseid, that then the wife of hym wiche nowe dwellyth in the Cocke shall have the house that the said John Hall nowe dwellyth in, of suche condytions as Mr Deane and Mr Pye shall thynke reasonable.[306]

161. *Same day. Further leases.*

Anno 1554 xv die Decembris. It is decreyd that Agnes and John Grene shall have a lease of Bagnall mylles for the space of xxxj yers.[307] Item it is decreyd that Thomas Collynes shall have a revertione of the parsonadge of Godmanchester aftere Bushis lease be expyrid, by the space of xxxj yers, and if Bushis lease be forfetyd before his lease be expyrid, the sayd Thomas Collenes shall nat tak any advantedge therof excepte he aggre with Mr Deane and the chapyter.[308]

Signed: H. Weston, Griffith, Perne, Mallet, Baker, Pye, Cole, Ramridge, T. Wood, Richarde, de Salinas.

162. *December 18. Advowson of Otford and Shoreham.*

[f. 93] Memorandum that it [is]^{a} aggreyd by Mr Deane and the chapiter the xviij daye of December 1554 that Mr Thomas Aynesworthe shall have the presentatione of Otforde and Shorame if Mr Cole dothe nat accept it.[309]

Signed: H. Weston, Griffith, Perne, Baker, Pye, Ramridge, de Salinas, Cole.

^{a} Ellipse in MS.

163. *1555. February 6. Leases granted.*

[f. 93v] Sexto die Februarii anno domini 1554. It is decreed by Mr Deane and the chapiter that the lease of the Castell taverne in Westm' made in the name of Kateren Stafferton for terme of yeres as in the same it is contayned, that the

---

[306] Hall, cook, granted the Cock and Tabard, Tothill St, for 41 years from Midsummer 1565 at £3 rent 18 December 1554: WAM Reg. III, ff. 279v–280v. For some previous tenants see Rosser, 127, 132–3, 375.

[307] *Alys* Grene, widow of John, and John their son, husbandman, granted the tucking mills in Bagnor, Berks., for years stated from Michaelmas following at £2 rent 4 December 1554: WAM Reg. III, ff. 274–5.

[308] Collyns, yeoman, granted the rectory (reserving the advowson to the dean and chapter) from the end of lease to Bush (above, n. 133) for years stated at £50 rent, with requirement to reside and many other special provisions, 6 December 1554: WAM Reg. III, ff. 252–4.

[309] See above, no. **157** & n. 303.

same lease shall*a* stande and be in his force notwithstondyng the covenauntes and grauntes therin conteyned to Rychard Drury of Westm' abovesaid, baker, for the yeres in the lease yet to come, the same condytions observyd and kepte.[310] Also it is further decreed that Thomas Smalebone shall have the mylle close and the grounde wher*b* the olde mylle stode nere to the scite of the mannor of Stevyngton, for terme of lj yeres,*c* paying therfor by the yere xxx s., the terme to begynne at Myhelmas next.[311]

Signed: H. Weston, Griffith, Baker, Cole, Ramridge, Reynolds, Richarde, de Salinas.

a Word altered and seven following inserted repl. 'shalbe renewyd accordyng to' ('to' not deleted).   *b* Altered from 'wherin'.   *c* Word repeated then deleted.

164. *March 2. The earl of Arundel*[312] *appointed high steward. Leases granted.*

[f. 94] Secundo die Martii *a* anno domini 1554. It is decreed by Master Deane and the chapiter that my lord of Arrundell shalbe highe stuard of the churche and landes of Westm' and have fyve poundes by patent dueryng his lif.

Also that John Savage, boucher, shall have [a lease]*b* of the house he nowe dwellyth in, paying a fyne as Mr Perne and Mr Pye therin shall agree, for terme of fowrescore yeres and ten.[313] Also it is further agreed by the said Mr Deane and chapiter that my lord Sturton shall have his lease renewyd, and to have so many yeres as he had at the fyrst tyme in the same.[314]

Signed: H. Weston, Griffith, Perne, Cole, Baker, de Salinas, Smith.

a MS. 'Maii'.   *b* Ellipse in MS.

165. *March 14. House for a canon.*

Anno domini 1554 mense Martii 14. It is decreid by Mr Deane and the chapiter that Mr Doctor Cole shall have the hoole howse that he dothe nowe dwell in, for the space of xx yers, providyd that if the sayde Mr Doctor Cole shalle deye before the sayde terme, that then in that case the prebendarie that shall succede him shall paye for suche thinges as the sayde Henrye Cole dyd bye of Doctor

310 For grant to Stafferton see above, n. 45.
311 Smalbone, yeoman, granted terms as stated, and to build a new corn mill at his charge within a year, 14 February 1555: WAM Reg. III, f. 264v.
312 Henry FitzAlan, 12th earl, lord president of the council and lord steward.
313 Savage granted a tenement in King St on the corner of Thieving Lane, lately occupied by John Henbury, ale brewer, for years stated from previous Michaelmas at £2 6s 8d rent 10 November 1554: *ibid.*, ff. 235v–236.
314 Charles, [8th Baron], granted a tenement in Tothill St for 72 years from Christmas 1552: *ibid.*, ff. 188–9; renewed for 72 years from previous Michaelmas at £1 6s rent 29 November 1554: *ibid.*, f. 266. Three years later he was hanged for murdering his (country) neighbours: M.A.R. Graves, *The House of Lords in the Parliaments of Edward VI and Mary I* (Cambridge 1981), 26.

Barnarde, his predecessor, as iiij men indifferently chosyne by bothe parties*a* shall then pryse them, then the sayde lease to be voyde and nat otherwyse.*b* [315]

Signed: H. Weston, Griffith, Perne, Baker, Pye, T. Wood, de Salinas, Smith, Cole.

   a Three words inserted. *b* Followed by 'except a prebendary folowith' deleted.

166.   *Same day. Accommodation for the king's confessor.*[316] *Leases granted.*

[f. 94v] 14 die Martii anno domini 1554. It is agreede by Mr Deane and the chapter that father confessor to the kinges majestie shall have and injoie the vaultt that is next to Mr Allonnce his house, for so long tyme as he shall remaine in this realme, and after his departure the saide vaultt shall remaine to the forsaide Mr Allonce and to his successors prebendaries there.*a*

It is decreyd that Robert Langryshe shall have the revertione of the howse and the tenement of the Bores heade that William Geniges now dwellythe in, with the apportynance, bearinge all maner of reparationes and pavinge, for the terme of lx yers.[317] Item it is decreyd that Lentall shall have [a lease for]*b* lx yers [of the house]*c* in that Lane dwell in in the Kynges streate*d* bearinge all maner of reparationes and pavinge.[318]

Signed: H. Weston, Griffith, Perne, Mallet, Baker, Pye, T. Wood, de Salinas, Smith.

   a Followed by line deleted and illegible. *b* Ellipse in MS. *c* Ellipse in MS. *d* Four words inserted.

---

[315] Cole granted the tenement, on the south of the church wall, for years stated from Christmas following, with provision for valuation as in act, at 8d rent 10 March 1555: WAM Reg. III, ff. 254–254v.

[316] Either Alfonso de Castro, O.F.M., who in the previous month had preached a controversial sermon *against* the heresy executions: *CSPV* vi, 49 & n. D.M. Loades, *The Oxford Martyrs* (1970), 158 & n. 64, following Foxe (ed. Pratt), vi, 704; or Bernardo de Fresneda: PRO, SP 11/5, nos 21, 37 (*CSPDM*, 175, 192).

[317] No lease for Langryshe for this property, in King St, is found (but cf. below, no. **168** & n. 322). Letter from the king and queen to the dean and chapter requesting a grant of a new lease of the Boar's Head to Jennings, groom of the chamber, in recognition of service (accommodation, stabling), 11 January 1555; grant of the same from the end of his lease from the abbot and convent for 70 years at £8 13s 4d rent 12 March 1555: WAM 18056; Reg. III, f. 267v. Jennings was M.P. for Westminster; had acquired the Boar's Head from his first wife, widow of John Bate, and held much other local property; d. Aug. x Nov. 1558, requesting the then abbot to attend his funeral in the Abbey, and erection of memorial brass (not extant): *Hist. Parl. 1509–1558*, ii, 441–2. Rosser, 383 (for Jennings), 129–31 (for the property), 369 (for Bate), 60 n. 83, 332 n. 39, 372, 374, 404 (for other previous tenants).

[318] Philip Lentall, cutler, granted the tenement where Robert Lawne, surgeon, dwelt, for years stated from previous Midsummer at £1 6s 8d rent, to rebuild it with good oak etc. at his charge within six years, 10 February 1555: WAM Reg. III, ff. 241v–242v. For Lentall (and Thomas Massey his son-in-law) see Rosser, 386–7.

167. *March 23. Leases granted. Houses for canons.*

[f. 95] xxiij° die Martii anno domini 1554. It is decrede by Mr Deane and the chapiter that William Weston shall have the revertion of *ᵃ* Vaughans house for the terme of lx*ᵇ* yeres, paying for a fyne xx li. and the yerely rente.³¹⁹ And that John Jemes and Margaret his wif shall have their ij tenementes in Tothill strete.³²⁰ Item it is also decreed that the greate brycke house over and agaynst Mr Deanes house shalbe from hensforthe ij prebendaryes houses, that is to saye for Mr Griffithe and Mr Baker, and so for ther successors prebendaries. Also that Polley shall have Otford and Shorham for the terme of fourscore and tenne yeres, paying the rent of fyftye and fyve poundes by yere, and the fyne of xx*ᵗⁱ ᶜ* li.³²¹

Signed: H. Weston, Griffith, Perne, Mallet, Baker, Cole, Pye, T. Wood, Richarde, de Salinas, Smith.

ᵃ Word inserted. *ᵇ* Altered from 'lxxxx'. *ᶜ* Repl. 'l'.

168. *March 30. Lease granted.*

[f. 95v] xxx*ᵐᵒ* die Martii anno domini 1555. It is agreed by Mr Deane and the chapiter that Robert Langryshe*ᵃ* shall have a lease of the parsonage of Swaffham Markett for terme of xl*ᵗⁱ* yeres, to begynne at the feast of thannunciaton next followyng after the ende and determinaton of the yeres comprysid in the lease that is nowe in ure, paying therfore yerly to the deane and chapiter and their successors*ᵇ* xviij li. iij s. iiij d., and to the bysshope of Norwytche iij li vj s. viij d., and to the archedeacon of Norfolk x s.³²²

Signed: H. Weston, Griffith, Perne, Mallet, Baker, Pye, Richarde, de Salinas.

ᵃ Repl. 'Layngridge'. *ᵇ* Three words inserted.

169. *? Same day. House for a canon.*

And it is furder decreed by Mr Deane and the chapter that Mr Docter Mallett shall have the hole house that he now dwellith in, under the same forme and conditions that Mr Docter Cole hathe*ᵃ* his grantid, as aperithe by the decree hertofore wrytten.³²³

---

319 Weston, gent., of London granted the tenement then occupied by George Vaughan, gent., in the close of the deanery, from the end of lease to Frances Vaughan for *90* years at £3 6s 8d rent 22 March 1555: WAM Reg. III, ff. 256v–257v, where deleted but with explanatory notes as to its validity.

320 James, yeoman, of Hampstead and Margaret granted the premises for 40 years from previous Christmas at 13s 4d rent 10 March 1555: *ibid.*, ff. 255–255v. This must be a second generation John and Margaret James: cf. above, n. 212.

321 Thomas Polley, yeoman, granted rectory of Shoreham only, reserving the advowson to the dean and chapter, for years stated from previous Lady Day at £30 rent; the dean and chapter to acquit the lessee against the king and queen and all others, 28 March 1555: WAM Reg. III, ff. 238v–239v.

322 Langrishe, yeoman, granted rectory on terms stated in act, same day: *ibid.*, ff. 263–263v.

323 Above, no. **165** & n. 315.

Signed: H. Weston, Griffith, Perne, Baker, Pye, Richarde, de Salinas.

ᵃ Word inserted.

170. *March 30. Lease granted.*

[f. 96] xxx Martii 1555. It is decreyd thatJohn Perne shall have aᵃ lease of Peakes ferme*ᵇ* aftre the expiratione of his lyve or lease, for the space of fower score and nynetene*ᶜ* yers, payinge therfor the usiall rentes as Mr Peke dothe nowe.³²⁴

Signed: H. Weston, Griffith, Perne, Baker, Pye, Richarde, de Salinas, Smith.

ᵃ Word inserted repl. 'Pekes'. *ᵇ* Two words inserted. *ᶜ* Four words inserted repl. 'thre score'.

171. *Undated. Houses for canons.*

[Itᵃ is decreyde that Mr Gryffithe and Mr Baker shall have Vahanes tower for the space of xx yers if thaye lyve.³²⁵

Signed: H. Weston, Perne, Pye, de Salinas.]

ᵃ Repl. 'It is decreyde that Master [*illegible word*]'. Whole entry then deleted.

172. *Undated. Leases granted.*

[f. 96v] Yt ys to be notyd that the ij Whyttes, Sir Wylliam and Edwarde,*ᵃ* shall have on howse havyng now iij dwellers therin, to have for the space of l yeres, paying the accostomyd rent with the reparatyons.³²⁶

Signed: H. Weston, Griffith, Perne, Baker, T. Wood, de Salinas.

[Ytᵇ ys agredd by the deane and chapyter that John Gruffyth shall haveᶜ the tenemente callyd the Lampe, syttyng, lyeng and beyng in Newgate marke, for [*blank*] yeres, the olde rent to be yerely answeryd, and the said Gruffyth and his assignes shall bere all reparations, with a clause of renovaton of the same leasse.]³²⁷

ᵃ Four words inserted. *ᵇ* Whole entry deleted. *ᶜ* Two words inserted.

173. *October 28. Leases granted.*

[f. 97] Anno domini 1555 28 Octobris were sealid theise indenturis folowyng. 1,2.*ᵃ* It is decreyd by the deane and the chapiter that Corridon of Poffley shall have the woode and underwode at his fearme acordinge to his indentur made

---

³²⁴ Perne, yeoman, of Balsham, Cambs., granted the manors of Holme and Langford, [Beds.], from the end of the lease to Edward Pecke, gent., for *40* years at £8 rent, with remission of 6s 8d, 20 March 1555; another lease for same rent but for 99 years (as in act) 13 December 1555: WAM Reg. III, ff. 251v–252 (where deleted), 264v–265.

³²⁵ No lease registered. But cf. account of charges in securing possession and repairing Vaughan's tower: WAM 37565.

³²⁶ Not traced. 'Sir' no doubt indicates clergy not knighthood.

³²⁷ Not traced.

therupeone,[328] and Sir William Warren a certen copes of woode at Priers Cowrte, acordinge to a payer of indenturs made therupeone.[329] 3. It is decreyd at the same tyme that Mr Henry Chanci shall have the revertione of the parsonadge of Sabridgeworthe for the space of lx yers.[330] Mr Deane have brought it in ageyne. 4. A leasse renewed of a tenement grauntid to Sir Raffe Rowlett.[331] 5. A leasse renewed of a tenement grauntid to Henrie Mekys.[332] 6. A leasse renewed of a tenement grauntid to Dyrik Coster.[333] 7. A leasse renewed of a tenement grauntid to John Albert.[334]

Signed: H. Weston, Griffith, Perne, Baker, Pye, Ramridge, T. Wood, Richarde, de Salinas.

[a] Numeration marginated.

174. *December 16. Leases granted.*

[f. 97v] Anno domini 1555 16 Decembris.[a] 1. It is decreid by Mr Deane and the capiter that Mr Richarde Westone shall have the revertione of Mr Persi lease callyd Tollshont, Essex[b] for fyvetye and one[c] yer, paynge for a fine xx li.[335] 2. It is decreyd that Sorell shall have the portion of[d] tythe in Heyghe Ester for xx marces, for[e] the tyme of xxxxj yer; this is payd to Russell the survayer for the churchis behove, as apperithe by his byll.[336] [*Margin (to 1 and 2)*: Thes 2[f] be to be answerid to the churche as apperithe in the auditors boke.][337] 3. It is decreyd that Sir Richarde Bridgis shall have the close and ij acres and a halve for lj yers,

---

[328] For the Poughley lease see above, no. **114** & n. 231.

[329] See below, no. **175** & n. 359. Warren [*alias* Warham; he was the former archbishop's nephew and heir] paid £7 for Prior's copse in 1555/6: WAM 37662, f. 2. For Warham see *VCH Hants.*, iv, 225.

[330] See above, no. **113** & n. 223.

[331] Rowlett, knight, of Holywell, near St Albans, Herts., granted a messuage in the parish of St Olave, Silver St, for 75 years from Michaelmas following at £2 6s 8d rent 11 June 1555: WAM Reg. III, ff. 276v–277. See *Hist. Parl. 1509–1558*, iii, 223–4; Heal, *Goldsmiths*, 235.

[332] Mekes, goldsmith, granted a tenement in St Martin-le-Grand for 55 years from previous Lady Day at £3 6s 8d rent 1 October 1555: WAM Reg. III, ff. 278v–279v.

[333] Coster, pouchmaker, granted a tenement in St Martin-le-Grand for 54 years from previous Lady Day at £4 rent 26 September 1555: *ibid.*, ff. 267v–268.

[334] Albert, shoemaker, granted a tenement in St Martin-le-Grand for 54 years from Lady Day following at £2 rent 4 October 1555: *ibid.*, ff. 293–4.

[335] Weston, esq., of London granted the prebend of Grove Hall (Grovenham) in Tolleshunt Knights (Chivelor), Essex, from expiry of lease to Thomas Percy of Islington [for 31 years from Michaelmas 1547: *ibid.*, ff. 81v–82] for years stated at 11 marks rent 1 January 1556: *ibid.*, ff. 290v–291v. He paid the £20 fine: see below, n. 337. The prebend had belonged to St Martin-le-Grand.

[336] William Sorrell, of High Easter, Essex, granted the tithes there for years stated from previous Michaelmas at £1 13s 4d rent [the 20 marks was the fine, for which see below, n. 337], and to certify the particulars because the rectory was owned by St Paul's Cathedral, 10 November 1555: WAM Reg. III, ff. 266v–267.

[337] WAM 37665, f. 2; 37710, f. 1v (fines from Weston and Sorrell).

xx s.[338] It is decreid that Richarde Sinderell, the carpenter, xx s.,[339] Edwarde Mason xx s.,[340] John Harte xx s.[341] and Gabriell Paulin xx s.,[342] Cole the goldes-mithe xx s.,[343] Hordene lease xx s.,[344] Antoni Campion xx s.,[345] Garret[g] Williamson xx s.,[346] Thomas Wilcokes xx s.,[347] White for Cutes lease [xx s.],[h] [348] Thomas Whale xx s.,[349] Mr Geninges xx s.,[350] Robert Godwyne xx s.,[351] Morgen xx s.,[352] Cowike for the wale v li.,[353] [Robert Wigeborne xx s.],[i] [354] and Cutberde

[338] Brydges, [knight], of [Great *alias* West] Shefford, Berks., granted land at Maidencourt there for years stated from previous Michaelmas at 12d rent [the 20s here and other sums in no. **174** are fines or fees], and to make a terrier, 10 December 1554: WAM Reg. III, ff. 291v–292. He was a receiver of the duchy of Lancaster, and cousin of the 1st Baron Chandos: *Hist. Parl. 1509–1558*, i, 534–5.

[339] Richard Sondryll, carpenter, granted a tenement and little backside in Tothill St for 80 years from Christmas following at £1 rent 10 December 1555: WAM Reg. III, ff. 295–6.

[340] Mason, glover, granted two tenements and a back yard under one roof in Tothill St for 40 years from Midsummer following at £1 12s rent 20 May 1555: *ibid.*, ff. 265–265v.

[341] Harte, yeoman, granted five messuages in the Sanctuary for 89 years from previous Michaelmas at £7 rent 10 December 1555: *ibid.*, ff. 268 (incomplete text), 270v–271v.

[342] Pawlyn, gent., of Little Stanmore, Middlesex, granted the manors of Fenne and Skreyne, Lincs., for 7 (*sic*) years from previous Michaelmas at £33 6s 8d rent 8 April 1555: *ibid.*, ff. 266–266v. See below, no. **218** & n. 117.

[343] Richard Coole, goldsmith, granted a tenement in the Great Sanctuary for 80 years from Midsummer following at £2 rent 3 June 1555: WAM Reg. III, f. 289v.

[344] Not traced. Cf. below, no. **190** & n. 8.

[345] Campion and Ellyn his wife granted a tenement in St Martin-le-Grand for 56 years from previous Midsummer at £3 rent 2 October 1555: WAM Reg. III, ff. 277v–278v.

[346] Williamson, shoemaker, granted a tenement in St Martin-le-Grand for 99 years from previous Lady Day at £2 rent 4 November 1555: *ibid.*, ff. 268–269v.

[347] Wylcockes, citizen and leather-seller of London, granted a tenement and shop in St Martin-le-Grand for 26 years from Christmas following at £2 3s 6d rent 10 November 1555: *ibid.*, ff. 282v–283v.

[348] Not traced. 'Cutes' was probably Sir John Cutte, under-treasurer of the exchequer, a substantial tenant of the abbey (WAM index) who was also of counsel to Lady Margaret Beaufort: Jones and Underwood, *King's Mother*, 223.

[349] Whall granted a tenement where Richard Johnson dwelt and a little house in the Queen's rents in the Almonry for 99 years from previous Michaelmas at £1 rent 26 November 1555: WAM Reg. III, ff. 294–294v.

[350] For William Jennings and his principal holding see above, n. 317. Another lease to him of a tenement and garden in the Sanctuary, to north of Henry VII's chapel, for 60 years from end of existing lease at £1 rent 14 March 1555: WAM Reg. III, ff. 305v–306v.

[351] Robert son of Henry Goodwyn, yeoman, granted five tenements and a garden in Long Ditch for 70 years from previous Lady Day at £2 8s rent, and to maintain the jakes, 10 December 1555: *ibid.*, ff. 283v–284v.

[352] Morgan Fourde, butcher, granted an under tenement and little back yard (below that of Sinderell [n. 339]) in Tothill St for 60 years from previous Michaelmas at 13s 4d rent 4 November 1555: WAM Reg. III, f. 290.

[353] John Cowyk, gent., of Stepney granted the walls of the Sanctuary gates, and the way through to King St, for 80 years from previous St Matthew's day [September 21] at quit-rent of 1s 8d, to rebuild at will, 20 March 1555: *ibid.*, ff. 284v–285v.

[354] Wygborne, tiler, granted three tenements and back house and yard in the Almonry for 60 years from Christmas following at £1 16s 4d rent 22 November 1555: *ibid.*, ff. 269v–270v.

Harberde shall have the Lambe in Negate marget for lxj yers, paynge xij li.,[355] Brian xx s.,[356] Francis[j] Mallett. xxxvij li. John Perne,[357] Roger Carter xx s.[358] [*Margin (to 3)*: Thes ar to be dyvidyd.]

> *Signed*: H. Weston, Ramridge, Perne, Griffith, Mallet, Baker, Cole, Pye, T. Wood, de Salinas, Smith.

> [a] Head to page, all which deleted. [b] Three words inserted. [c] Three words inserted repl. 'xxvj'. [d] Two words inserted. [e] Repl. 'the fine paynge' ('fine' not deleted). [f] Numeral inserted. [g] Repl. 'Gabriell'. [h] Deleted. [i] Deleted and marked 'stet'. [j] Repl. illegible name, 'xx s.' deleted.

175. *December 17. Leases granted.*

[f. 98] Anno domini 1555 17 Decembris.[a] It is decreid that William Weston shall have the ferme of [b] Priers Cowrte in the wiche Sir William Warran nowe dwell-lythe, for the space of lxx yers, payinge therfor for a fyne vj li. xiij s. iiij d.[359] [*Interlined*: I Andrewe Perne have receyvid the same and payd it in the divid<u>e</u>nt.] Item it is decreyd that John Cawod shall have[c] the tenementes in Westmynster and London whiche John Martyn of Walta[m][d] Crose hathe,[e] for the space of lx yers, payinge therfor a fyne vj li. xiij s. iiij d., and beringe all the reparationes duringe the terme.[f][360] Item it is decreyd that Raffe Henslowe, gentleman, shall have the revertion of Stevinton whiche Smalbon dothe nowe occapye, paynge for a fyne vj li. xiij s. iiij d. for the terme of lxx yers.[361] [*Margin*: This ar to be dyvidyd.] Roberte Dorset xx s.[362] Summa dividenda 18 Dicembris 1555 lix li. Singulis iiij li. iiij s.

355 Harbart, yeoman, of London granted a tenement in the parish of St Audoen, Newgate for 67 years from previous Michaelmas at £4 6s 8d rent 18 December 1555: *ibid.*, ff. 289v–290.
356 Brian Mourton, bricklayer, granted a tenement in the Almonry where John Coole, baker, dwelt, for 60 years from Midsummer following at £1 rent 20 May 1555: *ibid.*, ff. 296–296v.
357 See above, no. **170** & n. 324.
358 Carter, yeoman of the guard, granted three tenements and shops in the Little Sanctuary for 90 years from previous Michaelmas at £3 6s 8d rent 2 April 1555: WAM Reg. III, ff. 294v–295. One of this name, the king's servant, arrested in connexion with the Dudley conspiracy 1556: PRO, SP 11/8, no. 73 (*CSPDM*, 449). Keeper of the sanctuary: *CSPD* Addenda 1547–1565, p. 433.
359 Weston, gent., of London granted the manor, in Chieveley, Berks., now occupied by Sir William Warham, from Michaelmas following the end of grant to Edward Fetiplace (50 years from Michaelmas 1542) for years stated at £4 6s 8d rent, and to make terrier within two years, 3 February 1556: WAM Reg. III, ff. 286v–287v, duplicated ff. 298–298v.
360 Not traced, so it cannot be certain if the tenant was the queen's printer John Cawood, for whom see *DNB*.
361 Henslowe, gent., of West Boarhunt, Hants., granted the manor from the end of previous lease [cf. above, no. **96** & n. 175] for years stated at £27 rent 18 December 1555: WAM Reg. III, ff. 292v–293. For him see *Hist. Parl. 1509–1558*, ii, 335–6.
362 Robert Dosset granted a tenement on the south of the church, where William Woodhouse, gent., late dwelt, for 86 years from previous Midsummer at £3 rent 26 November 1555: WAM Reg. III, ff. 287v–288v.

Signed: H. Weston, Ramridge, Perne, Griffith, Baker, Cole, Pye, T. Wood, de Salinas, Smith.

Memorandum that Mr Doctor Cole, treasurar of Westmynster, have in his custodye the 18 daye of December 1555 the obligatione of Mr Lord of the Bell in Westmynster.³⁶³

Signed: Cole.

> ᵃ Head to page, all which deleted.   ᵇ Three words inserted.   ᶜ Word inserted.   ᵈ Word written to edge of page.   ᵉ Word inserted.   ᶠ Eight words inserted.

176.   *1556. January 17. A collector threatened with prosecution. Fines for slander. A minor canon punished for assaulting a lay vicar.*

[f. 98v] 17 Janewarii 1555. 1. It is decreid by Mr Deane and the chapiter that Mr Pye, Mr Doctor Mallet, Mr Perne, Mr Stapletone and Mr Bowland or any thre of thise shall have a comission sealyd by the chapiter seale of Westmynster and also*a* to call Rossye to accoumpte of his collectorshipe, and*b* to minister justice to him accordinge to the lawe. And if he do nat make present payment of his receptes, that then he and his ij suertyes to be suyd this terme nexte folowinge, being Hillari terme.³⁶⁴

[*Margin*: A decre for the commones.] 2. Also it is decreyd the same tyme that if anye of the petycanones, scolemasters or any other of the clarkes or other wyse in ther comones above the adge of xviij yers shall calle any of these before namyd in ther commones foole, knave or any other contumelius or slanderus worde, [they]*c* shall paye for every suche defaulte xij d. to the commones, the whiche shalbe set on by the chanter if he be ther, or in his absens by the stewarde of the commones.

Memorandum that wheras Sir Edmund*d* Hamonde, pryste, dyd breake John Wodes heade, beinge one of the clarkes, with a pote, he was commandyd to the gate howse for the space of iij dayes by Mr Deanes comandement and payde to John Wode for the healinge of his heade xl s. by the decree of Mr Deane and the chapiter. [*Margin*: Did imprison as deane.]

Signed: H. Weston, Ramridge, Perne, Griffith, Cole, de Salinas, Smith.

> ᵃ Ten words inserted, incl. 'and' repeated.   ᵇ Word repeated.   ᶜ Ellipse in MS.   ᵈ Repl. illegible word.

177.   *January 31. All leases to carry renovation clause.*

[f. 99] 31 Janewarii 1555.*a* It is decreid that no lease*b* shall passe here aftre by the deane and chapiter withowte the clawse*c* before usyd for the renovasione*d* of

---

³⁶³ The bond was for £40: *ibid.*, f. 303. See above, n. 298.

³⁶⁴ Payment for this commission and other expenses in proceeding against Rossey in WAM 37698*. Warrant for his arrest for debt of £208 18s 6d issued by Perne, Stapleton and Bowland 22 February 1556: WAM 33209. He was arrested (for his part in the Dudley plot) on March 18 and executed on June 9: Loades, *Conspiracies*, 267.

them at everi alionatiane, and that withowte that clause*e* all leasis hereaftre to be made shalbe voyde.

Signed: H. Weston, Ramridge, Perne, Griffith, Cole, de Salinas, Smith.

a Whole entry deleted. *b* Repl. illegible words. *c* Repl. illegible word. *d* Repl. illegible word. *e* Word inserted.

178. *February 1. Process for recovery of debt.*

Memorandum*a* that I Andrewe Perne have receyvid owte of the treasurye the obligation of William Rosye, Edwarde Trevor and William Clerke, suertyes of William Rosie for his collectione primo Februarii 1555. Thaye be*b* now delyverid to the receyver to sewe.

a Whole entry deleted. *b* Repl. words deleted and illegible.

179. *February 7. Provision of a house. Presentation to a benefice.*

[f. 99v] 7 Februarii 1555. 1. It is decrid that the howse in the whiche Mother Jone dothe dwell in shalbe a chapter howse, and that Mother Jone shall departe owte of it before owre Ladys daye next comynge, whiche is the feaste of thannunciation of owre blessyd Ladye, and that the dore shalbe mureyd upe that ys now open to the dore to Westm' halle.[365]

2. It is decreid that the vicaradge of Matharne shalbe gyvine to Richarde Gybbes, clerce, of this conditione, that if any of the peticanones will have it thaye shall have the preferment of it before thes Sir Richarde Gibbes, if thaye will dwell on it.[366]

Signed: H. Weston, Ramridge, Perne, Griffith, Baker, de Salinas, Pye.

180. *February 27. Note of sealing fees. Leases granted.*

[f. 100] The presentation of Matherne, nulla.*a* Richarde Stoneleye, xx s.[367] George Massye, xx s.[368] Mr Busbye, x s.[369]

365 This entry has been supposed to indicate that the Jerusalem Chamber was thus vacated and so became the chapter house: Stanley, 378 n. 3. But the topography and every likelihood is against this interpretation; see above, Introduction, p. xxiii.
366 Gibbes duly appointed, occuring as vicar 1558 x 1565: WAM 37819*, 38254.
367 Stonley, gent., of Aldersgate St granted five tenements in the Little Sanctuary and a messuage in Tothill St, from the end of several leases to Edmund Wilgrease [see n. 53 above] for 99 years at £4 8s rent 10 January 1556: WAM Reg. III, ff. 280v–281v.
368 Masseye, yeoman, the queen's servant, granted a tenement in King St [the Saracen's Head] and adjacent property for 41 years from end of his previous lease [19 years from Christmas 1551: *ibid*., ff. 170v–171] at £4 rent 3 February 1556: *ibid*., ff. 275v–276v, where 1551 lease is dated January 3 (*recte* 12) by repetition of previous entry at f. 170v. For the property see Rosser, 79 & n. 177.
369 Thomas Busbye, gent., of 'Mayford', Staffs., granted tithes of Langham, Rutland, granted to him 1544 for 41 years, and of Barleythorpe, granted in another lease of 1544 for 45 years [WAM Reg. III, ff. 55–6], from the end of these terms for 41 years, at £19 10s 1d (Langham) and £6 (Barleythorpe) rent 8 February 1556: *ibid*., ff. 272v–274.

27 Februarii 1555. It is decreyd that Mr Charche shall have his lease newe sealyd with the clause of renovatione under the payne of x li., and payenge xxvj s. viij d. for the fees continewally *b* and leave owte the payne of forfettynge for want of renovatione, and paynge for the change of this clause for a fyne vj li. xiij s. iiij d. This have I Andrew Perne receyvid.[370]

It is decreyd that Mr Busbye shall have his leasis renewid, withe an increase of fortye and one yers more then he have in his owlde leases, payinge for a fyne fortye marks.[371] It is decreyd that Mr Suttane shall have his lease renewid and have with those yers *c* that he have lxxj yers, paynge for a fyne fyve powndes and tene shillinges.[372]

Signed: H. Weston, Perne, Mallet, Baker, Pye, de Salinas, Richarde.

[*Margin (vertically)*]: These sumes dyd Mr Multon the receyvir receyve.]

a Repl. 'xx s.'   *b* Word inserted.   *c* Word inserted.

181. *March 6. Appointment of collector and verger.*

[f. 100v] 6 Martii 1555. It is decreyd that Mr Foscrofte shall have for terme of his lyve*a* the office of the collectorshipe whiche was grawntyd to Mr Rosye, the same Fosgrove layinge in to us the deane and chapiter sufficient suertyes, and bringinge firste in the sayde Rosyes patent, and as the sewertyes nowe layde in shall deye or decaye,*b* to bringe in frome tyme to tyme newe sufficient suertyes allowide by Mr Deane and the chapiter. It is lyke wyse decreyde by Mr Deane and the chapiter that the sayde Fostgrofte shall have the revertion of the vergareshipe for terme of his lyve,*c* grawntyd to one Gye Gaskoyne, the revertion wherof was grawntyd to the sayde William Rosye before by patent, whiche the sayde Thomas Foscrofte shall bringe in to the handes of the deane and chapiter, and also that the sayde Thomas Foscrofte shall exercise the office of the foresayde Gye*d* Gaskoyne duringe the naturall lyve of the sayde Gye Gascoyne, havinge for his paynes yerly xxvj s. viij d.

a Three words over erasure.   *b* Two words inserted.   *c* Five words inserted.   *d* Word inserted.

[f. 101 *excised*]

---

[370] John Churche, gent., of Maldon, Essex, granted the prebends of Keton and Cowpes, Essex, with the rectory of Maldon, for 80 years from previous Michaelmas at £24 1s 8d rent 25 November 1553 [but entered among business for 1555/6]: *ibid.*, ff. 271v–272v. Prebends formerly of St Martin-le-Grand: Harvey, *Estates*, 403.

[371] See above, n. 369.

[372] William Sutton, citizen and leather-seller of London, granted a tenement in Pouchmakers' court, and the hermit's lodging, St Martin-le-Grand, for 70 years from previous Michaelmas at £3 6s 8d rent 10 February 1556: WAM Reg. III, ff. 285v–286v.

182. *September 24. Note of sealing fees.*

[f. 102] Leasis sealyd 24 Septembris 1556. Nicholas Weston renewid xx s.[373] Edmond Chomeleye xx s. Johon Banches xl s. Agnes Bankes xx s. Robinson xx s. Sallet xl s. Marcial xx s. Farman xx s. Elizabethe Nicholson xx s. Johnson xx s.

[ff. 102v, 103, 103v *blank*]

The first collegiate church was determined by the resignation of the dean and chapter on September 26 [Reg. III, f. 307].

---

[373] Weston granted the manor of Letcombe Regis, Berks., for 71 years from expiry of previous lease [70 years from expiry of same previous tenure, 1554: *ibid.*, ff. 259–260v] at £60 rent 10 May 1556: *ibid.*, ff. 296v–298. Other leases mentioned in no. **182** not traced and probably lost by demise of the secular chapter.

MATERIAL OUTSIDE THE MAIN SEQUENCE OF ACTS

183. *1553. September 23. Fees for the chapter clerk.*

[f. 272] Die Sabato xxiij° die Septembris anno regni regine*a* Marie primo. [*In a later hand:* 1553. For the chapiter clark.] It is agreed by Mr Deane and the chapiter that William Browne, chapter clarke, and his successors for the tyme beyng shall have towardes the better mayntenaunce of his and their lyvyng, for the regestryng and doyng thoffyce of chapiter clarkshipe at thinstallation or admission as well of every deane and prebendarye as all other mynistres, almesmen and children of the fondatyon of this cathedrall churche all suche ffees as hathe byn hertofore accustomed, that is to saye for every deane x s., for every prebendarye v s., for every scolemaster of the grammer scole iij s. iiij d., of every peticannon, gospelar and pystoler xij d., of every ussher of the grammer scole and scolemaster of the querysters xij d., of every clarke and other officer belongyng to this churche viij d., of every almesman viij d., of every of the quenes scollars and querysters iiij d., of every payre of indentures wryting and regestryng xxvj s. viij d., of every patent xx s., of every advouson xxiij s. iiij d., for every presentatyon xx s., and for every saynctuary man that shalbe pryvelegyd wythin this saynctuary xiij s. iiij d.

a Repl. 'Marie'.

184. [ff. 272v–274] *Admission of canons 1547–54.*

[f. 272v] Westmynster. The admission and stallatyon of Mr Keble in to the rome and*a* prebend of Mr Edward Layghton, late prebendary there, was the xxj*th* daie of June in the fyrst yere of the reygne of our sovereygne lord Edward the syxt, by the grace of God kyng of England, Fraunce and Ireland, defendour of the faithe, &c.

Westmynster. The admission and stallatyon of Mr Gyles Eyre in to the rome and prebende of Mr Gerard Carleton, late prebendary there, was the third day of August in the third yere of the reygn of our sovereygne lord Edward the syxt, by the grace of God kyng of England, Fraunce and Ireland, defendour, &c.

Westm'. The admission and stallation of Mr Thomas *b* Bryckett in to the rome and prebende of Mr Gyles Eyre, late prebendary there, was the xx*th* day of October in anno Edwardi sexti quinto.

[f. 273] Westm'. The admission and stallation of Mr Andrewe*c* Nowell in to the

---

a Repl. 'of / and L'. *b* Word inserted. *c* *Recte* Alexander.

rome and prebende of Mr Docter Redman, late prebendary there, was upon Saterday the fyfte day of December*a* in anno Edwardi sexti quinto.

Westm'. The admission and stallation of Mr Edmonde Gryndall in to the rome of Mr William Bretten, late prebendary there, was upon Saterday the 30 day of July in anno Edwardi sexti sexto.

Westm'. The admission and stallation of Mr Androwe Perne in to the rome of Mr Symon Heynes, late prebendarye there, was the eight daye of November in anno Edwardi sexti sexto.

The admission and stallation of Mr Rychard Alveye in to the rome of Mr Anthony Bellasis, late prebendarye at Westm', was the xvj^th daye of December in anno Edwardi sexti sexto.

The admission and stallation of Mr Hughe Gryffithe in to the rome of Mr Nycholas Rydley, bysshope of London, late prebendarye at*b* Westm', was the fourthe*c* daye of July in anno Edwardi sexti septimo.

[f. 273v] Mr Mallat. The admission and stallation of Mr Mallatt in to the rowme and prebende of Mr Pekyns was the xxxj^th daye of Marche in the fyrst yere of the reign of our soveraygn lady Mary, by the grace of God, &c.

Mr Baker. The admission and stallation of Mr Baker in*d* to the rowme and prebende of Mr Edward Keble was the xij^th daye of Aprell in anno supradicto.

Mr Docter Cole. The admission and stallation of Mr Docter Coole in to the rome and prebende of Mr Docter Barnard Sandiforthe was the xxj^th daie of Aprill anno supradicto.

Mr. Pye. The admission and stallation of Mr Pye in to the rome of and prebende of Mr Byrkhed was the*e* thirde daye of Maye anno supradicto.

Mr Docter Ramridge. The admission and stallation of Mr Docter Ramrydge in to the rowme and prebende of Mr Rychard Alvey was the xij^th day of Maye anno*f* supradicto.

Mr Woode. The admission and stallation of Mr Woode in to the rowme and*g* prebende of Mr Edmonde Weston was the xij daie of Maye anno domini 1554.

Mr Rycardes. The admission and stallation of Mr Rycardes in to the rome and prebende of Mr Alexander Nowell was the xij daye of May anno domini 1554.

Mr Alphonsus. The admission and stallation of Mr Alfonsus in the rowme and prebende of Mr Docter Perkins was the xviij^th daye of Maye anno domini 1554.

Mr Docter Moureman. The admission and stallation of Mr Docter Moreman into the rowme and prebende of Mr Emonde Gryndall was the xxviij daye of Maye anno domini 1554.

[f. 274] The admyssion and stallatyon of Mr Smythe in to the rome and prebende of Mr Docter Moreman was the xj^th daye of September anno domini 1554.

a Repl. 'Nov[ember]'. *b* Repl. 'the[re]'. *c* Repl. 'xx^th daye of'. *d* Repl. 'was'.
e Word repeated then deleted. *f* Repl. 'in'. *g* Repl. 'of'.

185. [ff. 277v–282v] *Admission of inferior members of the foundation 1548–56.*

[f. 277v] Anno Edwardi sexti secundo. Anno domini 1548.[a]

Peticanons. Clarke. Upon Friday the xx[th] daye of September in the yere before wrytten ther was a chapiter holden by Mr Deane and certen of[b] the prebendaryes, at the whiche chapiter they dyd admitt ij peticanons and a clarke, that is to saye Syr John Thomas in to the rome of Sir Ellys Pecoke, Syr Wyllyam Laynborow in the rome of Syr Ludgolde, and John Marshall in to Fox rome.

Childerne. Also upon Tuysday the xij[th] day of December in anno supradicto Mr Docter Bellacys dyd admite a scoller in[c] to the kynges foundaton namyd [*blank*] Raynes in to the place of [*blank*] Raynes, his brother, accordyng to his lotte.

Childerne. Upon Wensday the xx[th] daye of Marche in anno tertio Edwardi vj[ti] Fletcher was[d] admittid, beyng a scollar, in to the kynges fondaton in[e] his brothers place, by Mr Weston.

Almesmen. This day the xj[th] daye of May in anno Edwardi vj[ti] tertio John Day and William Bowdeler was admittid in to the romes of almesmen by Mr Deane and the chapiter, accordyng to my lorde protectours graces letteres written unto the seid Mr Deane and chapiter in that behalfe.

[f. 278] Anno Edwardi vj[ti] tertio.[f]

Childerne. Upon Tuysdaye the xij[th] daye of June in anno Edwardi vj[ti] tertio there was ij scollars admittid to be of the kynges fowndaton by[g] Mr Docter Bellasis, Mr Docter Bretten and Mr Docter Barnard, wythe the consentes of Mr Docter Heynes, Mr Pekens, and Mr Keble, than beyng absent. The names of the childerne are theis: John Ponnte and Nicholas Broke, to[h] be placyd in to the seid Mr Heynes and Mr Barnardes lottes, and are pute in the romes of Cowell and Myllys, now beyng voyd.

Childe. Upon Saterday the xxij[th] day of June was a chapiter kepte at the whiche there was admittid a childe to be of the gramer scole[i] namyd Thomas Brune, in the rome of Laurence Nowell, being in the gyfte of Mr Deane.

Childe. Upon Thursday the xxvj[th] day of June was a chapiter kepte at the whiche was admyttyd on John Coxe to be on of the kynges scollars, in the rome of Brydgys, beyng of the gyfte of Mr Pekyns.

Peticanon. At the same chapiter also was admyttyd a prest namyd Syr Robert Jamys to be a petty cannon in the rome of Sir John Rychardes, latly decessid.

[Upon[j] Saterday the . . . day of . . . anno Edwardi vj[ti] . . . was on Robert/ Rychard . . . admittid to be of the kynges fondaton by divers of the prebendaryes, in the rome of on Lawton, than beyng in Mr Redmaynes lotte.]

[f. 278v] Anno Edwardi sexti tertio.[k]

Childerne. Upon Frydaye the seconde daye of August was admittid ij scollars,

---

[a] Head to page. [b] Two words inserted. [c] Repl. 'to'. [d] Repl. 'Sheperd'. [e] Repl. 'by'. [f] Head to page. [g] Repl. 'before'. [h] Repl. 'presentid by the'. [i] Two words inserted repl. 'kynges foundaton'. [j] Whole entry deleted. [k] Head to page.

namyd Hillary and Palmer, into the romes of John Hille and Badger, beynge of the lottes of Mr Haynes and Mr Carleton.

A scoller. Upon Mondaye the xij^th day of August was admittid by the consent of dyvers of the prebendaryes on Robert Kyng to be a scoller of the grammer scole of the kynges fondaton, in the place of on Lawton, whiche was in Mr Redmaynes lotte.

Scoller. Upon Fryday the xxv^th day of October Dennys Smythe was admittid to be a scoller of the kynges foundaton, in the place of on Mourton late the kynges scoller, which was Mr Redmaynes lotte.

Porter. Upon Fryday the xxx^ti daie of August was Raffe Pettit admittid to be on of the porters, in the rome of Rychard Bell, by Mr Deanes gyfte.

Clarkes. Upon Fryday the eyght daye of November in the thirde yere of the reigne of our soveraygne lord Edward the sixt, by the grace of God kyng of England, France, &c., was admittid by Mr Deane and the chapiter ij syngyng-men, whos names are Christofer Bryckett and Thomas Sandland. That is to saye the sayd Christofer Bryckett in the rome of William^a Alderston and^b the sayd Thomas Sandland in the rome of Thomas Roo, late decessid.

[f. 279] Anno Edwardi vj^ti tertio.^c

A peticanon. Upon Saterdaye the xvj^th daie of November Mr Deane^d dyd admitt Sir John Marcante^e to be a peticanon, in the rome of Sir Cowycke late a peticanon of Westm', who dyed the xviij^th day of October in anno predicto.

Scollars. Upon Saterday the xviij daie of January was admyttid by Mr Deane ij scollars to be of the kynges fondaton, the on namyd John Wolton, and the other John Denman, and are plasid in the lottes of my^f lord of Rochester and Mr Perkyns.

Almesman. Upon Monday the tenth day of February in anno Edwardi vj^ti quarto Patricke Maude was admittid into the rowme of an almesman by Mr Perkyns, subdeane, Mr Deane beyng at Oxford, and is put in to the rome of [*blank*] Cardif, this day departid, by vertue of the kynges graces byll assigned, and the cowncelles, in that behalfe.

[f. 279v] Anno Edwardi vj^ti 4°.^g

Scoller. Upon Tuysday the fyrst daye of Aprill Mr Weston dyd place a scoller namyd Edmunde Phynne to be on of the kynges scollars in the grammer scole, in the rome of on Grafton latly gonne awaye, who was in the said Mr Westons lott.

Clarke. Upon Tuesday the xxij^th day of Aprell was a syngyman admittyd in to the churche by Mr Deane, namyd John a Woode, in the place of William Becke, late decessid.

Clarke. Upon Saterday the seconde day of August was a singyngman admit-tid by Mr Deane, namyd John Holford, in the rome of William Innys.

Clarke. Upon Thursday the xvj^th daie of July in the fyfte yere of Kyng

---

^a Repl. 'Thomas'. ^b Repl. 'late'. ^c Head to page. ^d Word repeated. ^e Repl. 'Marckhant, prest' then 'Marchant' then 'March'. ^f Repl. 'Mr'. ^g Head to page.

'Edward the sixt &c., was a syngyngman admittid by Mr Deane, namyd*ᵃ* [*blank*] Kellam, in the place of John Holford.

Peticanon. Upon Thursday the xxijᵗʰ of October in anno Edwardi sexti quinto was a petycanon admittid by Mr Deane, namyd Alexander Bull, in to the rome of John Marcant, prest.

Peticanon. Upon Saterday the 13 of Februar' in anno Edwardi sexti sexto Sir William Doughty was admittid by Mr Deane in to the rome of Sir Horne, late decessed.

Cater. Upon Sonday the xvᵗʰ day of Maye in*ᵇ* anno Edwardi sexti sexto William Browne was admittid by Mr Deane in to the office of John Hill, decessid, late cater to the commens of the cathedrall churche of Westm'.

[f. 280] Anno Edwardi vjᵗⁱ sexto.*ᶜ*

Belrynger. Upon Fryday the xxiiijᵗʰ day of June in anno Edwardi sexti sexto Harry Holland was admittid by Mr Deane in to the rome of John Carpenter, decessed, late belrynger in the mynster of Westm'.

Scoller. Upon Fryday the xxixᵗʰ daye of July was John Rushton*ᵈ* admittid in to the rome of Robert Wyllott to be on of the kynges scollers placyd by Mr Nowell.

Clarke. Upon Fryday the xxjᵗʰ daie of October in anno supradicto Thomas Damporte was admittid by Mr Deane in to the rome of Kellam, syngyngman, late decessed.

Pystolar. Upon Saterday the xvijᵗʰ daye of December in anno domini 1552 Mr Deane dyd admit Mr Rogerson into the rome of [Odnell]*ᵉ* Haybourne, late*ᶠ* pystolar in the churche at Westm'.

Petycannon.*ᵍ* Upon Mondaye the xvᵗʰ daie of Maye in anno Edwardi sexti septimo Sir William Banne was admittid by Mr Deane in to the rome of Sir Dowghtye, late peticanon in*ʰ* the churche of Westm'.

[f. 280v] Westm'. Scoller. Upon Mondaye the xvᵗʰ daye of Maye in anno Edwardi sexti septimo Mr Deane dyd admitt Peter Shethe in the rome of Dennys Smythe to be the kynges scoller there.

Anno regni regine Marie primo. Upon the*ⁱ* xviijᵗʰ of July George Hetherley was*ʲ* admittid by Mr Deane to be on of the kynges scollars, in the rome of Philpott, late scoller in the gramer scole at Westm'.

Scollar. Upon Saterdaye the xxxᵗʰ daie of July anno supradicto Thomas Robson was admittid by Mr Deane to be on of the kynges scollars in the rome [of]*ᵏ* Smyth,*ˡ* late scollar in the grammer scole at Westm' in Mr Pekyns gyfte.

Scoller. At the same tyme John*ᵐ* Lewys was admittid in the rome of Nycholas, in Mr Kebles gyfte.

ᵃ Word repeated. *ᵇ* Repl. word deleted and illegible. *ᶜ* Head to page. *ᵈ* Followed by 'was' interlined (otiose). *ᵉ* Blank in MS. *ᶠ* Word inserted. *ᵍ* Repl. 'Anno regni regine Marie [primo]. Upon Tuysdaye the xviijᵗʰ daye of July' (anticipation of entry on next page). *ʰ* Repl. 'at'. *ⁱ* Repl. 'Tuysdaye' (though correct). *ʲ* Word repeated then deleted. *ᵏ* Ellipse in MS. *ˡ* Repl. 'Nycholas' (anticipation of next entry). *ᵐ* Word inserted.

Scollar. Upon the xth daie of August in anno regni Marie regine primo Thomas Wylkynson was admittid in to the rome of Nevynson, in Mr Alveys gyfte.

Almesman. Upon Mondaye the xviijth daye*a* of September in the fyrst yere of the reign of our soveraygn lady Mary, by the grace of God, quene of England, Fraunce and Ireland &c., Thomas Bronger was admittid by Mr Weston, deane of this churche, in the rome of John Robynson, late almesman here, by vertue of the quenes highnes byll signed wyth her owne hande beryng date the xxj of August in the yere above wrytten.

Scoller. Upon Monday the xvjth daie of October in the first yere of the reigne of our soveraygne lady Mary, by the grace of God quene of England, Fraunce and Ireland &c., Mr Deane dyd admitt Thomas Cotton to be one of the kynges scollars, in the rome of John Wolton, beyng Mr Nowelles scoller.

[f. 281] Anno regine Marie primo.*b*

Peticanon. Upon Fryday the xxth daye of October in anno regni regine Marie primo Mr Deane dyd admytt Sir Cheltham to be a peticanon of this churche in the rome of Sir John Smythe, late deceasyd.

Scollar. Upon Fryday the ixth daye of October anno supradicto [*blank*] Rogers[374] was admittid by Mr Deane to be one of the kynges scollars, in the rome of Wolton, late the*c* kynges scollar there.

Scollar. Upon Tuysdaye the xxjth daye of November anno supradicto Mr Deane dyd admytt Hawkys to be one of the kynges scollars, in the rome of Cotton.

Scollar. Upon Monday the xviijth daye of December in anno supradicto Welles was admittid by Mr Deane to be one of the kynges scollars, in the rome of Poyner.

Peticanon. Sir Rychard Devynys *d* was admittid by Mr Deane a peticanon, in the rome of Sir Harford, the ij^{de} daye of February in anno domini m^ldliij.

---

a Repl. 'of O[ctober]'.   *b* Head to page.   *c* Repl. 'sco[llar]'.   *d* Repl. 'Denyell'.

---

374 Archbishop Cranmer, by letter to the dean and chapter dated at Lambeth June 29 (no year) requested a place at Westminster School for 'one Roger' the stepson of a friend; endorsed 'this letter shalbe sped at Myhelmas': WAM 43047; printed in L.E. Tanner, *Westminster School* (1934), 4, noting the appearance of 'Rogers' among the scholars in October 1553. It will be seen that in an earlier entry in these acts the same vacancy is filled by a boy named Cotton, while a later entry mentions in turn the replacement of Cotton *alias* Rogers – an identity accepted by *ROW*, though perhaps meaning only that Cotton *or* Rogers had been the previous scholar. However, the archbishop's nominee could have acquired an *alias* by his parent's remarriage. A date of 29 June 1553 would place Cranmer still at Lambeth (although he must have been at Greenwich on July 6 when Edward VI died); but he is documented at Lambeth on June 23: *Thomas Cranmer. Churchman and Scholar*, ed. P. Ayris and D. Selwyn (Woodbridge 1993), 147; date of 1552 or 1553 suggested for WAM 43047 in Ayris and Selwyn, *op. cit.*, 298.

' Scollars.^a The fourthe day of February in anno supradicto Mr Deane dyd admitt Syr^b John to be one of the kynges scollars, in the rome of Scarlett.

Peticanon. Upon Sonday the fyrst of Apryll in anno domini m^ldliiij^{do} ^c Mr Deane dyd admytt Sir John Mekyns, pryst, to be one of the peticanons of this churche, in the rome of Sir John Thomas.

Pystoler. Sir [*blank*] Harryson was admitted by Mr Deane to be pystoler in Mr Rogers place the^d xxvij day of Marche anno regni regine Marie primo.

[f. 281v] Scollar. Robert Broke was admittid by Mr Deane Weston^e to be one of the qwenes^f scollars the xvjth daye of January anno^g domini 1553.

Scollar. Cotton alias Rogers was admittid by Mr Deane the ixth daie of October to be on of the quenes^h scollars anno domini 1553.

Scollar. Hawkes was admittid by Mr Deane to be on of the quenesⁱ scollars, in the rome of Cotton, the xxj daie of November anno^j domini 1553.

Scollar. Welles was admittid by Mr Deane to be one of the quenes scollars, in the rome of Poyner, the 18 daie of December anno domini 1553.

Scollar. Thomas Dormar was admittid by Mr Deane to be on of the quenes scollars, in the rome of Wytney, the 14 daie of February anno domini 1553.

Scollar. Wylliam Penson was admittid by Mr Deane to be one of the quenes scollars, in the rome of Penson his brother, the xvij daie of Marche anno primo regni regine Marie.

Scollar. Davy Rowland was admittid by Mr Deane to be on of the quenes scollars, in the rome of Russheton, the vj daie of Aprill anno domini 1554.

Scollar. Preston was admittid by Mr Deane to be one of the quenes scollars, in the rome of Peter Shethe, the xijth daie of Maye anno domini 1554.

Scollar. Mathewe Skydmore was admittid by Mr Deane to be one of the quenes scollars, in the rome of Runingers place, the first daye of Aprill anno domini 1554.

Petycanon. Sir Pedder was admittid by Mr Deane in to Sir Cromes place the vj daye of Aprill anno domini 1554.

Peticanon. Sir Scideat was admittid by Mr Deane in to Sir Langborough place the viij daye of Aprill anno domini 1554.

ij ^k clerkes. Richarde Vale and John Smyth were admittid by Mr Deane, viz. Vale in the rome of Damport and Smythe in the rome of Wynson, the viij daie of Aprill anno domini 1554.

[f. 282] Peticanon. Sir Sanden admittid by Mr Deane in the place of Sir Perryn the xxvij daie of Aprill anno domini 1554º.

Almesman. Stevyn Bull admittid by Mr Deane in the rome of Fynche, late almesman, the 7 day of Maye anno domini 1554º.

Peticanon. Sir Parker admittid by Mr Deane in to Sir Scooses rome the xxviijth daie of Maye anno domini 1554º.

---

^a *Sic.* ^b *Sic* (?anticipation of next entry). ^c 'domini' and figure inserted repl. 'supradicto'. ^d Word repeated. ^e Word inserted. ^f Repl. 'kynges'. ^g Repl. 'in'. ^h Repl. 'kynges'. ⁱ Repl. 'k[ynges]'. ^j Repl. 'in'. ^k Repl. 'Peticanon'.

Almesman. Davy Lewys admittid by Mr Deane in to Longes rome the vij daie of June anno domini 1554°.

Scollar. Richard Hodgeson was admittid by Mr Deane to be one of the quenes scollars, in the place of Bolton, the xxviij daie of June anno domini 1554°.

Scollar. John Wyckes was admittid by Mr Deane to be one of the quenes scollars, in the rome of Rychard Arkynstall, the first daie of June anno domini 1554°.

Peticanon. Sir Edmonde Haman admittid by Mr Subdeane in to the place of Sir Pedder the 4ᵗʰ daie of July anno domini 1554°.

Peticanon. Sir [*blank*] Blackwood was admittid the 17 daye of Marche anno 1554.

Peticanon.ᵃ Sirᵇ Jackson was admittid the 4 daye of October anno 1554.

Clerke. Noddell was admittid xxjᵗⁱ day of October anno domini 1554.

Clarke. William Pollatt was admittid 25 day of Marche 1555.

Almesman. John Dytton was admittid in to [*blank*] rome theᶜ 7 daye of January anno 1554.

Almesman. John Elton was admittid 27ᵈ day of Marche in to [*blank*] rome anno 1555.

Clerke. Carleton was admittid 31 daie of October anno 1554°.

[f. 282v] Peticanon. Sir Robert Nele was admittid the xij daie of Marche anno 1554.

Peticanon. Sir William Hamon was admittid 25 day of Aprill anno 1554.

Clerke. [*blank*] Pampyan was admittid 5 day of August anno domini 1555.

[Scolemaster.ᵉ Mr Udale was admittid to be scolemaster 16 Decembris anno 1555.]

Peticanon. Sir William Bunting was admittid the 11 daye of Januarii anno 1555.

Fausecrofte. Upon Sondaye the eight daie of Marche anno 1555 Thomas Fausecrofte was admittid by Mr Deane and the chapter in to Roseys romes, that is to saye toᶠ the collecters rome for the rentes of Westm' and Knyghtes bridge, and the verges rome whiche Gye Gascoyne holdithe for terme of his lif, and afterwardes to the said Thomas Fauscroft.

Pystoler. The sixt daie of Aprill anno 1556 Sir William Cappe alias Cope was admittid by Mr Deane to be pystler, in the rome [of]ᵍ Sir Bull then made peticannon.

Clerkes. Roger Coffen and [*blank*] Shackstone was admittid by Mr Deane to be syngyngmen in ij prystes romes the xxᵗʰ daie of Aprill anno 1556.

Almesman. John Foster was admittid by Mr Deane to be one of the quenes graces bedman wythin this cathedrall churche of Westm' the fyrst daye of Maye anno 1556, in Thomas Audelowes rome.

ᵃ Repl. 'Clarke' (anticipation of next but one entry).   ᵇ Repl. 'William' (ditto).   ᶜ Word repeated then deleted.   ᵈ Repl. '26'.   ᵉ Whole entry deleted (perhaps inadvertently by line separating entries).   ᶠ Word inserted.   ᵍ Ellipse in MS.

186. *1553. May 20. Goods seized by the crown.*

[f. 299] Be it knowen to all men to whome this present wryting shall come that on the ix^th daie of the monethe of Maye the yere of our lord God 1553° and of the reigne of owre soveraygne lord Edward the vj^th kyng of England &c. the vij^th yere, Syr Roger Chamley, knyght, lord chief justice, and Syr Robert Bowes, knyght, master of the roolys, the kyngyes commyssyoners for the^a gathering of ecclesiasticall goodes,[375] sate at Westm' and callyd before theym the deane of the cathedrall churche of Westm' wythe certen other of the same howse, and theym commawndyd by the vertue of their commyssion to bryng to theym a trewe inventorye of all the plate, cuppes, vestmentes, and other ecclesiasticall goodes whiche belongyd to their churche, whiche done the xij^th daie of the same monethe, they sent John Hodges of the cittie of Westm', Robert Smalwood of the same citie, and Edmonde Beste of the same citie, whome the said commissioners had made their collectors, with a commawndement to the deane and chapiter for the delyverye of the said goodes, whiche were by Robert Crome, clerke, sexten of the said churche, delyveryd to the said collectours, thies parcelles of plate, cussins and other thinges^b the names wherof be here subscribyd only left to the use of the said churche.

In primis ij cupps wythe the covers all gylte. One white sylver pott. iij herse clothes. xij cussins. On carpett for the table. viij staule clothes for the quyre. iij pulpyt clothes. A litle carpett for Mr Deanes staule. ij tabull clothes.

All other savyng the^c above namyd parcelles the said collectors by the commawndement of the said commissioners hadd and caryed awaye wythe them. In witnes wherof the deane and prebendayes of the said cathedrall churche with other mynysters of the same have to thies lettres testimoniall subscribyd their handes the xx^th daie of Maye in the yere above wrytten.

Signed: Cox, Bricket, E. Weston, J. Pekyns, Nowell, Grindal, Perne, Alvey.

^a Word inserted. ^b Repl. 'then'. ^c Word inserted.

187. [Rear of volume (upside down)]

I. *Register of sealing fees begun 10 February 1543 but not continued.*

[Cover]   William Browne
                           chapiter clarke

Westmynster. The boke of receptes of the chapter sealles ffrom the ffyrst sellyng the x day of February anno xxxiiij° Henrici viij by thandes of Wyllyam Russell.

[f. 313 *pen trials*] [f. 312v] Mr Brokett. Item delyverid a seall of Mr Brokettes and

---

[375] *CPR 1550–3*, pp. 392–3. Bowes and Cholmley were joint lords-lieutenant of Middlesex: *Hist. Parl. 1509–1558*, i, 471–3, 644–6.

he must pay ffor a ffyne'xx li., wherof rec' ᵃ x li., and x li. to be paid at Myhelmas anno xxxvº Henrici viij, the seall pardonid by the chapter.³⁷⁶

Mr Curry. Item delyverid a seall of Mr Cury, maister coke for the prynce, soll'ᵇ to William Russell x s.³⁷⁷

Richard Fuller. Item delyverid a seall of Richard Fuller, servant to my lord prynce, soll' to William Russell x s.³⁷⁸

Sampson Audley. Item delyverid a seall of Sampson Audley for iij tenementes on the brode gattes, soll' x s.³⁷⁹

Ric. Bulloke. Item delyverid a seall of Bullokes whiche was pardonyd by the chapter by reasone of costes don on pavyng in Fayter Lane – nulla.³⁸⁰

James Tylson. Item delyverid a seall to James Tylson, rec' per Russell x s.³⁸¹

John Wrenford. Item delyverid a seall to John Wrenfford, rec' per Russell xl s. Rec' in party payment of ₗhis fyne xxvj li. xiij s. iiij d.³⁸²

Edward Bawgh. Item delyverid a seall to Edward Bawgh, rec' per Russell for the seall xl s. Item rec' of the same Bawgh for a ffyne – x li.³⁸³

[*Sum*] ˣˣₓₓₓₓ xiiij li. xiiij s. viijd.

   ᵃ 'recepta' or 'received'. ᵇ 'soluta' (paid).

[bottom of page (correct way up) *pen trials*]

II. *Note about an almsman 1553.*

[f. 312] [*pen trials*] Stevyn Bull hathe the next rome of an almesmanᵃ that shall falle voyde in this churche, by vertue of the quenes graces byll assigned with her owne hand beryng date the vjᵗʰ daye of September anno primo regni Marie regine.

   ᵃ Three words inserted.

³⁷⁶ See above, no. **7** & n. 21.
³⁷⁷ See above, no. **7** & n. 22.
³⁷⁸ See above, no. **7** & n. 27.
³⁷⁹ See above, no. **7** & n. 24.
³⁸⁰ Bullock of London and Alice his wife granted five cottages and other property in Fetter Lane for 40 years from previous Lady Day at £1 10s rent 9 May 1543: WAM Reg. III, ff. 23–4.
³⁸¹ Tyllson, clothworker, and Cecillie his wife, granted a tenement in Tothill St for 50 years from Michaelmas following at £1 10s rent 14 March 1543: *ibid.*, ff. 24–5.
³⁸² See above, no. **5** & n. 18.
³⁸³ See above, no. **5** & n. 16.

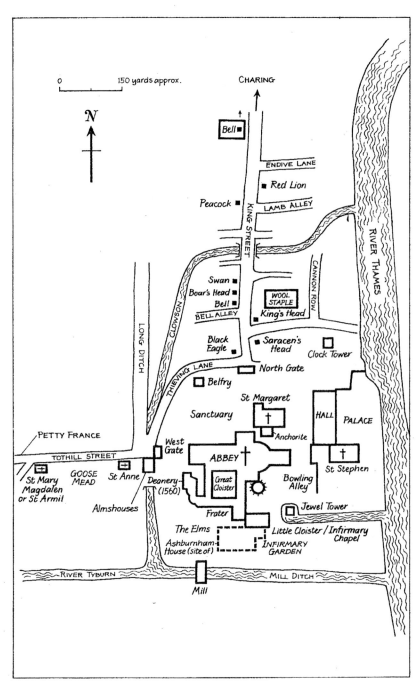

Map 1. Westminster Abbey and its surroundings
(Sources: Rosser, 124–5; Harvey, *Living and Dying*, p. [xvii])

110

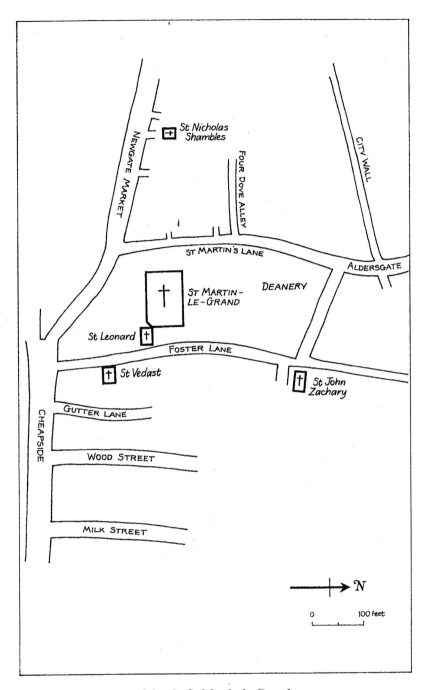

Map 2. St Martin-le-Grand
(Sources: M.B. Honeybourne in *JBAA* (1932–3); Pepys, x)